Insurgent Intellectual

The **Strategic and Defence Studies Centre (SDSC)** in the School of International, Political and Strategic Studies, College of Asia and the Pacific, at the Australian National University, is Australia's leading centre for the study of strategic, defence and wider security issues. SDSC conducts research and teaching on the role of armed force in international affairs, especially as it affects Australia and its region. It aims to use good scholarship to illuminate strategic and defence policy questions faced by Australia and other countries. Its research therefore seeks to contribute to policy and public debates as much as to academic discourse. SDSC's research and teaching priorities are the conceptual and historical foundations of strategy and policy, global and Asian regional developments that shape Australia's strategic environment, and Australia's defence policy, strategic posture, military capabilities and operations.

The **Institute of Southeast Asian Studies (ISEAS)** was established as an autonomous organisation in 1968. It is a regional research centre dedicated to the study of socio-political, security and economic trends and developments in Southeast Asia and its wider geostrategic and economic environments. In addition to stimulating research and debate within scholarly circles, ISEAS endeavours to enhance public awareness of the region and facilitate the search for viable solutions to the varied problems confronting the region.

ISEAS Publishing, an established academic press, has issued more than 2,000 books and journals. It is the largest scholarly publisher of research about Southeast Asia from within the region. ISEAS Publishing works with many other academic and trade publishers and distributors to disseminate important research and analyses from and about Southeast Asia to the rest of the world.

Insurgent Intellectual

Essays in Honour of **Professor Desmond Ball**

EDITED BY
**BRENDAN TAYLOR
NICHOLAS FARRELLY
SHERYN LEE**

INSTITUTE OF SOUTHEAST ASIAN STUDIES
Singapore

First published in Singapore in 2012 by
ISEAS Publishing
Institute of Southeast Asian Studies
30 Heng Mui Keng Terrace
Pasir Panjang
Singapore 119614

E-mail: publish@iseas.edu.sg
Website: http://bookshop.iseas.edu.sg

All rights reserved. No part of this publication may be reproduced, stored in a retrieval system, or transmitted in any form or by any means, electronic, mechanical, photocopying, recording or otherwise, without the prior permission of the Institute of Southeast Asian Studies.

© 2012 Institute of Southeast Asian Studies, Singapore

The responsibility for facts and opinions in this publication rests exclusively with the authors and their interpretations do not necessarily reflect the views or the policy of the publishers or their supporters.

ISEAS Library Cataloguing-in-Publication Data

Insurgent intellectual : essays in honour of Professor Desmond Ball / edited by Brendan Taylor, Nicholas Farrelly and Sheryn Lee.
1. Security, International.
2. Security, International—Pacific Area.
3. Australia—Strategic aspects.
4. Australia—Defenses.
5. Australia—Military policy.
6. Nuclear warfare—Prevention.
I. Taylor, Brendan, 1974–
II. Farrelly, Nicholas.
III. Lee, Sheryn.
JZ5588 I59   2012

ISBN 978-981-4414-62-3 (soft cover)
ISBN 978-981-4414-64-7 (PDF)

Typeset by Superskill Graphics Pte Ltd
Printed in Singapore by Mainland Press Pte Ltd

CONTENTS

The Contributors   vii

Acknowledgements   ix

Introduction
1. Introducing the insurgent intellectual   3
   Brendan Taylor, Nicholas Farrelly and Sheryn Lee

2. From the beginning   8
   Robert O'Neill

Global Strategy
3. Nuclear war and crisis stability   17
   President Jimmy Carter

4. Our first obligation   19
   Brad Glosserman and Ralph Cossa

5. Shining a light on the world's eavesdroppers   30
   Jeffrey T. Richelson

6. Controlling nuclear war   43
   Robert Ayson

7. Avoiding Armageddon   57
   Ron Huisken

Asia-Pacific Security
8. Challenging the establishment   69
   Alexander Downer

9.	Rumblings in regional security architecture *Pauline Kerr*	75
10.	Constructive criticism and Track 2 diplomacy *Brian L. Job and Anthony Milner*	88
11.	Gazing down at the breakers *Euan Graham*	112
12.	A regional arms race? *Tim Huxley*	122
13.	Securing a new frontier in mainland Southeast Asia *Nicholas Farrelly*	132
14.	"Big Brain" on the border *Phil Thornton*	147

Australian Strategic and Defence Policy

15.	A national asset *Kim Beazley*	165
16.	The defence of Australia *Ross Babbage and J. O. Langtry*	175
17.	American bases in Australia revisited *Richard Tanter*	191
18.	Cyber security and the online challenge *Gary Waters*	212
19.	Pressing the Issue *Hamish McDonald*	222

Bibliography   231

CONTRIBUTORS

Robert Ayson is Head of the Centre for Strategic Studies at Victoria University of Wellington.

Ross Babbage is founder of the Kokoda Foundation and Managing Director of Strategy International (ACT).

Ambassador Kim Beazley is the Australian Ambassador to the United States of America and former Australian Minister for Defence.

President Jimmy Carter is former President of the United States of America and founder of The Carter Centre.

Ralph Cossa is CSIS Trustee at Pacific Forum, Center for Strategic and International Studies.

Alexander Downer is former Australian Minister for Foreign Affairs and Visiting Professor of Politics and Trade at the University of Adelaide.

Nicholas Farrelly is a Research Fellow at the School of International, Political and Strategic Studies at the Australian National University.

Brad Glosserman is Executive Director at Pacific Forum, Center for Strategic and International Studies.

Euan Graham is Senior Fellow at the S. Rajaratnam School of International Studies, Singapore.

Ron Huisken is Senior Fellow at the Strategic and Defence Studies Centre at the Australian National University.

Tim Huxley is Executive Director at the International Institute for Strategic Studies — Asia, Singapore.

Brian L. Job is Professor of Political Science and Director of the Security and Defence Program of the Center of International Relations at the University of British Columbia.

Pauline Kerr is former Director of Studies at the Asia-Pacific College of Diplomacy at the Australian National University.

Lt. Col. J. O. Langtry is former Executive Officer at the Strategic and Defence Studies Centre at the Australian National University.

Sheryn Lee is a Ph.D. student in Political Science at the School of Arts and Sciences, University of Pennsylvania.

Hamish McDonald is a journalist for Fairfax Media.

Anthony Milner is Basham Professor of History at the School of Culture, History and Language at the Australian National University.

Robert O'Neill is former Chichele Professor of the History of War at the University of Oxford.

Jeffrey T. Richelson is Senior Fellow at the National Security Archive.

Richard Tanter is Senior Research Associate at the Nautilus Insitute.

Brendan Taylor is Head of the Strategic and Defence Studies Centre at the Australian National University.

Phil Thornton is an independent journalist.

Gary Waters is Head of Strategy at Jacobs Australia.

ACKNOWLEDGEMENTS

Producing an edited volume to mark Professor Desmond Ball's 25th year as a Special Professor at the Australian National University (ANU) has been a tremendous honour. We will be forever impressed by the devotion of Des' collaborators, co-authors and contemporaries to the tasks of writing their chapters and providing other assistance. Through our editorial responsibilities we came to know Des in a new light and hope that the chapters presented here adequately reflect the simply remarkable career of Australia's home-grown Strategic Studies giant. Des has friends all over the world and many played a role in making this volume possible. From Wellington to Washington, and Mae Sai to Melbourne, they have jostled to be part of Des' story.

A volume of this magnitude also required significant institutional support from across the ANU. The College of Asia and the Pacific, the School of International, Political and Strategic Studies, and the Strategic and Defence Studies Centre, have provided the intellectual and logistical space for this volume. Colleagues from across these enmeshed academic units, especially Professor Paul Hutchcroft, Professor Andrew MacIntyre and Professor Hugh White, were early and enthusiastic supporters of a *festschrift* to mark Des' contribution to the university. Along with Paul Hutchcroft, Emeritus Professor Paul Dibb, Professor William Tow and Professor Robert Ayson — each longstanding friends and colleagues of Des — have provided invaluable guidance and advice along the way. We are also indebted to Darren Boyd, James Giggacher, Raoul Heinrichs, Ingram Niblock and Sarah Norgrove for their exemplary support as we have finalised this manuscript for publication, and to Olivia Cable for her superb stewardship of the logistics related to this and so many other projects.

It is a little known fact that Des arrived in Canberra as a teenager, relishing the opportunity to test himself against Australia's best and brightest. And now, after more than four decades, here he enters a new stage in his great Australian romance with this great Australian institution. For Des, the ANU is home and we hope this volume appropriately recognises the institution's affection for one of its most famous sons.

The Institute of Southeast Asian Studies (ISEAS) has also proved a worthy partner in the publication of this volume. It is especially appropriate that we thank Triena Ong and Rahilah Yusuf for their support as we progressed towards completion of this volume to a standard befitting the scholar whose work it honours.

A further note of thanks is due to the subject of this book himself. We are delighted that he agreed to a volume that recognises his impeccable service to Strategic Studies, the Asia-Pacific region and the Australian community. His good humour as we went about the quiet task of editing this volume deserves our thanks.

Finally, we want to acknowledge Des' family — Annabel, Katie, Matthew and James — for their gracious support of such a unique man. We appreciate that life with someone as busy and talented as Des is not always easy. It is with them that we share Des. We hope that in the words of this volume they can further appreciate his career and the overwhelming respect of his grateful academic friends.

Brendan, Nicholas, Sheryn
Canberra
November 2012

Introduction

1

INTRODUCING THE INSURGENT INTELLECTUAL

Brendan Taylor, Nicholas Farrelly and Sheryn Lee

Denis Healey, the former British Labour MP and one of the founding fathers of the International Institute for Strategic Studies (IISS), observed in his memoirs that "from the middle fifties Australia has contributed far more to international understanding of defence problems than any country of similar size".[1] Healey was almost certainly referring here to the likes of Coral Bell, Hedley Bull, Paul Dibb and Robert O'Neill — all of whom Professor Desmond Ball has worked closely with at various times during the course of his illustrious career. Yet it would be difficult to contest the proposition that Des was actually foremost in Healey's mind as he made this observation, writing as he was in the late 1980s. As the Cold War began its unexpected retreat into the shadows of history, Des Ball stood as the leading Australian Strategic Studies scholar of his generation. Or as Brad Glosserman and Ralph Cossa more eloquently put it in their contribution to this volume, Des had by this time earned the respect of "every high church in the nuclear priesthood".

Those who know Des most intimately will readily anticipate how he would respond to such acclaim. On the one hand, he is a scholar who is quietly proud of his momentous achievements, and justifiably so. At the same time, one can imagine the manner in which the man who colleagues affectionately refer to as a "gentle giant" would bashfully wince at such flattery. This is just one of the many contradictions to Des Ball, more of which are drawn out in this volume. Some of the contributors write, for example, of a scholar possessing a remarkable grasp of the 'big picture' who at the same time is almost obsessively preoccupied with the devil in the detail. Others characterise him as a realist and slightly hawkish scholar with strong idealistic, dovish proclivities. Some policy elites have routinely detested his work, while others describe him as an "academic gem" and have forged longstanding friendships with this "insurgent intellectual".

Amidst these apparent contradictions, one constant in Des' career has been his longstanding association with the Strategic and Defence Studies Centre (SDSC) at the Australian National University. As O'Neill details in the next chapter of this volume, Des was appointed at the SDSC in the early 1970s and became its first tenured academic in 1980. He has spent the remainder of his career at SDSC, including as Head of the Centre from March 1984 to July 1991. As a number of the contributors to this volume rightly observe, he has been the heart and soul of the SDSC throughout this period. And it has been his intellectual home. Consistent with this, the volume is structured around the three areas, which have traditionally provided the primary focus for the Centre's research efforts — global strategy, Asia-Pacific security and Australian strategic and defence policy.

Former US President Jimmy Carter, with whom Des collaborated during the 1980s, offers the introduction to the section of this volume addressing Des' contribution to the study of global strategy. In this introduction, President Carter discusses the positive contribution that Des' work made during the 1980s to the collective goal of avoiding nuclear war. Glosserman and Cossa subsequently identify four main themes that are apparent in Des' writings on global strategic issues — the influence of extraneous (i.e. non-rational) factors upon strategic decision-making; the dangers associated with failing to understand the practical concerns of warfighting; a fierce nationalism; and respect for the fundamental principles of democracy. Jeffrey Richelson then reviews Des' contribution to the literature on signals intelligence — a substantial contribution that Richelson estimates extends beyond thirty books, monographs, academic articles and book chapters. Robert Ayson follows with an examination of Des' scholarship on nuclear strategy, providing a detailed analysis of three key works produced by Ball during the early 1980s — a period where Ayson regards Des as having been at the height of his powers. Juxtaposed with Ayson's chapter, Ron Huisken concludes the section on global strategy with a review of Des' contributions to scholarship on arms control and arrives at the somewhat paradoxical conclusion that this intellectual giant in the field of Strategic Studies — an area of study traditionally dominated by realists, hawks and hardliners — is something of a dove.

The section dealing with Des' even more extensive contributions to the study and practice of Asia-Pacific security is introduced by Australia's former Minister of Foreign Affairs, Alexander Downer. Downer describes Des as both a generator and a challenger of ideas. Pauline Kerr then surveys the contribution to the study both of security and security architecture that Des has made over the last two or more decades. Kerr dissects the logic of his thinking about regional security, demonstrates how his distinctive analytical approach accounts for the significant contribution of his work, canvasses critiques of his approach and examines the implications of Des' analysis for how we think about regional security architecture today. Focusing on a particular element of regional architecture, Brian Job and Anthony Milner examine Des' practical efforts to build a stable and enduring Asia-Pacific region through his direct involvement in the establishment and maintenance of so-called 'Track 2' mechanisms for multilateral dialogue, such as the Council for Security Cooperation in the Asia-Pacific (CSCAP). Euan Graham then reviews Des' scholarly contributions in the area of maritime security, examining specifically his work on nuclear strategy at sea, naval arms racing, confidence building, and technical intelligence gathering. Drawing out the 'arms race' theme, Tim Huxley analyses the contribution of Des' work addressing the dynamics of military procurement and capability development in the Asian region. Finally, Nicholas Farrelly and Phil Thornton each discuss Des' contribution to the study and practice of security in Southeast Asia, paying particular attention to his more recent work along the Thailand-Burma border.

The final section of the volume dealing with Australian strategic and defence policy is introduced by Australia's former Defence Minister and current Ambassador to the United States, Kim Beazley. In this introduction, Ambassador Beazley outlines Des' contribution to Australian strategic thinking in the 1970s and 1980s, during which time such issues were at the very heart of Australian politics. As Beazley recounts, Des' work explored the two central strategic preoccupations of that time — what should Australia contribute to the American alliance and what national defence posture it should adopt? Interestingly, such preoccupations continue to resonate strongly in Australia's contemporary defence debate. Ross Babbage and J. O. Langtry in the first chapter of this section recount the highly influential research they undertook with Des on the "Defence of Australia (DOA)" during the 1980s, focusing in particular upon his scholarly modes of operation, the key themes underpinning Des' thinking on DOA and his personal style as a project leader. Richard Tanter discusses Des' path breaking work on the United States' strategic installations in Australia, which markedly expanded the contours of public debate on this subject. Gary Waters then highlights the more recent contribution that Des has made in raising Australian public awareness of cyber security issues. Finally, Hamish McDonald discusses Des' interactions with the Australian media, particularly with reference to his collaboration with Des on a widely acclaimed book examining the killing of five Australian newsmen in Balibo during the covert Indonesian invasion of Portuguese Timor in 1975.

Viewed in their entirety, the reader of these contributions honouring the work of Des Ball will begin to see that the apparent contradictions in his scholarship and approach are less paradoxical than first meets the eye. Instead, they are much more a product of Des' uncanny capacity to transcend conventional academic, political and even personal boundaries. Huisken's chapter captures this wonderfully when he makes the point that "it is not easy to attach a familiar label to Des. He is not an ideologue of any kind and labels like hawk, realist, constructivist and so on seem quite out of place". In similar vein, Ambassador Beazley observes that "he was and essentially is a man of the left. But he also transcended the left. His intellectual curiosity compelled him to seek a deep understanding of the global military distribution of power."

Des' crossing of these conventional boundaries is as much a reflection of his generosity — to which Babbage and Langtry refer in their contribution — as it is a product of the intellectual curiosity of which Beazley writes. As editors, we have and continue to be the fortunate beneficiaries of his immense intellectual generosity as, indeed, have each of the contributors to this volume. Yet as Ambassador Beazley astutely observes, we each remain destined to stand in the shadow of his remarkable career — a very long shadow, and one that has indelibly left a remarkably positive impression on our lives and individual academic careers. As we honour Des, we are reminded of President John F. Kennedy — whose administration proved formative in Des' understanding of strategy and politics — when he observed that "as we express our gratitude, we must never forget that the highest appreciation is not to utter words, but to live by them".[2] Readers of this volume will almost certainly concur that Professor Desmond Ball's life and work has been, and continues to be, the epitome of this proposition.

Notes

1. Denis Healey, *The Time of My Life* (London: Michael Joseph, 1989), p. 192.
2. Robert M. Gates, "Veteran's Day Message" (speech Washington DC, 8 November 2010), US Department of Defense.

2

FROM THE BEGINNING

Robert O'Neill

"You might want to think about the guy who wrote that", said Hedley Bull as we sat together in his office just after my return from ten months study leave in the United Kingdom, in December 1973. Hedley was, of course, referring to Des Ball's doctoral thesis. And the need to think about Des had arisen because in my absence the Defence Minister of the day, Lance Barnard, had awarded the Strategic and Defence Studies Centre (SDSC) two non-tenured posts. We now needed to think hard about candidates for them, at Research Fellow and Senior Research Fellow level.

I did not know Des very well at all in 1973. In 1970, when I first came to the ANU, and he was finishing his Ph.D., we were on very different tracks. He was a young, free, radically inclined man who had been prominent in opposing Australia's part in the Vietnam War. I was a decade older with thirteen years of service in the Australian Army behind me, including a year in Vietnam as an infantry officer, 1966–67.

When Hedley asked me early in 1970 if I would take on the Headship of the Centre, my initial reaction was to refuse. By entering academia I was expressing a desire to be free and, if need be, to be critical of national foreign and defence policies. But in taking on responsibility for the Centre, which inevitably had some dealings with the Defence Department and the armed services, I would have to tread very carefully in order to sustain the

Centre's existing relations without becoming too circumscribed by them. After talking Hedley's offer over with my wife, Sally, that evening in early 1970, I changed my mind. It was probably going to cause some serious disappointment if I was to refuse to take the Centre on, and perhaps I could do the necessary balancing act and make a success of the responsibility. So I told Hedley next morning that I would accept the post. The die was cast — and it was an excellent outcome for me too in the longer term.

But my first years as Centre head were a somewhat lonely experience. The air of student and collegial disapproval of the Centre's existence was palpable on the ANU campus. We were going to get no breaks in terms of funding and new posts from the University, and in some ways I was always on the defensive. There was not a lot of specific criticism of the Centre or its activities, but there was enough to make me tread carefully and avoid provocation, especially at times of major student activism. Therefore those two new posts that Lance Barnard had offered the Centre were hugely important both to the Centre and to me personally. They meant company and a chance to show what an academic team could do with contentious policy issues.

Thus it was particularly important that the first holders of those posts were outstanding researchers and writers. Once they were advertised Des applied at the Research Fellowship level, and after a review of the field of applicants, he was by far the strongest and was appointed. Peter Hastings, Foreign Editor of *The Sydney Morning Herald*, was appointed at the Senior Research Fellow level. What the Centre got in Des was a young scholar, still in his twenties, with a proven track record of high quality analysis in one of the central fields of international studies at that time — the strategic arms competition between the two super-powers. I was particularly keen that the Centre should have a capacity to speak on the international level and not be simply an Australian-focused organisation. Hedley had told me of Des' capacity to engage with and gather very interesting information from senior defence analysts, both official and unofficial, in the United States. His thesis was proof of his skills in this direction. As well, Des' dissent regarding the Vietnam War was not driven by an over-riding ideology. What mattered to Des was evidence and rigorous analysis of the relevant factors that a policy had to address. Through personal interaction with Des I quickly gained confidence that we could work together effectively. We took things gradually and, I think, developed a very open, confident and trusting relationship from 1974 onwards.

In one special way Des gave rise to a new set of problems for me. Some members of the Department of Defence, particularly the permanent head, Sir Arthur Tange, thought Des was too close to highly classified information, and he would cause them problems. Defence people were worried about Des' capacity to investigate difficult and complex subjects, such as the United States facilities in Australia at Pine Gap and Nurrungar, and to produce politically uncomfortable conclusions. Des was amazingly good at trawling though what was publicly available, especially in the United States, and then assessing what was happening in terms of United States activities in Australia and how far these were under Australian control. Because Des knew so much about the full scope of Pentagon policies, weapons, equipment and deployment, he was better placed than most to fathom the implications of what he was reading. What he published certainly caught the public eye, especially when it became apparent that the Australian government initially had ceded too much freedom to the United States to use its signals facilities in Australia for its own purposes.

Every now and then I would receive a message from Sir Arthur to say that he wanted to see me. In the privacy of his office he would voice his unhappiness over some of Des' activities, and occasionally remind me that Des' work was being supported by the Defence Minister's funding. I had to stand my ground as an academic and tell Tange that, whether he approved of the output or not, Des was doing what a good scholar should do. Occasionally I then had to put those thoughts onto paper and send Tange a letter. I will not say that this diplomacy ended the problem but it kept the frictions at a relatively low level, and Des was able to get to know some of the Defence analysts further down the bureaucratic pyramid and impress them with his knowledge, his breadth of expertise and his commitment to contributing to a more effective Australian defence policy. Gradually the fuss died away and I did not have to face a growing crisis.

This turn of events was helped by the international attention which Des' work was receiving. His writings were being published by very prestigious international journals, and he soon established a profile on the international conference circuit. His work on strategic weaponry, command and control systems and intelligence gave him a capacity to analyse very complex and consequential questions such as whether nuclear war could be controlled once it had been initiated. This was a major topic of debate around the world in the late 1970s, and the International Institute for Strategic Studies (IISS) offered Des a research associateship to work on this question. The

Adelphi Paper he produced, *Can Nuclear War Be Controlled?*, quickly became cited as a major source in this debate and did much for the reputations of both Des and the IISS. In 1983 he followed this Adelphi with another: *Targeting for Strategic Deterrence*. This one also made a strong impact and established Des as an international expert on strategic targeting.

In parallel with this work on global nuclear strategy, Des was opening up other lines of research which he was to follow with increasing success over the next four decades, such as Australian defence industry, especially the aircraft industry, the air defence of Australia, and the basic strategies and force structure required for a more self-reliant defence of Australia. This direction of work was strengthened by the arrival in the Centre of Ross Babbage, then a Ph.D. student, and J. O. Langtry, one of the brightest colonels in the Australian Army. In 1976 the Centre took a bold new direction in the topic of its annual conference. Moving from the stability of the global nuclear balance, our topic in 1974 and 1975, we focussed on a controversial and consequential topic much closer to home: the future of tactical airpower in the defence of Australia. Des planned the framework of the conference and edited the resulting volume of papers. The rest of us worked together to produce contributions that were both within the scope of our expertise and relevant to the major questions which the conference had to examine. Over 200 people took part, and from then on the Centre's conferences required the main theatre of the Coombs building, not merely a room in University House as before. We had seven papers, including a 53-page masterpiece by Des, and a wide-ranging and very interesting debate on each of them.

On the basis of that success, we became even bolder the following year and addressed the basic defence strategy that Australia should employ in the new international context in the decades ahead. This produced a volume titled *The Defence of Australia: Fundamental New Aspects*.[1] It began a series of debates in the media, the wider academic community, the Department of Defence, the major political parties and the Government itself. Building on that foundation, our annual conferences became major events with some 300 people usually participating, resulting in excellent media coverage for the Centre and the presenters, and a commercially produced book. All of these developments did the reputation of the Centre much good in a more general sense both within Australia and abroad.

Since the mid-1970s, the Centre was in receipt of a major grant from the Ford Foundation for work on arms control issues in the Asia-Pacific region. This enabled us to bring to the Centre two Asian experts annually, who stayed for six months each. They strengthened our knowledge of regional political and strategic issues and our conferences and publications programs benefited accordingly. At the same time Des' research interests widened further, taking him into the mainstream of regional security analysts on Asia-Pacific security matters.

The Centre became busier and busier; it held more seminars and conferences and launched many new publications. Soon it commenced its own publication program. Subscription sales built up due to Langtry's efforts, and the Centre thereby had a new source of funds as well as an expanded impact on the national debate.

In the late 1970s I began to urge the leadership of the Research School of Pacific Studies to create a tenured post in the Centre, to which Des could aspire. This involved a challenge to existing principles because Centres were meant to be collapsible bodies which could be folded up when demand for their services weakened or the University was in financial difficulties. My own post, certainly tenured, was in the Department of International Relations and not the Centre. Regarding Des' future, he was doing so well that I could imagine him receiving some very tempting invitations from prestigious universities, especially in the United States, and unless he had something to anchor him to the ANU, he could be gone very quickly and probably for a long time.

I discussed these matters with him and a very helpful result emerged. Despite the attractiveness of some of the invitations he was already beginning to receive, he did not really want to leave the ANU, and certainly not Australia. Hence the establishment of a tenured post in the Centre was all the more important. After batting the problem around the Faculty Board and other high level tables at the ANU, I was able to get the right decision. When Des returned from his year at the IISS in October 1980, he was appointed a Fellow in the Centre.

Des' activities from then on took a turn in the direction of signals intelligence and regional security problems. He had an amazing capacity to discover the antennas usually associated with foreign signals intelligence programs on the roofs of embassy buildings around the world. Soon we all came to know much more about what was happening out in cyber-space as the electronic warfare era burgeoned. Des also became expert in issues relating to Thailand and Burma — a very difficult field in which to work and one where he is regarded as one of the world's foremost experts.

Altogether, as this book makes clear, Des has had a remarkably productive and significant career. He has been an assiduous field-worker, travelling extensively every year and investigating extremely interesting and important issues ranging from global nuclear strategy to paramilitary organisations in Southeast Asia. He has tackled subjects requiring a huge span of expertise, from technology to human behaviour. And his many published works have always been superior. No wonder he was made a Fellow of the Academy of the Social Sciences in Australia — a very appropriate vindication of Hedley Bull's judgement of Des in late 1973!

For me personally it was a great pleasure to work with Des. He is a fine scholar and a good team player. His easy, unassuming, relaxed but focused nature has always been a great strength, both for him and for whatever organisation he was working in. I have kept a highly valued friendship with him for some forty years. Sadly our lives have been on different trajectories for much of the past thirty years. Therefore as two busy people on different sides of the world, Des and I have not had as much opportunity to exchange thoughts as I would have liked. But I still have much to look back on with the greatest satisfaction and happiness. I am very grateful to Des for his friendship and to the editors of this volume for their invitation to contribute.

Note

1. Robert O'Neill, ed., *The Defence of Australia: fundamental new aspects: the proceedings of a conference organised by the Strategic and Defence Studies Centre, The Australian National University, October 1976* (Canberra: Australian National University, 1977).

Global Strategy

3

NUCLEAR WAR AND CRISIS STABILITY

Jimmy Carter

When I became president of the United States I inherited the awesome threat of a nuclear holocaust during the later years of the Cold War, when the United States and the Soviet Union confronted each other with arsenals of an indescribable power. I knew the entire time I was president, that twenty-six minutes after we detected the launching of an intercontinental ballistic missile, that the missile would strike Washington D.C. or New York or any other target that the Soviets had chosen. Soviet President Leonid Brezhnev and I knew that we had an equally strong retaliatory capability centred primarily in the intercontinental ballistic missile submarines. They were almost invulnerable to any kind of surprise attack. Just the nuclear warheads from one of those ships could have destroyed every city in the Soviet Union with a population of 100,000 or more.

This nuclear threat strengthened our commitment to peace. After I left the White House and formed the Carter Center, President Gerald Ford joined me in chairing our first major international conference, which included the foremost experts and political leaders from the Soviet Union and the United States. Our goal was to analyse the existing nuclear threat and the opportunities to reduce these remaining dangers to human existence on the face of the earth.

Desmond Ball was one of those experts we invited to that Consultation on International Security and Arms Control in April 1985: we already knew that his stature and the recognition accorded to his positions would add significantly to the strength of the enterprise. That was a particularly dangerous period in United States-Soviet Union relations, a time when the prospect of nuclear war was no distant fantasy. Ball's ideas were very valuable and contributed to the success of the project, and I was grateful for his participation.

In the following two or three years I met with Ball on a number of occasions, both privately and in relation to a project by the American Academy of Arts and Sciences on nuclear war and crisis stability. I was asked on a number of occasions to bring a presidential input into that work, to give a sense of what would have been in my mind in certain situations. Desmond Ball's work on the vulnerability of the crucially important United States and Soviet Union nuclear command, control and intelligence facilities, indicated that in all likelihood they would be high priority early targets in the event of nuclear war. This work demonstrated the degree of wishful thinking behind concepts of controlled nuclear escalation. Ball's work raised the possibility that if both sides were "blinded" early in a nuclear exchange by the loss of those facilities, a catastrophic slide into uncontrolled escalation and all-out nuclear war was a realistic possibility. This was in one of the darkest periods in the Cold War, when theories of planned graduated escalation and using nuclear "signalling" were most talked about as part of planning for nuclear war-fighting.

I had been aware of these vulnerabilities of nuclear command and control when I became president, and ordered a thorough review of these issues. Since then, there have been some improvements, at least on the American side. In technical terms, these facilities are now less vulnerable through built-in system redundancies. Desmond Ball's counsel and cautionary advice based on deep research made a great difference to our collective goal of avoiding nuclear war.

While that period of extreme tension has passed, with many thousands of nuclear weapons still in the hands of the nuclear powers, and with the door to proliferation still not closed, the threat of nuclear war has not disappeared. The fundamental lesson learned was that nuclear war is inherently uncontrollable, and that our fundamental goal must be to reach a world without nuclear weapons, and to eliminate every single nuclear weapon from the face of the earth.

4

OUR FIRST OBLIGATION

Brad Glosserman and Ralph Cossa

In truth, Des Ball does not look much like one of the world's leading strategic thinkers. In a world dominated by sharply pressed creases (military planners) and the precision that comes with scientific equations — think overpressure, single shot kill capability, circular error probability, and other detailed calculations — Des is, well, "rumpled". And apparently, he has always been somewhat "rumpled". In his interview for the Australian National University's (ANU) *Mentors* series, he tells of showing up at a dinner party at the house of his mentor, the distinguished Australian strategist Hedley Bull, "probably not wearing shoes, because I rarely wore shoes in those days."[1] Before leaving for the United States in 1970, Bull slipped Des some additional pocket money "to buy a pair of shoes and to buy a suit, and insisted that when I was seeing his colleagues … that at least I wore those shoes."[2]

As Des tells it, he sort of fell into his career, graduating from digging trenches and laying building foundations to working on Asia-Pacific economic cooperation (after a chance meeting with Sir John Crawford at the ANU, who noticed his sunburnt neck) and then being nudged into Bull's orbit by Crawford. Bull took the youngster under his wing and opened doors for him in the United States where he did research on his Ph.D. thesis on the strategic force levels of the United States.

That launched an extraordinary career that took Des to every high church in the nuclear priesthood. He clocked time at Harvard's Center for International Affairs, Columbia's Institute of War and Peace Studies, the ANU's Strategic and Defence Studies Centre (SDSC), think-tanks like the International Institute of Strategic Studies (IISS) in London and the RAND Corporation, and even enjoyed stints at the Pentagon and the underground Command and Control Centre in Cheyenne Mountain. He explored the particulars of strategic thinking with luminaries such as Bull, Robert O'Neill and Robert McNamara. It has been a rich and rewarding (and sometimes infuriating) journey — for Des and his audience, a group that includes policymakers and analysts, students and the countless Australians who have enjoyed (sometimes without knowing) the benefits of his insights and fierce nationalism.

This chapter attempts to tease out key themes that animate Des' writing on strategic issues. We identify four main currents: the "bending" of strategic analysis by considerations other than those of the national interest; the dangers created by the failure to appreciate the practical concerns of war fighting and their potential to prevent the realisation of core strategic objectives; an enduring nationalism; and a demand for respect for the fundamental principles of democracy.

"BENDING" STRATEGIC ANALYSIS

Des' first major work was *Politics and Force Levels: The Strategic Missile Program of the Kennedy Administration*. This 1980 publication was the outgrowth of his Ph.D. dissertation, and supplemented by annual fieldwork in the United States and Europe. Des explored the rationale for the massive build-up of United States strategic forces during the early years of the Kennedy administration, a drive that was spurred by reports of a "missile gap" with the Soviets. Bucking conventional wisdom — an activity he has made into an art form — Ball noted that by 1961 Defense Secretary Robert McNamara could admit that there was no unexpected program by the Soviets to build missiles and that the missile gap did not exist. Still, the United States went ahead with its procurement efforts and developed a 1,000-missile Minuteman Inter Continental Ballistic Missile (ICBM) program.

Extensive interviews led Ball to conclude that the missile procurement decisions of the early 1960s were "arbitrary" and "made in haste." His judgment was that:

> All of the missile decisions of the Kennedy-McNamara Administration, throughout the years of the missile build-up (1961–64), were, in some senses at least, political. In other words, the outcomes of the decision-making process were not wholly or solely the results of objective and systematic analysis, but rather resulted from a reconciliation both of a diversity of values and goals and of alternative means and policies, with the actual outcome reflecting, more than anything else, the relative power of the participating groups. ... But strategic doctrine in the Kennedy-McNamara Administration was never decisive with regard to the missile program; it appears to have served as no more than a rationalization for decisions taken on political grounds.[3]

That conclusion was disturbing on several levels — not least of which was the prospect of a new arms build-up being launched by the Reagan administration, which was taking office as *Politics and Force Levels* was being published. Des concluded that his study "causes much sense of déjà vu",[4] although he was then referring to the debates over targeting options during the Carter administration in the 1970s. The United States was again deliberating over the numbers of new Inter Continental Ballistic Missiles (the *MX*) and submarines (*Tridents*, this time, instead of *Polaris*) that would be deployed. Moreover, the readiness to develop weapons systems that did not reflect strategic concerns resulted in "excessively high stockpiles of vulnerable systems".[5] If, as should be the case, newer systems have a higher capability than older ones, then modernisation should yield force level reductions, not a static number or an increase — especially if earlier decisions were "arbitrary" and resulted in vulnerable systems. Yet that did not appear to be on the horizon. Instead, once again, strategic concerns were being subordinated to 'extraneous' factors.

THE PERILS OF WARFIGHTING

Des' subsequent work explored the resulting vulnerabilities in more detail. His assertion that "there are good reasons for believing that the first use of nuclear weapons could take place at sea" and the concern that "escalation dynamics of nuclear warfare in this theatre are far less constrained" than those on land yielded his 1985 assessment, "Nuclear War at Sea".[6]

In his next major effort, Des took up strategic nuclear targeting. This study was part of a broader reconceptualisation of strategic issues that had seized the field: until the mid-1980s, most discussions of strategic concerns remained painfully general, exploring such concepts as minimum deterrence or flexible response; these did not examine the ways that nuclear weapons would actually be employed in a conflict. At this stage, steadily improving Soviet capabilities were erasing United States strategic supremacy; American planners were losing the margin of error that allowed them to "distort" strategic planning by incorporating nonstrategic issues in their decision-making. To put it bluntly, strategic decisions had to better match capabilities to intentions and objectives. As Des explained, the loss of United States strategic superiority has meant that "U.S. strategic decision makers have been forced to be much more consistent and efficient with respect to the alignment of weapons acquisition policy, declaratory policy and nuclear weapons employment policy".[7]

This new approach also reflected a growing emphasis on escalation control — a continuing focus of Des' work — and a consequent deep appreciation and understanding of technology. Those twin concerns were evident in his conclusion that developments in strategic command, control, communications, and intelligence systems, which expand targeting options "offer the promise of controlling the escalation process in such a way that limits might be maintained on a nuclear exchange".[8]

But if technological advances were seen to facilitate escalation control, doctrine itself might work at cross-purposes to that objective. United States war planners were busily devising new targeting options that, in their minds, provided opportunities to bargain, leverage, and communicate with the Soviet leadership about goals and intentions during a conflict. So, for example, counterforce options were articulated that would permit "limited" nuclear exchanges as the United States tried to contain a nuclear conflict and slowly increase pressure on Moscow to sue for peace. The problem, as Des noted in various works,[9] was that Soviet ICBMs were located across the entire country — unlike the United States, which located its ICBMs west of the Mississippi River — and an attack against them would be difficult, if not impossible, to differentiate from a counter-value strike. This "might pose insuperable problems for the Soviet attack assessment system".[10] Particularly problematic were the ICBM fields located near Moscow. As Des laconically noted, this "increases the difficulties of persuading the Soviet leadership to accept the notion of limited counterforce nuclear warfare".[11] Des concluded that "much of the discrimination that has been programmed in to United States nuclear war plans in recent years is probably significant only to United States target planners themselves; it is most unlikely to be unmistakably obvious to the adversary".[12] In fact, he noted that "strategic policy makers and planners in no other country with strategic nuclear weapons capabilities have proved willing to seriously entertain the imposition of such restraints on their employment policies and plans".[13]

His assessment led Des to the conclusion that there was, for all the time, money and effort devoted to strategic targeting, little understanding of escalatory dynamics. In the abstract, that failure is troubling: in real terms, it was horrifying. Des noted that "any large scale use of nuclear weapons would be catastrophic. An all-out strategic nuclear exchange could well result in about a quarter of a billion fatalities in the United States and the Soviet Union from the direct blast, fire and prompt radiation effects, together with another quarter billion in Europe and Asia from the same effects".[14] Such sobering analysis helped to feed the anti-nuclear movement; an unintended (or intended?) consequence of his analysis.

Des remained focused on strategic targeting, and his next major article, written with *Los Angeles Times* reporter Robert Toth, took aim at the war-fighting doctrine articulated in the Single Integrated Operational Plan (SIOP) that came into effect in October 1989.[15] As the article points out, United States strategic war planning involved a continuing effort to make nuclear weapons more usable. Technological developments ostensibly facilitated doctrinal changes that would permit escalation control as a conflict progressed; the United States sought to maintain the ability to coerce its enemies while ensuring that there was always a choice short of an all-out nuclear exchange. But the authors' assessment of the (then) most recent changes in the SIOP — "the most radical change in both the substance and structure of the United States strategic nuclear war plan since the preparation of SIOP-63 in 1961–62" — was that they threatened to be "wasteful and dangerous ... ineffective as well as destabilizing to the nuclear balance."[16]

While acknowledging that there are "sound grounds" for some war fighting plans and force capabilities, Des and Toth concluded that the evolution of the SIOP during the 1980s took those arguments to "dangerous extremes." Identifying and finding leadership (or other mobile) targets was hard enough. But given their size and number, and the fact that they would be dispersed, a decapitating or "limited" strike would be virtually indistinguishable from a more general attack. In addition, threatening the Soviet leadership could push Moscow to decentralise weapons use authority, making control of nuclear assets more difficult. In short, the authors could find "no strategic justification for expensive weapon systems designed primarily for such challenging, perhaps impossible, tasks as locating and destroying a significant portion of Soviet relocatable targets and leadership targets."

This study again confirmed Des' previous insight that strategic doctrine is rarely driven by strategic concerns. The review of targeting during the Reagan years, the product of extensive interviews with the civilian and defence officials that developed United States strategic nuclear employment policies and plans, concluded that "in general, strategic concepts and doctrines have played very little role in the development of United States strategic force structures. Rather military technical innovation has been more determinate."[17]

STRATEGIC CULTURE TO THE FORE

Des recognised that American strategic thinking reflected its particular strategic culture; as noted, no other possessor of a strategic arsenal entertained the notion that a limited nuclear war could or should be fought. The end of the Cold War and the reduced salience of super-power dynamics allowed Des to focus more on the forces shaping strategic thinking in the Asia-Pacific region.[18] He laid out his conclusions in "Strategic Culture in the Asia-Pacific Region", a seminal article that explored the evolving regional security architecture at the dawn of the post-Cold War era.[19] He began by pointing out that most literature on strategic culture dealt almost entirely with United States and Soviet/Russian thinking, and there was little investigation of non-Western or even European thinking about strategic affairs. While acknowledging that "cultural factors will be less important than economic, technological and strategic developments in determining the new architecture of regional security", his article provides a long list of details that differentiate Asian and Western strategic culture (while conceding that Asia cannot be treated as a single entity, that some attributes rest more on myth than practical respect, and none are absolute or immutable). His key factors include:

> Longer time horizons and policy perspectives than those which characterize Western thinking and planning; reliance on bilateral rather than multilateral

approaches to conflict resolution and security planning; an Asian way of war which places less emphasis on the holding of territory, and greater emphasis on the exercise of other forms of military, economic, and cultural hegemony, commitment to the principles of non-interference in the internal affairs of other countries; styles of policy making which feature informality of structure and modalities, form and process as much as substance and outcome; consensus rather than majority rule and pragmatism rather than idealism; multidimensional or comprehensive approaches to security; and roles for the military that go beyond national defence to include politics, economic development and social affairs.[20]

This outlook has powerful implications. For those who may recall, the early 1990s was a period of considerable fever and fervour for the Asia-Pacific region. The region's economic dynamism was accelerating. The Soviet presence was being reduced, and this produced a parallel (but by no means as extensive) drawdown of United States forces in the region. Regional governments were embarking on a round of defence modernisation programs. These changes demanded a response. For Des, these "cultural traditions should be regarded as providing the raw materials for new political constructions".[21]

Those new constructs would be informal, pragmatic and evolutionary, focusing on dialogue rather than the creation of 'hard' new institutions. Patience would be the handmaiden of this process. He knew well how much patience would be required: in the late 1980s, Des was working to help set up Strategic Studies centres in various Southeast Asian capitals. And as his article came out, Des was putting those words into practice and helping to form the Council for Security Cooperation in the Asia-Pacific (CSCAP), a multilateral track two organisation that anticipated the ASEAN Regional Forum (ARF), and continues to serve as the premier nongovernmental forum for security discussions in the Asia-Pacific region. It promoted multilateralism at a time when few others saw its value and some openly and vigorously resisted the trend.[22] CSCAP is based on the principles articulated in Des' analysis and continues to this day to struggle to balance Asian and Western approaches to security.

"OUR FIRST OBLIGATION IS TO THE AUSTRALIAN PEOPLE"

A fourth and perhaps the most powerful and enduring theme in Des' work is a fierce nationalism. Indeed, while some have excoriated him for exposing secrets that undermined Australian security, Des is foremost an Australian nationalist whose work has struggled to identify the best way to secure his country's national interests. Critics typically point to his opposition to the Vietnam War (or the first Gulf War or the Iraq War or Australia's continuing involvement in Afghanistan) or his exposure of United States signals intelligence facilities in Australia as proof of his pacifism or "unreliability". Neither charge could be further from the truth. As for Vietnam, as Des explained in an interview, "it was not a war which I thought had any real strategic utility in terms of Australia's interests". While conceding that he has opposed all wars Australia has been involved with since Vietnam, his rationale for that stance is simple: "they have damaged our ability to defend ourselves…we've damaged our relations with our neighbours, Indonesia in particular…we've damaged our ability to influence our local strategic environment."[23] His calculus is simple: Des is an advocate of a "robust Australian defence posture … which would secure Australia in a very fundamental sense".[24]

The analytical foundation of this nationalism is evident in one of his first publications, *A Suitable Piece of Real Estate: American Installations in Australia*.[25] This study was the first exposé of the extensive United States intelligence facilities on Australian territory and his readiness to reveal the facilities, their purposes and the lack of Australian insight into and oversight of their operations infuriated many people, particularly in the Australian defence establishment. The inclusion of a number of classified memos in the book was especially galling for officials who in them appeared uninformed and dependent on the United States for basic information. To be fair, there are leaks and there are leaks. Some put actual lives in jeopardy. Others, the ones Des focused on, may have caused embarrassment but, more significantly, they also forced the establishment to concede and then deal with weaknesses. Des' real disdain was for the politicians, not the uniformed officers, although they were inclined to suspect anyone who seemed eager to reveal secrets, much less someone doing it while sporting a ponytail.

In his introduction to the book, Des refers to the "disdain" with which the Australian people and the country's national interests have been treated when it comes to those United States facilities. "Australia has simply been taken for granted by the United States."[26] While he is plainly offended by that treatment — "secrecy, evasion and deception" are his characterisation of United States policy — he is equally troubled by the way those facilities undermine Australian strategic interests. Of course, the relationship is not all bad for Australia. The presence of the facilities reinforces the United States commitment to Australia's defence; they help ensure a flow of intelligence from Washington to Canberra; they also provide information that was critical to arms control agreements between the United States and the Soviet Union, treaties that were in Australia's national interests. Besides, some of his best friends — hopefully us among them — are Americans. Again, it is United States policy and Canberra's apparent deference to Washington that most upset Des.

While there are positives associated with the facilities for Australia, Des did not hesitate to point out that those facilities also impose real costs on Australia. First, to take on the presumptive arguments in favour of the facilities: the United States commitment to Australia's defence also worked against the development of a self-reliant defence posture in the event that United States support was not forthcoming; while information flowed from the United States to Australia, Australian intelligence collection was "distorted" to satisfy United States global intelligence collection needs; and the independence of Australian foreign policy was limited, as when, for example, Indian Prime Minister Indira Gandhi dismissed one of Canberra's diplomatic initiatives because of the presence of United States facilities.[27]

In addition, the facilities make Australia a target in the event of a conflict since an adversary would likely try to eliminate them, especially given their vital role in information collection. Moreover, and perhaps most troubling, Des concluded their presence "constrains any independent Australian policy" and gives the United States "a dangerous degree of influence over Australian decision making".[28]

It is this last item that should be seen as the cornerstone of Des' work on strategy and strategic issues. The way that extraneous considerations or mistaken assumptions distort strategy is an enduring theme and we are all indebted to him for his relentless pursuit and exposure of the short-sighted thinking and short cuts that undermine rigour in this field. Policy makers must maintain a clear understanding of and focus on national interests if they are to serve their country.

The Australian government is not the only institution discomforted by his relentless digging. It was Des who shined light on the link between North Korea and Myanmar, not based on leaked memos but on field interviews with refugees. In truth, he is much more at home and comfortable (not to mention more suitably dressed) when he is out in the field, searching for new facts and insights that would otherwise elude not only the general public but even the otherwise well-informed. *A Suitable Piece of Real Estate* was published to spark an informed public debate on a controversial but critical subject. That purpose has animated all of Des' work — a conscious desire to serve the Australian people, to be critical and frame and develop alternatives that better his country and protect its national interests.

Notes

1. Desmond Ball, interview by Nicholas Farrelly, *The Australian National University Mentor Interview Series*, transcript, 18 May 2011, p. 8.
2. Ibid.
3. Desmond Ball, *Politics and Force Levels: The Strategic Missile Program of the Kennedy Administration* (Berkeley: University of California Press, 1980), p. 269.
4. Ibid., p. 265.
5. Ibid., p. 278.
6. Desmond Ball, "Nuclear War at Sea", *International Security* 10, no. 3 (Winter 1985-86): 3-31.
7. Desmond Ball, "Toward a Critique of Strategic Nuclear Targeting", in *Strategic Nuclear Targeting*, edited by Jeffrey Richelson and Desmond Ball (Cornell: Cornell University Press, 1986), p. 16.
8. Ibid.
9. For example: Desmond Ball, "Research Note: Soviet ICBM Deployment", *Survival* 22, no. 4 (July/August 1980): 167–70.
10. Ibid., p. 169.
11. Ibid., p. 170.
12. Ball, "Toward a Critique of Strategic Nuclear Targeting", p. 19.
13. Ibid. This theme is taken up later in this review.
14. Ibid., p. 31.
15. Desmond Ball and Robert C. Toth, "Revising the SIOP: Taking War-Fighting to Dangerous Extremes", *International Security* 14, no. 4 (Spring, 1990): 65–92.
16. Ibid., p. 66.
17. Ibid., p. 86.
18. Of course, no Australian strategist worthy of the name can ignore developments close to home and Des was no exception; he conducted extensive fieldwork throughout the Asia-Pacific region starting in the late 1970s.
19. Desmond Ball, "Strategic Culture in the Asia-Pacific Region", *Security Studies* 3, no. 1 (Spring 1993): 44–74.
20. Ibid., pp. 46–47.
21. Ibid., p. 68.

22. The authors are also participants in CSCAP; Cossa worked with Des to establish CSCAP, meeting in Lombok in December 1993 to draft its charter.
23. Desmond Ball, interview with Nicholas Farrelly, 18 May 2011, p. 11.
24. Ibid.
25. Desmond Ball, *A Suitable Piece of Real Estate: American Installations in Australia* (Sydney: Hale and Iremonger, 1980).
26. Ibid., p. 16.
27. Ibid., pp. 150, 151, 147.
28. Ibid.

5

SHINING A LIGHT ON THE WORLD'S EAVESDROPPERS

Jeffrey T. Richelson

There are assorted ways to describe the writings of Desmond Ball with respect to signals intelligence. One is to note the volume or types of publications. Even without including working papers, many of which became the basis for articles or book chapters, an examination of Ball's vita yields evidence of over thirty books, monographs, articles, and book chapters explicitly focusing on signals intelligence. In addition, there are a number of works — for example, *A Suitable Piece of Real Estate, The Ties that Bind,* or *The Intelligence War in the Gulf* — in which a discussion of signals intelligence activities is a key element.

An alternative, somewhat hybrid approach, is to focus on the targets of his research as well as some other common aspects of his output. One can identify a number of works that might be grouped under "SIGINT History" — that is, signals intelligence activities during World War II or during the early Cold War. A second group is the one in which Soviet/Russian intelligence activities were the focus. In addition, there is his work concerning various aspects of UKUSA SIGINT operations. Then there are two variants of what might be called the "SIGINT in…" effort

— one of which focuses solely on the signals intelligence organisations and activities of the target nation, and another which concerns both allied and host country SIGINT efforts.

Those do not exhaust the categories that can be used to describe his SIGINT research. Another group of writings reflect the expansion of the SIGINT field to include information warfare and, now, cyberwar. Finally, there are those works concerning relatively contemporary events that might be grouped under the heading "SIGINT in Action". The books, articles, and other publications that fall in that category involve the collection of SIGINT (usually, communications intelligence) in support of specific military activities or to provide intelligence to political leaders.

SIGINT HISTORY

Among Ball's major works in the "SIGINT History" category is one that he co-authored with David Horner. Published in 1998, *Breaking the Codes: Australia's KGB Network, 1944–1950* is a significant addition to the literature on Soviet World War and early Cold War espionage networks stimulated by the VENONA declassification. Relying, *inter alia*, on VENONA material as well as declassified Australian Security Intelligence Organisation (ASIO) documents, Ball and Horner describe the role that signals intelligence, as well as the assistance of the British Security Service, had in unravelling Soviet intelligence activities in Australia during the last years of the Second World War and the beginning of the Cold War.[1]

Specifically, the authors discuss a group of about ten individuals "all of whom were members of the Communist Party of Australia or close acquaintances of communists", who provided the Soviet state security service with "information about domestic Australian political matters, foreign policy, and the structure and activities of the Australian wartime Security Service". In addition, they provided American and British documents concerning post-war strategic planning that the British had provided to Australia.

Breaking the Codes was not Des Ball's first work relating to the history of SIGINT. In 1978, *Australian Outlook* published his article on "Allied Intelligence Cooperation Involving Australia During World War II". While the article deals in part with the Allied Intelligence Bureau, as well as British special operations and human intelligence operations directed from Australia, the primary focus of the article is on Australia's role in signals intelligence. Ball notes how such operations were one of the antecedents of the post-war UKUSA SIGINT alliance.

"Allied Intelligence Cooperation," also identifies "a number of general points which remain to be made concerning allied radio intelligence activities during this period". The discussion focuses on the value of SIGINT in the war, and particularly in the Pacific theatre. Ball also argues that much of the effectiveness of Allied SIGINT activity was the product of the cooperative arrangements established in 1940-1941, but that cooperation was rarely complete. He also focused on two points relevant to Australia and the UKUSA relationship in the post-war era — intelligence sites as potential enemy targets as well as the aspects of SIGINT that require secrecy and the aspects where secrecy is likely to be counterproductive. He concludes by proposing "some general guidelines for Australian policy with regard to the collection and assessment of electronic intelligence" — which include a completely independent Australian assessment capability, Australian operational control of intercept stations on Australian soil, and safeguards to prevent Allied monitoring of Australian communications.[2]

A more recent contribution focuses not on Australia, but New Zealand. Co-authored with Cliff Lord and Meredith Thatcher, *Invaluable Service: The secret history of New Zealand's signals intelligence (SIGINT) during Two World Wars*, examines the origins of New Zealand SIGINT activities, the collection activities at a variety of stations, New Zealand SIGINT in Fiji, the monitoring of enemy radio broadcasts, and New Zealand Army SIGINT activities.[3]

SOVIET AND RUSSIAN SIGINT

Ball's production with regard to Soviet and Russian SIGINT can be tracked across several decades and a multitude of formats, including monographs, articles in scholarly journals, and book chapters. Monographs on Soviet SIGINT include an overview, *Soviet Signals Intelligence (SIGINT)*, published in 1989, as well as *Soviet Signals Intelligence (SIGINT): Intercepting Satellite Communications* (1989), and *Soviet SIGINT: Hawaii Operation* (1991). All were published as part of the Canberra Papers on Strategy and Defence series.[4]

As the title *Soviet Signals Intelligence (SIGINT)* would suggest, the monograph is an overview of the Soviet effort. Over approximately 150 pages, the reader is informed of Soviet SIGINT organisations, as well as the capabilities of Soviet ground stations, diplomatic and trade establishments, vehicular systems, naval systems, aerial platforms, and satellites for intercepting signals of interest.

The monograph on intercepting satellite communications, approximately 130 pages, focused on the extensive Soviet effort in targeting diplomatic, military, and civilian communications transmitted via satellite. After treating the subject of the acquisition of signals from communications satellites, and the interception of defence and intelligence satellite communications, the author then turns to three different approaches the Soviets used to intercept such communications. The shorter *Hawaii Operation* monograph, as its title suggests, concerns one geographic target of the Soviet SIGINT effort. It examined the expansion of Soviet efforts against that target, the signals of interest, the purposes of monitoring specific signals (for example, monitoring national/strategic communications or monitoring intelligence operations), and possible means for countering that effort.

UKUSA SIGINT

It was in his 1978 *Australian Outlook* article that, I believe, Des first explored the UKUSA SIGINT relationship. At the time, that relationship's very existence was neither confirmed nor denied — as indicated by a 1982 letter from the National Security Agency in response to a Freedom of Information Act request for documents pertaining to its formation. But that did not prevent his co-authorship of *The Ties that Bind: Intelligence Cooperation between the UKUSA Countries — the United Kingdom, the United States of America, Canada, Australia and New Zealand*.

The book covered more than the SIGINT relationship between those countries — examining their intelligence communities, liaison, discord, and the treatment of dissent, among other topics. But it was the SIGINT relationship that was the core of the book. Beyond the two chapters on collection (8 and 9, covering over 50 pages), which examined the multitude of facilities and systems used to gather the targeted signals other portions of the book — including those on organisation, exchange, and discord — also dealt with aspects of the allied SIGINT effort.

That book was certainly noticed by various authorities, and came up in the legal effort directed against Peter Wright and the publication of *Spycatcher*. Another work dealing with the allied SIGINT effort that was noticed by the authorities was *Pine Gap: Australia and the US geostationary signals intelligence satellite program*.[5] The Air Force Space Command certainly took note, describing the work in its 1988 history as "yet another study of the US-Australian space-related installations in the country authored by perennial critic Desmond Ball" — a comment that suggests they did not notice the book's support for maintenance of the facility.[6]

Four of the topics covered by *Pine Gap* included: Pine Gap, the National Reconnaissance Office and the CIA, the development of American geostationary signals intelligence systems such as RHYOLITE and ORION, geostationary signals intelligence capabilities and missions, and the link between espionage and arms control verification. But the centrepiece of the book is the fifth topic examined — the Pine Gap ground station. The chapter is about history and technology. Based on interviews, parliamentary and other Australian documents, and open source reports, it examines how Pine Gap came to be, the details of the station from the building of radomes over the years to its internal organisation, as well as the issue of Australian sovereignty and access.[7]

Australian and allied SIGINT was also the subject of another Desmond Ball product published in 1988 — the monograph *Australia's Secret Space Programs*.[8] The space programs are space programs in the sense that they are Australian/allied programs involved in intercepting satellite communications from a variety of sites. Three chapters involve projects designated Kittiwake, Larswood, and Sparrow. What readers learned about in those chapters are details of the facilities in Hong Kong; Shoal Bay, Northern Territory; and Watsonia Barracks, near Melbourne and their missions — the interception of Chinese and Indonesian satellite communications and the provision of communications links for sites in Australia and between Australia and Ft. Meade, Maryland.

Another chapter concerns the Australian Defence Signals Directorate (DSD) satellite signals intelligence station in Western Australia, near Geraldton — a part of what was known as the ECHELON network. While the Australian government acknowledged the existence of the station, it was less forthcoming about its mission. In *Australia's Secret Space Programs*, Ball tries to provide some answers, providing a four-page table listing all the geostationary satellites within the purview of the dishes at Geraldton.

Allied SIGINT operations in Hong Kong was also subject of another Ball product — a July 1996 article in *Intelligence and National Security* — "Over and Out: Signals Intelligence in Hong Kong". As is often the case in his work, Des traces the origins of the SIGINT effort to World War II and then its development in subsequent years. Subsequently, the article focuses on U.S. SIGINT operations, problems at Britain's Little Sai Wan station, its performance during the Chinese invasion of Vietnam, Project Kittiwake, and several other sites.[9]

SIGINT IN....

For almost two decades Des has been producing studies of foreign signals intelligence organisations and operations in Asia. The July 1995 issue of *Intelligence and National Security*, for instance, carried his article on "Signals Intelligence in India".[10] The essence of the article is its focus on the Indian SIGINT establishment (twelve distinct organisations) and their collection activities. That is followed by an assessment of the effectiveness of those activities — including those directed at Pakistan, Sri Lanka, and Kashmir — as well as the treatment of a number of other issues concerning Indian SIGINT, including cost-effectiveness and politicisation.

In several other articles, published in *Jane's Intelligence Review*, Ball has reported on the product of his research on the SIGINT efforts of North Korea, Taiwan, Burma, and China.[11] Aside from covering SIGINT in a particular part of the world what they have in common is their approach. Each identifies the relevant intelligence organisations in each nation as well as discussing the purposes of their activities and their collection operations.

Further work on SIGINT in the Asian area was contained in articles in *Strategic Analysis*. The May 1995 issue included "Signals Intelligence (SIGINT) in Pakistan",[12] which covered origins, as well as the U.S. connection (particularly the Bada Bier station and airborne collection) — but focused mainly on Pakistan's own SIGINT organisation, capabilities, and operations as well as its value to Pakistan during the Soviet intervention in Afghanistan. Later that year, the November issue, carried "Signals Intelligence (SIGINT) in Sri Lanka".[13]

At least two further works that begin with 'Signals Intelligence [or SIGINT] in' should be mentioned. One of those works, published in 1993, focuses on the Asia-Pacific Region.[14] In approximately 100 pages Des examines developments involving key players in the region — including both organisation and operations. Specifically, American and Russian SIGINT are each the subject of a chapter and in the case of the latter, one topic is the change that had taken place in the Russian effort as a result of the collapse of the Soviet Union. Another chapter focuses on the SIGINT efforts of a number of Asian states — China, Japan, South Korea, Singapore,

Thailand, Australia, New Zealand, India, and Pakistan. Beyond examining organisation and capabilities the article explores characteristics of the regional SIGINT effort — including the increasing attention to collection of economic and commercial information, increasing regional self-reliance, the monitoring of regional conflict, and maritime surveillance.

The other is a 1995 monograph, *Signals Intelligence (SIGINT) in South Korea*.[15] The heart of the monograph is about the United States' effort there — from its history, to the ground stations and deployments, to advanced battlefield systems. The reader is informed of the variety of units and sites that the U.S. has operated in the south for decades, as well as the capabilities of assorted collection equipment — both ground and airborne.

INFORMATION WARFARE AND CYBERWAR

Signals intelligence is closely related, but not identical to two other disciplines — electronic warfare and cyber-warfare. The electronic intelligence component of signals intelligence, particularly the identification and characterisation of radar systems, can support electronic warfare operations — which can include meaconing, intrusion, jamming, and interference (MIJI) directed against a variety of electronic systems, including radars and aircraft. Some cyberwar activities, such as the Stuxnet virus, may be more closely related to covert action than SIGINT. But other aspects of cyber-warfare include activities that either are similar to electronic warfare (the interruption of computer networks, including the Internet) or signals intelligence (intrusion into computers to gather data — only rather than 'data in motion' the target is "data at rest").

In one very detailed paper in 2002 and 2003, Ball examined the triad of signals intelligence, electronic warfare, and cyber-warfare. Here his focus was on China. The paper explored the evolution of the People Republic's capabilities in all three areas, and then examined, in detail, its SIGINT capabilities — its ground stations, satellite communications intercept operations, its space, airborne (manned and unmanned), and naval intercept platforms. He then turned to its electronic warfare capabilities, also providing a detailed breakdown of the various platforms employed, before turning to Chinese cyber-warfare — a subject in which interest and concern has grown in recent years.[16]

The paper explores Chinese policy, capabilities, and activities — including a variety of Chinese hacker attacks on foreign (including Taiwanese) computer networks. The concluding section contains an assessment of China's information warfare capabilities — asking the question whether China could "be expected to achieve 'information superiority' over its potential adversaries" in large-scale or intensive military operations? Des argues that China would possess inferior information warfare capabilities for decades and to be effective in a conflict they would have to be employed in a pre-emptive manner.[17]

SIGINT IN ACTION

The purpose of developing and deploying intelligence capabilities is to provide warning of hostilities, an accurate portrayal of foreign developments and capabilities, and to support policymakers and those who implement policy. Three particularly interesting works by Ball examine the collection, analysis, and use (or non-use) of intelligence (including signals intelligence) with regard to countries of significant interest to Australian policy-makers.

Burmese SIGINT is the subject of a 1998 book Des authored for Bangkok's White Lotus Press — *Burma's Military Secrets: Signals Intelligence (SIGINT) from 1941 to Cyber Warfare*. A review of the book that appeared in the CIA's *Studies in Intelligence* journal, described Des as "a widely respected observer of Southeast Asian political developments and a long-time commentator on intelligence". The reviewer notes that the book "makes its real contribution to Burma studies in its blow-by-blow account of the *Tatmadaw's* (Burmese Army) successful siege of the insurgent Karen National Union (KNU) headquarters ... in January–February 1995".[18] That account (in chapter 8) involves a description of the role of communications intercepts in the fighting.[19]

Two studies focus on Indonesia and East Timor. One study focuses on events from 1975, when Indonesia invaded East Timor. As Des, and co-author Hamish McDonald, discuss in *Death in Balibo, Lies in Canberra*, the Australian Defence Signals Directorate (DSD), along with other intelligence organisations, particularly the Australian Secret Intelligence Service (ASIS), monitored Indonesia's preparations for its invasion and DSD obtained evidence that Indonesia's armed forces had murdered five Australian-based journalists at Balibo on 16 October 1975.[20]

A key chapter in the book does more than simply reveal the existence of an intercept disclosing the Indonesian complicity in the journalists' deaths. It is a case study of "SIGINT in Action" — SIGINT collection, dissemination (or non-dissemination), analysis, the use (or non-use) of the data by policy-makers, and the consequences. *Death in Balibo* reveals a key intercept that provided warning of Indonesian intentions to eliminate the journalists, where it was intercepted (Shoal Bay), that it was processed by the DSD in Melbourne five hours before the Indonesian attack, and that it was apparently withheld from intelligence analysts with the Joint Intelligence Organisation's Office of Current Intelligence.[21]

The authors write that there was time "for the Australian government to have made an effort to save the newsmen. It allowed 12 hours, half a day, before the final Indonesian advance into Balibo during which the newsmen were killed". The certain consequence of the failure to confront the Indonesians was summarised in another intercepted cable, which noted, "Among the dead are four [sic] white men," and asked, "What are we going to do with the bodies?"[22]

The book also provides a specific case study of the reluctance to reveal the product of SIGINT collection for fear of target countermeasures — even when continued secrecy can result in the deaths of innocents. The Balibo case is particularly noteworthy because, according to the authors, the decision to withhold the intercept was made *within* DSD, and not by elected leaders. The politicians were informed of the intercepts that revealed the deaths, but not of the ones warning of the journalists' peril.[23]

More recent developments concerning Indonesia and East Timor — those of 1999 — were the focus of "Silent Witness: Australian Intelligence and East Timor", an article first published in 2001 and subsequently updated.[24] Key elements of the study are the intercepts of Indonesian armed forces communications by the DSD, what those intercepts revealed about Indonesian attempts to prevent East Timor from achieving independence, and the extent to which Australian officials did their best to ignore the secret intelligence.

APPRECIATION

One can note, as clear from the discussion above, that Ball's scholarship on the subject of signals intelligence is extensive — indeed, his SIGINT publications would constitute a good career in themselves. It can also be observed that those publications are diverse with respect to the periods of time covered — from World War II to the 1970s to today — and also range over a wide number of countries.

It is also clear that they are based on extensive research. In his *Mentors* interview with Nicholas Farrelly for the Australian National University, Des talks of his extensive collection of material for future work,[25] evident in his SIGINT scholarship. To take one example, his 52-page "Information Warfare in Asia" paper contains 188 footnotes and, it would seem, 250–300 different sources. But beyond discussing the breadth and depth of his research there are several, some related, even more important aspects. One is an interest in, and a willingness, to explore areas of national security activities, whether allied or strictly Australian, that decades ago were, to a great extent, off-limits to scholars and academics. Those areas include nuclear targeting and intelligence collection, particularly SIGINT. Des has been one of the pioneers, to put it mildly, in moving the detailed study of modern-day SIGINT into the academic and scholarly communities.

Moving beyond generalities and the study of just historical cases, Des' SIGINT research focuses on providing details of a multitude of nations' SIGINT organisations and their collection systems — including space, air, ground, naval, and submarine. Readers learn the technical details, the capabilities, and, to the extent feasible, the targets of these collection systems. And as noted above, at times, they also learn of what intelligence has been produced by those systems and how it has been (or not been) employed.

This detail is a product of more than an "inside-baseball" interest in the workings of Australian or allied intelligence. It also reflects an appreciation that intelligence activity is an integral part of national security, and thus understanding intelligence capabilities and alliances is an integral part of assessing national security policies — past and present. Further, there is also, I am sure, the belief that understanding the *details* of intelligence organisations, capabilities, and alliances are necessary for outside experts (including watchdogs) or concerned citizens to make informed judgments about government actions in the intelligence and national security area. Thus, knowing that Pine Gap is a ground station for United States geosynchronous SIGINT satellites and what types of targets those satellites gather intelligence on, is crucial to evaluating the significance of Pine Gap (and for Australians for judging the desirability of having the facility on Australian territory). Thus, in his introduction to *A Suitable Piece of Real Estate*, Des writes "the choices which the Australian public must make with regard to the installations, and the conditions which should be imposed upon their operations, must be the product of informed public debate. This book is a contribution to that debate".[26]

And, understanding the activities of the KGB and GRU SIGINT efforts in Canberra, Melbourne, and elsewhere is crucial to deciding and how much of a threat those efforts represent and asking about how effectively they are being neutralised.

There are two further implications of such a view that is apparent from Ball's SIGINT research. One is that while extensive research into the published literature is a part of the process of scholarship, there is also a need to be an 'investigative scholar' — which can involve either interviewing confidential sources with special knowledge or obtaining documents that government officials have stamped "Secret" and want to keep from one's hands. Thus, his work on Pine Gap has been aided by interviews with confidential sources, while in his *Mentors* interview Des notes that in *A Suitable Piece of Real Estate* "I go public with a lot of classified memos which show the ignorance of the government" about some of the activities at U.S. facilities in Australia.[27]

Of course, a willingness to engage in such investigative scholarship, and publish material that government officials preferred to remain confidential, requires a willingness to be the target of ire from intelligence and government officials. And Des has noted, that "Sir Arthur Tange, Head of the Department of Defence at the time that I was head of [the Strategic and Defence Studies Centre], took a vehement dislike to me" and that there were those in the "Australian intelligence community ... who hated me".[28]

Possibly, they have changed their minds — or hate Des even more for the profound impact he apparently has had on reducing secrecy about Australian intelligence, the United States-Australian intelligence relationship, and American facilities in the country. Of course, there are a number of reasons why secrecy has declined over the years in all these regards and change did not come overnight — some aspects of official acknowledgment, such as the National Reconnaissance Office presence at Pine Gap or the release of documents concerning the UKUSA agreement — have taken over two decades since Ball first wrote about those topics.[29] But it would be difficult to believe that the continued discussion of these topics in open sources and the lack of detrimental consequences to American and Australian intelligence capabilities did not help make it easier for those in favour of disclosure, both inside and outside the respective government, to chip away at the secrecy that was an impediment to public understanding about this crucial area of national security activities.

Notes

1. Desmond Ball and David Horner, *Breaking the Codes: The KGB's Network in Australia, 1944–1950* (Sydney: Allen and Unwin, 2000). Other works based substantially on VENONA material include; John Earl Haynes and Harvey Klehr, *Venona: Decoding Soviet Espionage in America* (New Haven: Yale University Press, 1999); and Nigel West, *Venona: The Greatest Secret of the Cold War* (Chicago: Trafalgar Square, 2001).
2. Desmond Ball, "Allied Intelligence Cooperation Involving Australia During World War II", *Australian Outlook* 32, no. 2 (December 1978): 299–319.
3. Desmond Ball, Cliff Lord and Meredith Thatcher, eds., *Invaluable Service: The Secret History of New Zealand's signals intelligence (SIGINT) during Two World Wars* (Auckland: Resource Books Ltd, 2011).
4. Desmond Ball, *Soviet Signals Intelligence (SIGINT)*, Canberra Papers on Strategy and Defence no. 47 (Canberra: Strategic and Defence Studies Centre, Australian National University, 1989); *Soviet Signals Intelligence (SIGINT): Intercepting Satellite Communications*, Canberra Papers on Strategy and Defence no. 53 (Canberra: Strategic and Defence Studies Centre, Australian National University, 1989); *Soviet SIGINT: Hawaii Operation*, Canberra Papers on Strategy and Defence no. 80 (Canberra: Strategic and Defence Studies Centre, Australian National University, 1991).
5. Desmond Ball, *Pine Gap: Australia and the US geostationary signals intelligence satellite program* (Sydney: Allen and Unwin, 1988).
6. United States Air Force Space Command, *History of Air Force Space Command, January – December 1988* (Peterson AFB: AFSPACECOM, n.d.): p. 34.
7. Ball, *Pine Gap*, pp. 55–82.
8. Desmond Ball, *Australia's Secret Space Programs* (Canberra: Australian National University, Strategic and Defence Studies Centre, 1988).
9. Desmond Ball, "Over and Out: Signals Intelligence in Hong Kong", in *Intelligence and National Security* 11, no. 3 (July 1996): 62.
10. Desmond Ball, "Signals Intelligence in India", *Intelligence and National Security* 10, no. 3 (July 1995): 377–407.
11. Desmond Ball, "Signals intelligence in North Korea," *Jane's Intelligence Review* 8, no. 1 (January 1996): 28–33; "SIGINT strengths form a vital part of Burma's military muscle", *Jane's Intelligence Review* 10, no. 3 (March 1998): 35–41; "Signals intelligence in Taiwan", *Jane's Intelligence Review* 11, no. 1 (November 1995): 506–10; "Signals Intelligence in China", *Jane's Intelligence Review* 7, no. 8 (August 1995): 365–70.
12. Desmond Ball, "Signals intelligence (SIGINT) in Pakistan", *Strategic Analysis* 18, no. 2 (May 1995): 195–214.
13. Desmond Ball, "Signals intelligence (SIGINT) in Sri Lanka", *Strategic Analysis* 18, no. 8 (November 1995): 1077–1108.

14. Desmond Ball, *Signals Intelligence in the Post-Cold War Era: Developments in the Asia-Pacific Region* (Singapore: Institute of Southeast Asian Studies, 1993).
15. Desmond Ball, *Signals Intelligence (SIGINT) in South Korea*, (Canberra: Strategic and Defence Studies Centre, Australian National University, 1995).
16. For example: United States-China Economic and Security Review Commission, *Occupying the Information High Ground: Chinese Capabilities for Computer Network Operations and Cyber Espionage*, 7 March 2012.
17. Desmond Ball, "China and Information Warfare (IW): Signals Intelligence (SIGINT), Electronic Warfare (EW) and Cyber-Warfare", paper prepared for ASC '03: Asian and Chinese Security Issues in the Decade 2001–2011, New Delhi, 25–29 January 2003.
18. Jon A. Wiant, "Burma's Military Secrets: Signals Intelligence (SIGINT) from 1941 to Cyber Warfare", *Studies in Intelligence* 44, no. 1 (Spring 2000): 95–96.
19. Other chapters, in addition to the ones concerning World War II, include examination of Burma's SIGINT operations, SIGINT and the Insurgents, Kuomintang SIGINT Operations in Burma, Russian and Chinese SIGINT related to Burma, Burma as a SIGINT Target, and SIGINT in Conflict.
20. Desmond Ball and Hamish McDonald, *Death in Balibo, Lies in Canberra* (Sydney: Allen and Unwin, 2000).
21. Ibid., pp. 115–17.
22. Ibid., p. 117.
23. Ibid., pp. 119–20. The collection and use of SIGINT with regard to other aspects of Australian reaction to Indonesia's military actions in East Timor during that time are discussed elsewhere in the book, including an appendix "Signals Intelligence After Balibo".
24. Desmond Ball, "Silent Witness: Australian Intelligence and East Timor", *Pacific Review* 14, no. 1 (March 2001): 35–62. The article was subsequently updated.
25. Desmond Ball, interview by Nicholas Farrelly, *The Australian National University Mentor Interview Series*, transcript, 18 May 2011, p. 22.
26. Desmond Ball, *A Suitable Piece of Real Estate: American installations in Australia* (Sydney: Hale and Iremonger, 1980), p. 17.
27. Ibid., p. 14.
28. Ibid.
29. Scott F. Large, Director, National Reconnaissance Office, Memorandum, Subject: Declassification of the "Fact of" National Reconnaissance Mission Ground Stations and Presence Overseas, 24 September 2008, Freedom of Information Act Release.

6

CONTROLLING NUCLEAR WAR

Robert Ayson

Desmond Ball made his name as an internationally recognised scholar with an impressive body of work on aspects of American nuclear strategy. This had its origins in his graduate studies at the Australian National University (ANU) in the late 1960s and early 1970s. He had first undertaken a study of ballistic missile defence for his Honours thesis in the Faculty of Arts, drafts of which he had shown to a recently arrived Professor of International Relations, Hedley Bull,[1] who had come to the ANU from the London School of Economics via a two years stint as Director of the Wilson government's Arms Control and Disarmament Research Unit (ACDRU) at the Foreign Office. With his impeccable contacts in the United States strategic studies community, Bull was a demanding but ideal lead supervisor for Ball's subsequent Ph.D. thesis on the Kennedy administration's strategic missile program. Geoffrey Jukes, an authority on Soviet forces and a former ACDRU colleague of Bull's, and Arthur Lee Burns, one of the only Australians to have published work on nuclear strategy in American journals, were also on Ball's panel in the Research School of Pacific Studies.

That this research was the platform for Ball's outstanding career in strategic studies is confirmed by the content of the academic works he was writing at the very height of his career. For me that apex comes in

1980 and 1981, some eight years after the completion of Ball's Ph.D., a period of intense intellectual productivity represented by three significant pieces of writing. While these only represent a small fraction in numerical terms of Des Ball's mountainous output, they are clear demonstrations of his scholarship at its most powerful and influential. The first was the extensively revised and extended version of Ball's Ph.D. thesis, which was published by the University of California Press in 1980 under the title *Politics and Force Levels*.[2] The second was a short but significant article on counterforce which first appeared in the journal of the American arms control community, *Arms Control Today* and reprinted elsewhere in the 1980s.[3] And the third is a very widely cited Adelphi Paper on the dismal prospects of controlling a nuclear war once it had begun, published in London by the prestigious International Institute for Strategic Studies (IISS) in 1981.[4] As I will seek to show in this chapter, some of the thematic connections between these three pieces of writing tell us a great deal about the issues and themes which preoccupied Ball in the first two decades of his academic career.

POLITICS AND FORCE LEVELS

A reader of *Politics and Force Levels* who knows anything about Ball's work will not be surprised to see the characteristic emphasis on the empirical details of the development of weapons systems. As occurs with a good deal of his extensive writing on America's nuclear forces, one comes away with a close knowledge of force numbers, force structure options chosen and foreclosed, and the targeting plans which explain how the Kennedy administration's rapidly expanding nuclear arsenal would have been used had a nuclear war with the Soviet Union began. But there is even more. Today's reader might in fact be a little taken aback by Ball's interest in positioning his work in the context of rival *theoretical* explanations for foreign policy decisions. I do not think many of the students who have listened to Des speak about his favourite contemporary subjects, including Thailand-Burma border relations or military applications of satellites, would quite take him for a scholar engaged directly in such matters. But as he explained in the preface to his first of many books to come:

> This study is intended to have both theoretical and policy import. It is a contribution to the current debate among students of national security policy as to how to explain foreign and defense policy decisions and events.[5]

It is not evident that a great deal of Ball's subsequent work has been similarly designed. Nor as an established scholar has he often felt the need to cite the theoretical literature on the particular subject he is writing about. But in this earlier case he had a particular part of that debate he wished to target, and that was the bureaucratic politics model which was most famously on show in Graham Allison's widely read *Essence of Decision*. Soon after the completion of his Ph.D., Ball had devoted his first article in an academic journal to criticise that model of thinking which "credits executive agencies and bureaucrats with virtually total control over the development of American policy abroad"[6] and he had only become less fond of it in the ensuing years. As he observed in *Politics and Force Levels*:

> Earlier drafts of the work argued along lines similar to that which has since become publicly identified with the "bureaucratic politics" school of, in particular, Graham Allison and Morton Halperin. The present argument does not accept so crude a bureaucratic determinism. Rather, it sees the decision-making process as complex, the key relationships being those between McNamara and Kennedy, and between them and the military and Congress.[7]

The complexity of those influences on policy comes through clearly in the book whose author is critical of just about every explanation which had been proffered for the massive nuclear build-up put in place by Kennedy, his Defense Secretary Robert McNamara and their advisors. These explanations included the widely held view that American intelligence estimates (or misestimates) of the infamous missile gap favouring the Soviet Union were responsible for the early 1960s build-up. Ball's contending view is right there in the title: the importance of politics in shaping force levels, and by the former he meant the domestic political processes, which shaped American government decisions. As Ball explains in his conclusion to the book:

> All of the missile decisions of the Kennedy-McNamara Administration, throughout the years of the missile build-up (1961–64) were, in some senses at least, political. In other words, the outcomes of the decision-making process were not wholly or solely the results of objective and systematic analyses, but rather resulted from a reconciliation both of a diversity of values and goals and of alternative means and policies, with the actual outcomes reflecting, more than anything else, the relative power of the participating groups.[8]

Ball's argument that the empirical reality of America's nuclear force development was not a direct reflection of "objective and systematic analyses" offers an especially important insight to his way of thinking about strategic questions, or more particularly to the types of strategic questions which Des feels are important for scholars to ask. In my own interactions with Des I have rarely seen him get excited (or even that interested) about statements of strategic objectives or the development of strategic concepts. About these he is generally dismissive. But he has forever been interested in what was going on in the development and positioning of forces, in the details of command and control systems, and in the hardware which intelligence gathering relied on, and with the limits to all of these systems. And in many cases the only way to find this information was to go there. Anyone doubting this commitment to on-the-spot research should note that in his curriculum vitae Des lists more than 150 field work episodes he has been involved in, beginning with eight months in the United States as part of his Ph.D. research in 1970. The majority of this first foray Ball spent as Visiting Scholar with Columbia University's Institute of War and Peace, an arrangement made possible due to Hedley Bull's contacts with Warner Schilling and W. T. R. Fox.[9]

Politics and Force Levels offers one reason for Ball's doubts about the real value of big theoretical arguments and the common practice amongst academics to look at what states say rather than what they do (something which I suspect Ball regards as lazy scholarship in which case I plead guilty on many and various occasions). "U.S. strategic policy" during the early 1960s, he writes in one chapter, "was continually in a state of flux…and never stood long enough to provide a precise base for determining the strategic-forces requirement. Strategic policy never served as a direct criterion for deciding U.S. missile numbers".[10]

It is abundantly clear in *Politics and Force Levels* that the big ideas of strategic policy and academic theory are much less important to the author than the myriad specific decisions about what forces and other systems have been acquired and how they might be employed. This is revealed in the close attention given to America's nuclear targeting plans. A particular interest here for Ball was the extent to which the evolving Single Integrated Operational Plan (or SIOP) revealed preferences for attacks on enemy nuclear forces (counterforce strikes) and what this told us about the tendency towards notions of fighting a nuclear war. Here Ball was getting to the heart of some big questions. Was it sensible or fanciful to think of nuclear strategy in terms of a series of discrete options (reflected in specific packets of forces and targets), which allowed decision-makers the (illusory) possibility of controlled escalation? Was it rational or simply dangerous to limit the damage an opposing force could threaten by preparing to conduct (first) strikes on their forces? And in this book is the judgment that the United States had sunk such massive policy costs in a rapidly expanding nuclear arsenal that the force structure and targeting plan was more likely to tell us about what the country would really do in a serious crisis and conflict than the pull-me-push-you public explanations of what was intended: "it is apparent", Ball argues, "that strategic policy provided a rationalization for the missile decisions"[11] that were being, or already had been, made.

THE COUNTERFORCE TENDENCY

Ball's first book, published the same year (1980) as his first monograph on the joint facilities in Australia,[12] ran to over 300-tightly argued pages. But what we might regard as the second very significant international publication on the nuclear strategy theme from that period consisted of just nine pages of argument. Ball's short essay on counterforce is a concentrated extract of the distinctive and elsewhere extremely detailed observations (and criticisms) that he was making about contemporary nuclear strategy. The first of these comes in the very opening passage when Ball explains to his readers that:

> US strategic nuclear policy can usefully be divided into several different facets, of which the most important are declaratory and action policy. Declaratory policy is the set of public pronouncements made by the President, the Secretary of Defense or sometimes other senior Administration officials regarding the requirements of deterrence, targeting policy, and strategic doctrine. Action policy, on the other hand, comprises the actual war-fighting strategy that the United States would adopt in a nuclear exchange.[13]

This was perhaps the most careful and theoretical refinement of Ball's argument that things are often not what they are made out to be. You cannot know strategy if you simply listen to what governments *say* they are doing. You need to know what they are doing and intend to do. This means probing more deeply, almost making the job of a scholar akin to an educated investigative journalist, blowing the lid on things governments would rather we did not know. As Ball continues in this opening section to the short article, the action policy was revealed not in the public statements of Presidents and others (such as Robert McNamara's famous "no-cities" speech at Ann Arbor which Des had covered in his first book). It was instead revealed in private and often classified documents such as memoranda from the President, the Secretary of Defense's Nuclear Weapons Employment Policy (NUWEP) and the SIOP in its various forms. These would be the main sources for so much of Ball's writing on nuclear strategy for years to come, including a series of articles in *International Security*,[14] the leading American journal on strategic issues.

In another one of these earlier studies, Ball admitted to a set of four types of policy: as well as declaratory and action policy, there was the force development policy which laid down what nuclear systems would be acquired, and the arms control policy which explained where restraints on some of this development might be discussed and agreed.[15] For Ball, it was action policy, a concept he had borrowed from a 1956 *Foreign Affairs* article by none other than Paul Nitze, who became the dean of American arms control negotiations, and was the unchallenged king of strategy.[16] And in this short article from 1981 Ball makes it clear that in his view the action strategy showed that the United States was committed to a course where counterforce strikes would be central in a nuclear exchange. Ball observed this emphasis did not make deterrence redundant: indeed some of the targeting options reflected in the SIOP, including the ability to bring nuclear pressure directly upon the Soviet leadership and the quest to strengthen inadequate American command and control systems "are intended not just to improve the US capability to actually fight a nuclear war, in a tightly controlled fashion, but in so doing enhance the US deterrence posture".[17]

That was the point of this analysis in Ball's view. Attempts to accelerate counterforce abilities along with enhanced command, control and communications systems, which had become part of the Carter Presidency's legacy for nuclear strategy and which in Ball's view would be pursued "to even further extremes" under President Reagan,[18] and which Ball had observed in all of the administrations since Kennedy,[19] incorrectly assumed that a nuclear exchange could be managed in that "tightly constrained fashion". A range of very practical factors made that assumption dangerously flawed. Civilian casualties could easily run into the tens of millions even if civilian targets were deliberately avoided, meaning that Soviet decision-makers would hardly see the difference. And as it would take two to tango in limiting a nuclear war, the Soviet predilection for launching a single massive and coordinated nuclear strike at the outset ran completely counter to these hopes.[20] Moreover, command and control systems could never be robust enough to guarantee the level and fidelity of management in the fog of nuclear war that the fool's errand of controlled escalation would require.[21]

THE MYTH OF CONTROL

The most developed form of Ball's argument against the idea that a nuclear war could be controlled once it had begun is found in the third of these important and representative publications from the first two years of the 1980s. The IISS had already published a number of his empirically rich articles on nuclear weapons systems in its journal *Survival*.[22] Ball joined that organisation in October 1979 as a Research Associate for twelve months. The main product of that association was a fifty-page essay on the near impossibility of controlling a nuclear war, issued as one of the Institute's Adelphi Paper monographs. It was this work which clearly established Ball as quite likely the world's leading authority on this question. His verdict was delivered in a typically blunt and precise manner, revealing along the way Ball's view on the array of real-world factors that any informed student of strategic affairs should focus on. As he argued in the middle of the document:

> The notion of controlled nuclear warfighting is essentially astrategic in that it tends to ignore a number of realities that would necessarily attend any nuclear exchange. The more significant of these include the particular origins of the given conflict and the nature of its progress to the point where the strategic nuclear exchange is initiated; the disparate objectives for which a limited nuclear exchange would be fought; the nature of the decision-making processes within the adversary governments; the political pressures that would be generated by a nuclear exchange; and the problems of terminating the exchange at some less than all-out level. Some of these considerations are so fundamental and so intemperate in their implications as to suggest that there can really be no possibility of controlling a nuclear war.[23]

To this unambiguous and eminently readable warning is connected some of the mainstays of his work on this and related subjects. There is the by now familiar theme that strategic policy can just as easily be shaped by force structure as shape it. "What technology permits", Ball writes at one point in the monograph, "is often difficult to turn down".[24] The importance of strategic policy tended to be exaggerated:

> The lead-times for the design, development and deployment of modern sophisticated command-and-control systems are such that the rare periods when the guidance has been clear enough have generally been too brief for any systematic overall relationship to be established.[25]

And the Ball theory of what goes into decision-making, including in a crisis, is on powerful show as he rejects what he sees as the conventional wisdom. "Among strategic analysts", he writes in his conclusion, "the ascendant view is that it is possible to conduct limited and quite protracted nuclear exchanges in such a way that escalation can be controlled".[26] But that was simply the wrong view to take. It demanded far too much clarity, simplicity and focus in national security decision-making systems on both sides of the Iron Curtain which were characterised by none of those features:

> In neither the United States nor the Soviet Union are these establishments unitary organizations in which the decisions are made and executive commands given on the basis of some rational calculation of the national interest.[27]

Ball's intention at this point was not to establish a position within the various strains of international relations theory. It was to demonstrate empirically that the idea of a controlled nuclear war was so flawed as to be impossible to maintain, and that the stakes were so high as to make this conception as dangerous as it was dubious. Here Ball drew attention to problems that other scholars would be likely to overlook, or not notice in the first instance. This included the fact that controlled nuclear war relied on command and control systems whose physical features, including the antennae and other communications devices they relied on, could never be as hardened as the missiles that would carry the nuclear weapons. It included the prospect that these same systems could be vulnerable to "jamming" by the adversary,[28] an idea which set a precedent for Ball's study of cyber warfare some decades later. Even in 1980, Ball is already talking about the bandwidth of these communication systems, which he notes would be easily overwhelmed by "the extremely heavy demands of a strategic nuclear exchange".[29] Anyone puzzled by the notion of a scholar writing in longhand about complex information technology issues might be reminded that Desmond Ball has been doing so for a generation and a half.

And then there was the Australian connection to these problems. While some might be tempted to argue that Desmond Ball was drawn to the study of the joint facilities because of the sheer controversy and secrecy that surrounded them, and while Hedley Bull might have wondered if these subjects were of sufficient scholarly importance to merit such close attention, there is logic here. The American satellite systems were one of the most vulnerable parts of the complex required for any control of nuclear war, Ball argued, because of their reliance on just a couple of ground stations, one of which was in Australia.[30]

In this third study, then, one sees the intersection of so many of the themes, which were to dominate Ball's subsequent writing. Not all of these related to nuclear strategy but in the next few years quite a few of them did. For example, the continuing focus on what American targeting plans said, and how the Soviets were likely to use their weapons, was a feature of his work later in the same decade.[31] His expertise on the immense difficulty in achieving any measure of sustained control in a serious United States-Russia confrontation was in demand internationally including for an American Academy of Arts and Science study where his illustrious co-authors included Bruce Blair, Paul Bracken, Ashton Carter, Richard Garwin, Condoleeza Rice, Richard Ned Lebow and John Steinbrunner.[32] That publication coincided with Ball's consideration of career opportunities at Harvard and in Washington DC, and it was Ball's reputation in this area of policy-relevant scholarship which helps explains the reference from former President Jimmy Carter (among other luminaries) supporting his appointment as one of the ANU's small band of Special Professors, a post which has seen him remain in Australia.[33]

ENCOUNTERING AN INTELLECTUAL GIANT

It was very much this Professor Desmond Ball, the renowned international expert on nuclear forces, which I encountered soon after my arrival in Canberra in early 1988 to undertake the SDSC's recently established Masters program. The mainstay of that program was a core course on Strategic Studies where the backbone was a set of consecutive lectures on nuclear strategy, which Des provided. He was not, I have to admit, naturally suited for teaching large groups of students, and I understand his decision not to continue with that practice in what was a very short tenure at the University of Sydney directly after his Ph.D. But we were a group of a dozen or more graduate students from across the Asia-Pacific region and from throughout Australia, and Ball's mastery of the empirical details of nuclear strategy struck a chord with at least a few of us. A number who were braver than me and got to know Des as much as a person as they did as an academic quickly developed close friendships which were to last for decades. That approach has continued down the years including the army of fellow travellers (using that term in a non-political sense) who accompany Des on his regular Thailand-Burma border expeditions.

But in 1988 I was too serious, and also too intimidated, to strike up that sort of friendship. My focus was on the intellectual content of Ball's teaching which closely mirrored the work he had been writing: if there ever was a case of research-led teaching this was it. In fact I am not sure that I have ever heard Des teach on a subject he has not written on, including when he addressed students in the later Masters program, which was established by the SDSC in 2002. Fourteen years earlier the intimidation factor was not caused by Des Ball's personality, which was self-effacing and even shy. It was my sense of wonder at the content and sheer quantity of his writing on nuclear issues.

I still recall a sense of minor personal accomplishment in that core course when I was able to explain during one of the seminar-style lectures that Des was delivering in one of the Coombs Building Seminar Rooms why the calculation of the Circular Error Probable for an intercontinental ballistic missile's landing area involved the square of a number. This was probably the one and only detail regarding nuclear targeting that Des did not have on the tip of his tongue, and it conveys a sense of how empirically focused and detailed his teaching on this subject was. Later that year I tried in my own way to copy his research style. I was doing an essay and then a sub-thesis on Soviet fishing activities in the South Pacific and Des lent me his folder on the subject. He had a folder on everything, and he told someone, tongue in cheek I think, that when a folder got to a certain size it was time for a book. I tried in vain to replicate his assembly and syntheses of vast arrays of data points, building up long lists of footnotes to small and seemingly insignificant newspaper items and other sources. It was great fun but it was not an approach I would continue. The reason for my change in tack was not the comment from one of the external examiners that I had presented enough information for a Ph.D. but not nearly enough analysis even for a good MA. It was instead that a few months after submission in the first half of 1989 the Berlin Wall came down and the logic of studying the Soviet threat suddenly dissipated.

I expect Des himself must have wondered about what the end of the Cold War meant for the huge body of research he had built up on United

States (and to a lesser extent Soviet) nuclear strategy. That sudden and in many ways unexpected change in the international political and strategic landscape must certainly be a major explanation for his increasing focus on other issues for which he is often better known today. A quick look at his list of writings (the sheer number of which only a small handful of the world's scholars in the humanities and social sciences must come close to matching) indicates that while works on international nuclear strategy constitute the bulk of his work for at least a decade from the mid-1970s, by the early 1990s they have largely disappeared from the menu. This is not to say they were the only features in his work even in this earlier period: a number of works on Australian defence issues, discussed elsewhere in this volume, can also be found there. But today's readers who follow Des Ball's work on Asian security (both general topics including regional security cooperation and arms build ups and much more specific topics including the voluminous Thailand-Burma border material) may be surprised to find that such regionally focused work did not feature in his rise to international prominence as a scholar.

I found my own cure for the post-Cold War blues in the intellectual history of strategic studies. This allowed me to spend more time in that earlier era (and particularly the late 1950s and early 1960s) which in many ways is still more fascinating than what came immediately after the Soviet Union collapsed. That period featured in my doctoral studies and it was thanks in part to Ball's encouragement that I sought a place for this research at King's College London where I ended up working under Lawrence Freedman. My specific subject became the work of Thomas Schelling, an American strategic thinker from the height of the nuclear age who Des knew alongside pretty much everyone else in that community. I do not think I would have been brave or foolish enough to attempt this particular study without the background influence of Ball's lectures in 1988 including the long reading lists, which accompanied each one of them. I still recall my enthusiasm for one of the pieces he had just published in a volume amongst whose editors was Bernard Brodie, the most influential writer on strategy to have come out of the United States. That volume has "stability" lurking in its title:[34] this was the same concept which became the central focus for my work on Schelling, and it is with Des that my long interest in questions about stability really began. There is also a Ball connection to my second main effort at writing an intellectual biography. This time the subject is a contemporary of Schelling, a certain Hedley

Norman Bull. And it was Ball's very first conversation with Bull, held in the ANU's wonderfully confusing Coombs Building, that persuaded the young Victorian to opt for strategic studies.[35]

THE BALL APPROACH

If there is one thing that my work on Schelling and Bull has taught me, it is that a scholar's early writing, which can so often become overshadowed over time by better known works, is where one finds the true and most powerful origins of the work which is to come. This is certainly true of Ball's scholarship. Reading the three representative works from the 1980–1981 period which I have canvassed in this chapter reveals so much of the Ball essence: the emphasis on what the data tells us rather than what the big theoretical and policy explanations would suggest; the commitment to push boundaries to find that data (which sometimes got Des into controversial waters as he drew connections that others either do not agree with or would rather that he did not know); and the desire for the complete empirical picture which explains his insistence in some of his later work on photographing every aerial and antenna he can find. Des has never run out of subjects to study because there is always new information on new subjects which people have not bothered to go and find. And to go and find is quintessential Des: he does not believe in watching the world from a desk, and has no time at all for those who obfuscate issues by theorising rather than learning about them. But Des is aware that he possesses a rare gift, which helps explain his distinct methodology:

> It's an inductive process, it's a highly empirical process, it's one that involves bringing together data from all sorts of sources wherever one can find it, and it's only possible because I was blessed, and I have absolutely no knowledge or understanding of why or where it comes from, but blessed with a very, very good memory.[36]

Hard work also has a lot to do with it, and barrow loads of overseas trips, and the range of people who know of Des is quite formidable. When I was a colleague of his at the ANU for eight years and would travel overseas, as soon as people knew I was working at the SDSC the first question was almost inevitably about the person who is being honoured in this book. Des has remained for many people the core of the Centre, and I know that it was his early work on nuclear strategy around which so much of this reputation was built. In Australia, then, younger students and established scholars would do well to pay more attention to these important and powerful writings, which came in the early years of Desmond Ball's wonderfully prolific career.

Notes

1. Desmond Ball, interview by Nicholas Farrelly, *The Australian National University Mentor Interview Series*, transcript, 18 May 2011.
2. Desmond Ball, *Politics and Force Levels: The Strategic Missile Program of the Kennedy Administration* (Berkeley: University of California Press, 1980).
3. Desmond Ball, "Counterforce Targeting: How New, How Viable?", *Arms Control Today* 11, no. 2 (February 1981): 1–9, reprinted in *The Use of Force: International Politics and Foreign Policy*, edited by Robert J. Art and Kenneth N. Waltz, 2nd ed. (Lanham, MD: University Press of America, 1983), pp. 516–27. Citations in this chapter come from the latter version.
4. Desmond Ball, *Can Nuclear War Be Controlled?*, Adelphi Paper, no. 169 (London: International Institute for Strategic Studies, Autumn 1981).
5. Ball, *Politics and Force Levels*, p. xv.
6. Desmond Ball, "The Blind Men and the Elephant: A Critique of Bureaucratic Politics Theory", *Australian Outlook* 28, no. 1 (April 1974): 71.
7. Ball, *Politics and Force Levels*, p. xv.
8. Ibid., p. 269.
9. Desmond Ball, interview with Nicholas Farrelly, 18 May 2011.
10. Ball, *Politics and Force Levels*, p. 209.
11. Ibid., p. 211.
12. Desmond Ball, *A Suitable Piece of Real Estate: American Installations in Australia* (Sydney: Hale and Iremonger, 1980).
13. Ball, "Counterforce Targeting", p. 516.
14. See: Desmond Ball, "US Strategic Forces: How Would They Be Used?", *International Security* 7, no. 3 (Winter 1982/83): 31–60; Desmond Ball, "Nuclear War at Sea", *International Security* 10, no. 3 (Winter 1985/86): 3–31; Desmond Ball and Robert C. Toth, "Revising the SIOP: Taking Warfare to Dangerous Extremes", *International Security* 14, no. 4 (Spring 1990): 65–92. For a later article in the same journal which also approached force development issues but in the context of the Asia-Pacific region, see Desmond Ball, "Arms and Affluence: Military Acquisitions in the Asia-Pacific Region", *International Security* 18, no. 3 (Winter 1993/94): 78–112.
15. See: Desmond Ball, "Developments in US Strategic Nuclear Policy Under the Carter Administration", *SDSC Working Paper* 17 (Canberra: Strategic and Defence Studies Centre, 1979), p. 2.

16. Ball, "Developments in US Strategic Nuclear Policy Under the Carter Administration", p. 2.
17. Ball, "Counterforce Targeting", p. 522.
18. Ibid., p. 526.
19. In addition to Ball's work on the Kennedy Administration's strategy, see Desmond Ball, *Deja Vu: The Return to Counterforce in the Nixon Administration*, California Seminar on Arms Control and Foreign Policy no. 46 (Santa Monica California, December 1974).
20. See: Desmond Ball, "Strategic Culture in the Asia-Pacific Region", *Security Studies* 3, no. 1 (Autumn 1993): 44–74.
21. For these and other doubts, see Ball, "Counterforce Targeting", pp. 523-26.
22. See Desmond Ball and Edwin Coleman, "The Land-mobile ICBM System: A Proposal", *Survival* 19, no. 4 (July/August 1977): 155–63; Desmond Ball, "The Costs of the Cruise Missile", *Survival* 20, no. 6 (November/December 1978): 242–47; Desmond Ball, "The MX Basing Decision", *Survival* 22, no. 2, March/April 1980): 58–65; Desmond Ball, "Soviet ICBM Deployment", *Survival* 22, no. 4, July/August 1980): 167–70.
23. Ball, *Can Nuclear War Be Controlled?*, p. 36.
24. Ibid., p. 8.
25. Ibid., p. 6.
26. Ibid., p. 35.
27. Ibid., p. 36.
28. Ibid., p. 4.
29. Ibid., p. 4.
30. Ibid., p. 21.
31. See Desmond Ball and Jeffrey Richelsen, eds., *Strategic Nuclear Targeting* (Ithaca NY: Cornell University Press, 1986) and; Desmond Ball, "Soviet Strategic Planning and the Control of Nuclear War", in *The Soviet Calculus of Nuclear War*, edited by Roman Kolkowicz and Ellen Propper Mickiewicz (Lexington, MA: Lexington Books, 1986), pp. 49–67.
32. See Desmond Ball et al., *Crisis Stability and Nuclear War, A Report published under the auspices of the American Academy of Arts and Sciences and the Cornell University Peace Studies Program* (Ithaca NY: Cornell University, January 1987).
33. Desmond Ball, interview with Nicholas Farrelly, *The Australian National University Mentor Interview Series*, transcript, 19 May 2011.
34. Desmond Ball, "The Role of Strategic Concepts in US Strategic Nuclear Force Development", in *National Security and International Stability*, edited by Bernard Brodie, Michael D. Intriligator and Roman Kolkowicz (Cambridge, MA: Oelgeschlager, Gunn and Hain, 1984), pp. 37–63.
35. Desmond Ball, interview with Nicholas Farrelly, 18 May 2011.
36. Ibid.

7

AVOIDING ARMAGEDDON

Ron Huisken

I first met Des Ball in 1975, at the Australian National University in Canberra. We have been comfortable friends ever since. Our careers diverged and we lost contact several times, sometimes for years, but it was the sort of friendship that never had to be restarted, it was always there. In 1975, I was into my fifth year with the Stockholm International Peace Research Institute (SIPRI) and, in lieu of "home leave", had been allowed to attend a conference on nuclear disarmament in Fiji. En route to Fiji, I dropped into the Australian National University's (ANU) Strategic and Defence Studies Centre (SDSC) and, in addition to Des, met the then head, Robert O'Neill, and a bunch of other current and prospective doyens of the Australian strategic community including David Horner, Ross Babbage, Hedley Bull, Tom B. Millar, J. D. B Miller and Geoffrey Jukes. This could have turned the head of a young migrant economist from an (at the time) unfashionable extremity of the Commonwealth, and it did. When, a year later, O'Neill asked me to join SDSC as a visiting fellow for a year, I jumped at the chance. Later still, I had the good fortune to have O'Neill and Des as supervisors for my Ph.D. After more than two decades with the United Nations and the Australian Public Service (intersecting occasionally with SDSC and the newer ANU Peace Research Centre),

I re-joined SDSC (with Des still at the heart of it) in 2001 until I retired in 2012. In short, Des has been something of a constant in my professional life (although he is still evasive when I ask whether he ever read any draft chapters of my thesis, let alone the final product). He also lured me into my one and only (scouts honour) experiment with a "prohibited substance", but that's another story.

It is not easy to attach a familiar label to Des Ball. He is not an ideologue of any kind and labels like hawk, realist, constructivist and so on seem quite out of place. Des is what I would call a forensic analyst with a work ethic of Dickensian proportions. Indeed, I know of no other student of security affairs that comes close to matching Des' consistent and absolute faith in the capacity of diligent scholarship to unlock all doors, especially those guarded by official secrecy. Des has never held a security clearance. Nor, to my knowledge, has he ever used information conveyed confidentially prematurely, that is, before he was able to locate corroborating open source information or before the source agreed to its use. Despite this iron discipline, on every issue that piqued his curiosity and engaged his sustained attention, he ended up being justifiably confident that there were very few people in the world that had a more complete picture than he had. Given the international status that Des attained on several broad issues in the field of security studies, I recall on more than one occasion urging him to step back and write the occasional reflective piece, something devoid of footnotes. He essentially ignored this advice. It simply was not in him to have a paragraph let alone a page or several pages that was not referenced to something that he had seen, heard, touched, photographed or read. This is only a slight exaggeration. A glance through his list of publications reveals "Reflections of a Defence Intellectual", "The Blind Men and the Elephant: A Critique of Bureaucratic Politics Theory" and a few other pieces that one can reasonably infer were exceptions to my generalisation. But the list of his publications is itself a publication and these pieces look rather lonely.

The theme I want to explore in this chapter is whether, behind that formidable figure and the penchant for the forensic assembly of information, there is some other predisposition that informed Des' professional output. Specifically, I will explore the proposition that the appearance of a hawkish security and defence analyst is just that, an 'appearance', and that Des Ball is in fact something of a dove. At one level, this is not hard to do. He dabbled periodically with the subject of arms control, including in publications like *Arms Control Today*, and the *Bulletin of the Atomic Scientists*, and clearly not from the standpoint of a defence hawk seeking to highlight the dangers of arms control for an adequate and coherent defence effort. In the second half of the 1980s, Des, as Head of SDSC, developed an energetic and productive collaborative program with the ANU's Peace Research Centre headed at that time by Andy Mack, amongst other things, co-editing a 1986 book on *The Future of Arms Control*.[1] And all this was before the end of the Cold War when Des switched the focus of his work decisively toward the comparatively nebulous world of confidence building and multilateral security processes in East Asia.

But let's look more closely at the targeting of nuclear weapons, the theme that established Des' international reputation in the 1970s and did so much to put SDSC on the map. From the late 1950s, the United States strategic nuclear community had begun to look more critically at the posture of massive retaliation, America's first formal attempt to bring nuclear weapons into active service in support of foreign and security policy interests. It had been estimated that executing the massive retaliation plan in 1960 would have resulted in 360–425 million fatalities in the Soviet Union, China and other bloc states. Two decades later, when average warhead yields had declined and direct targeting of populations had fallen from favour, official United States estimates of fatalities from a full-scale nuclear exchange (including deaths from fallout in the first month after the exchange) were 50–105 million in the Soviet Union and 70–160 million in the United States. Des had reviewed "Armageddon scenarios" in a 2006 paper[2] and recalled using these numbers to suggest that "nuclear winter" proponents in the early 1980s were exaggerating the number and size, and therefore the effects, of the warheads that would be exchanged in a United States-Soviet nuclear war, in his view, an analytical sin fully comparable to belittling the consequences of such an event.

The nuclear weapons arena was particularly vibrant and dynamic in the 1960s and 1970s. Everything was on the move. For one thing, technological advances in the size, weight and yield of warheads and in the reliability and accuracy of delivery systems, and in early warning systems continually invited analysts to consider new missions or new ways of performing old ones. The thrust of technological change was inexorably in the direction of counterforce; that is, seemingly enhancing the ability to engage the opponent's nuclear forces rather than aspiring to simply crush the other side as a coherent economic and social entity. For another, it was clear that the Soviet Union was determined to become a formidable nuclear opponent, and with Sputnik in October 1957, looked for a moment as though they might surge ahead. Thirdly, simply living through the standoff called the Cold War was telling people that the black and white, good versus evil, scenario that the posture of massive retaliation seemed to require was utterly unrealistic. If things were to break down, it would almost certainly happen in a gradual, indirect and untidy fashion, adding further complexities to the deterrent signals that the nuclear arsenal should be tasked to emit. The Cuban missile crisis of 1962 had also driven home the point that deterrence not only had to work perfectly it also had to work pre-emptively. Making deterrence work in a crisis, as was the case in October 1962, was not an experience that either side wanted or, as it turned out, dared to go through again.

Des had cut his teeth on these issues in his research for his Ph.D. thesis on the strategic nuclear policies of the Kennedy administration, exposing a singular talent for unearthing crucial and sensitive information and being accepted as a peer amongst a small group of American analysts determined to supplement the ocean of arm-chair strategic analysis with hard information about how what a President, National Security Advisor or Secretary of Defense said about America's nuclear posture was connected to the way the deployed forces might actually be used if the President so instructed. In setting out to expose as far as possible the actual mechanics of nuclear deterrence, this group enormously enriched the strategic nuclear debate in the United States.

The Cold War nuclear competition was characterised by a curious discontinuity, an intellectual gap that was profoundly troubling but seemingly unbridgeable. The evidence suggested that, in a crisis, political leaderships found that nuclear threats became utterly compelling at the level of a single bomb on a single city. But this dread of the bomb also found expression in strong support for the development and preservation of nuclear capabilities that not only promised impenetrable general deterrence — that is, crushing retaliation in all imaginable circumstances of all out nuclear war — but which also endeavoured to preclude the enemy leadership making adventurous political moves in the belief that, on a particular issue in a particular place, it could generate a capacity to coerce and to prevail. This latter instinct, of course, the instinct to preclude crises, led to lavishly large and diverse nuclear arsenals that extended into every military domain and presented an existential threat to humankind.

The questions this group explored included the consistency of the relationship between declaratory policy and targeting practice, and whether

(1) ambitions to posture the nuclear forces to deliver more subtle and nuanced deterrent messages during as well as before a nuclear war or (2) whether the associated notions of positive control of an unfolding nuclear war were in any practical sense realistic. Des himself concluded that it would be heroic to assume that the Soviet leadership could be relied on to distinguish many of the 'limited options' that the United States' force had been programmed to deliver from an attempt to simply destroy that nation, and to react accordingly. The Soviet leadership, it could be noted, never conceded the slightest willingness to entertain notions of limited or controlled nuclear war. Similarly, in a particularly influential IISS Adelphi Paper published in 1981,[3] and discussed at length by Rob Ayson in the previous chapter, Des presented a compelling case that the vulnerability of the sensors and communication links in both protagonists made notions of positive control quite fanciful. He concluded that beyond a few days or a few tens of detonations (whichever came first) the leadership could not expect to have reliable intelligence on damage inflicted or sustained nor reliable control over the residual forces. Whether intentionally or not, this body of work compellingly reinforced the view that beyond the nuclear threshold lay an abyss that would render reason and strategy, or notions of victory, nonsensical. Inevitably, of course, the same material provided powerful ammunition to the anti-nuclear movement, which zeroed in on the risks of nuclear war starting by accident, unauthorised use or faulty intelligence and the strong probability of escalation in addition to the spectacular possible outcomes like a nuclear winter.

A few years later, in a 1985 article in *International Security*,[4] Des looked in particular at challenges for positive control posed by sea-based nuclear forces. Both superpowers, but especially the United States, deployed a major part of their strategic nuclear forces at sea. Communicating with submerged submarines is extraordinarily difficult and, as a result, the political and military leadership has been compelled to live with a greater measure of autonomy for these platforms than was the case with land-based missiles and bombers. Needless to say, the greater autonomy of and poor communications with such an important component of the nuclear forces reinforced the lack of confidence in a controlled nuclear exchange. Later still, in a 1989 article in the *British Journal of Politics*, he examined the prospects of controlling a theatre (or sub-strategic) nuclear war, reaching much the same conclusions.[5]

These arguments point to a contribution on a vitally important theme that is difficult to overvalue. A measure of the status that Des attained in this field is the calibre of the studies he was invited to contribute to. One example is the 1984 volume *National Security and International Stability*, edited by Bernard Brodie, Michael Intriligator and Roman Kolkowicz, some of the giants in the development of United States nuclear strategy. Another would be Kurt Gottfried and Bruce Blair, who in 1988 gathered fifteen leading analysts to collectively consider the issue of crisis stability and nuclear war, with Des being the only participant not from an American institution. Similarly, when he and Jeffrey Richelson edited a volume on strategic nuclear targeting in 1987, they were able to attract contributions from figures like Lawrence Freedman, Colin Gray and George Quester.

The quite extraordinary database and contacts (especially in the United States) on strategic nuclear targeting, early warning, communications with strategic forces that Des had developed had an important by-product in the form of books on the two key American military installations in Australia, Pine Gap (1980) and Nurrungar (1987). These installations — but Pine Gap in particular — were highly classified both with respect to the nature of the operations conducted and the agencies involved in running them and naturally attracted a lot of speculation, some of it quite bizarre. I do not believe that Des was opposed in principle to the presence of these facilities nor to the alliance with the United States that provides the political foundation for their existence. Nor was he opposed to secrecy as a matter of principle, only to the use of secrecy to preclude democratic processes of accountability and reasoned evaluation. He also simply regarded secrecy as an irresistible challenge and is probably a secret admirer of the fact that the United States strives to live by the proposition that government activities should be transparent unless secrecy is absolutely necessary, a proposition that few governments around the world are prepared to live by. The book on Pine Gap, *A Suitable Piece of Real Estate*, put Des' forensic skills on full display. Government took some time to catch up but in 1987–88 the Hawke Labor government saw political merit in demystifying Pine Gap and persuaded the United States to agree to say that it was a ground station for satellites that gathered intelligence useful to the Australian Defence Force (as well as the United States armed forces) and to the verification of international arms control agreements. This was not the whole story but it did not mislead. It was part of the real story, unlike the line that it was a space research facility that had been used for more than two decades. It would be hard to deny that this development had been facilitated by the fact that so much of the real story could be, and had been, pieced together from open sources.

Dipping selectively into Des' publications in this way to explore our particular theme may give the impression that Des is a normal professional academic who, in the 1970s and 1980s, produced a rich body of work focussed on nuclear weapons. This would be quite misleading. Des is in many respects a 'normal' person but he parts company with most of us in how utterly he has dedicated himself to his professional interests for every one of the past 45 years or so.

From the late 1980s, the thesis of this assessment of Des' output abruptly became something that was incontestable rather than something that could be (albeit readily) inferred. He remained focussed on the central strategic balance through to 1990 although, as intimated above, he had begun, occasionally, to dip his toe into the business of arms control. Just a year later, however, the thrust of his work changed dramatically. In 1991, he published pieces with titles like *Towards Arms Control and Reduction in the Pacific,* and (together with Sam Bateman) *An Australian Perspective on Maritime CSBMs in the Asia-Pacific.* This was not an aberration. Des had evidently determined that the apparent end of the Cold War would take the heat out of the strategic nuclear business and was attracted to the challenge of what greater East Asia would, could and should do to protect and strengthen stability and security in the still-amorphous post-Cold War era.

The Cold War ended dramatically in Europe. In the space of just 25 months (November 1989 to December 1991), the Berlin Wall fell, the Iron Curtain was lifted (through the dissolution of the Warsaw Pact and the withdrawal of Soviet forces from Eastern Europe), Germany re-unified and the Soviet Union dissolved into the Commonwealth of Independent States. It was readily apparent that two powerful multilateral agencies, the European Union and NATO, had been instrumental in keeping this compressed geopolitical transformation peaceful: not a shot was fired. Nothing comparable happened in Asia. Asia had not been hard-wired to the Cold War standoff to anything like the same degree as Europe. But as policy circles and academics began to survey the outlook for the newly liberated international system, it appeared to most that Asia could be headed for "interesting times" (to paraphrase that Chinese saying). A consensus developed that a major reason for the outlook being so indeterminate was the near complete absence of multilateral institutions and processes and the apparently weak instincts to put any in place.

Des launched himself into the slippery and indeterminate world of cooperative security, transparency and confidence building, publishing on maritime CSBMs, strategic culture in the Asia-Pacific, preventive diplomacy, and the outlook for arms control. Conceptually, cooperative security aspired to constrain national military capabilities so that destabilising threats of large-scale military aggression were out of reach. Cooperative security therefore sought to obviate the need to deter and, if necessary, defeat such threats, including through collective security arrangements. In any drive to nudge the region toward collective and collaborative solutions to security concerns, a key analytical question was to gauge the urgency of the requirement: as the basic parameters of the post-Cold War world began to take shape, what was happening to national security assessments and to what extent could this be inferred from military plans for capability development? This became an identifiable theme of Des' work in the early 1990s. He pulled this work together in an article in the winter 1993/94 edition of *International Security* in which he concluded that while there was no arms race underway in East Asia, at least as measured against the quantitative and qualitative characteristics that the United States-Soviet Union competition had given to this term, there were disturbing aspects to the region's defence acquisition programs that warranted urgent policy attention. These included emerging power projection aspirations, particularly on the part of China, and a region-wide aversion to transparency, particularly in respect of security perceptions and concerns. In a comparable net assessment a decade later he was less cautious, describing the Asia-Pacific region as in an "emerging complex arms race".[6] In between these two assessments, there was a steady flow of papers on multilateral security cooperation, the emerging architecture of security in the Asia-Pacific and on Australian perspectives, including ramifications for ANZUS and developments like the trilateral United States-Japan-Australia security dialogue. The context for all this work was whether cooperative approaches were making any inroads on the traditional unilateral (or collective) solutions to security concerns and what could be done to improve the balance.

Towards the end of the 1990s, Des acquired a new interest: Burma and the Thailand-Burma border. This was to become a consuming preoccupation in the new century with Des spending so much time up there that an award of honorary dual citizenship from Thailand would surprise no one. He once said to me that some of the largest conventional military operations since World War II had been conducted on and near the Thailand-Burma border but no one had ever taken any notice. Even as Des transitioned into the hazy world of cooperation, transparency, and multilateral dialogue, he never left that "forensic analyst" behind. All his publications bore the trademark characteristics of comprehensiveness and meticulous documentation. But the Thailand-Burma borderlands constituted virgin territory and presented the challenge of developing an entirely new body of information from the ground up, a challenge that he evidently found irresistible. Characteristically, when the nature of the Burma-North Korea relationship become the subject of high-level political speculation around 2009, particularly the improbable possibility that it included a nuclear dimension, it transpired that Des had interviewed the two defectors who were a primary source of this speculation.

I consider my case to be proven beyond any reasonable doubt. Des has never been an ideologue of any sort but neither has he been an agnostic. He much prefers to let facts and analyses speak for themselves rather than engage in conspicuous advocacy. He is not by any stretch of the imagination a pacifist but he has consistently displayed an instinct that addressing national security interests through giving full rein to national security programs cloaked in as much secrecy as can be sustained politically is likely to result in sub-optimal outcomes. As stressed at the outset, Des has been without peer in his commitment to the capacity of forensic scholarship to expose shortcomings and dangers and thereby set the stage for new ways of doing business, even if it remained for others to give substance to these new ways.

Notes

1. Desmond Ball and Andrew Mack, eds., *The Future of Arms Control* (Sydney: Australian National University Press, 1987).
2. Desmond Ball, "The Probabilities of *On the Beach:* Assessing 'Armageddon Scenarios' in the 21st Century". Working paper no. 401, Canberra: Strategic and Defence Studies Centre, Australian National University, 2006.
3. Desmond Ball, "Can Nuclear War Be Controlled?", Adelphi Paper no. 169 (London: International Institute for Strategic Studies, Autumn 1981).
4. Desmond Ball, "Nuclear War at Sea", *International Security* 10, no. 3 (Winter 1985/86).
5. Desmond Ball, "Controlling Theatre Nuclear War", *British Journal of Politics* 19, no. 3 (July 1989).
6. Desmond Ball, "Security trends in the Asia-Pacific region: an emerging complex arms race", Strategic and Defence Studies Centre Working paper no. 380, Canberra: Strategic and Defence Studies Centre, Australian National University, 2003.

Asia-Pacific Security

8

CHALLENGING THE ESTABLISHMENT

Alexander Downer

Australia's success has and will continue to depend at least in part on the strength of its intellectual and academic life. That may be fairly obvious in the fields of science and medicine but less so in political science. Yet political scientists play a central role in not just teaching but in generating debate based on evidence based research.

In the nearly twelve years I served as the foreign minister of Australia, I looked to our universities for creative ideas. The public service is efficient in the administration of public policy. The major departments of state such as the Treasury and the Department of Foreign Affairs and Trade (DFAT) employ able and dedicated people. They show a patient determination to implement government policy efficiently and within budgets. They are also dedicated to meeting the objective once articulated by a former DFAT Secretary, Nick Parkinson; making their Ministers look good. Nothing is forgotten, submissions are pored over by earnest desk officers and their superiors; Ministerial correspondence is carefully checked and rechecked and neatly presented.

There are two types of Ministers; those who need to be restrained by a cautious public service and those who need a good hard push.

The public service is by its nature an institution that errs on the side of caution. Ministerial enthusiasm for thought bubbles found in the columns of an ideologically sympathetic weekly magazine will be pricked. But the slothful Minister will be reminded of the heavy workload, which has to be completed.

That is what the public service does. But what it does not do needs to be contemplated. The public service is seldom a nerve centre of ideas. Yet good government needs a steady flow of positive ideas and a steady diet of criticism of what it is doing.

Professor Des Ball is one of those who has made an immense contribution to political thought and debate over several decades. He has inspired controversy, anger and not a little anxiety within the corridors of government. There has been many an occasion in recent years when I have disagreed with him. That is not the point. The point is: he has helped to generate ideas, to build the national conversation on foreign policy and security issues and to ensure decision-makers in government reflect on the decisions they are making, sorting out their arguments and at times questioning their own decisions.

My early interest in Des Ball was triggered by his work on Australia's spy agencies and our joint facilities with the United States at Pine Gap, Narrunga and Exmouth. These issues are worthy of substantial debate yet almost no one outside a very small group of government officials had, or has, any substantial knowledge of them.

There are two things to say about that. First, the public service, in the best traditions of its legendary caution, over classifies information and it has, therefore, over classified both the functions of the joint facilities and the work of our intelligence agencies, in particular, the Australian Secret Intelligence Service (ASIS), the Defence Signals Directorate (DSD) and the Australian Security Intelligence Organisation (ASIO). Secondly, it is only reasonable that the virtues, costs and risks associated with the agencies and facilities should be subject to public debate. Those, like myself, who believe they all contribute to Australia's national welfare, need to be prepared to make and explain the case, not just be reduced to an enigmatic ramble about sensitive national security issue. Some assume the public have no right to know what their money is being spent on and what the risks are which ultimately they incur through investments in espionage, counter-espionage and other activities undertaken by intelligence agencies.

This lack of transparency has been unhealthy. It has created the impression the intelligence community has something deep and dark to hide. If they do have something to hide, then it begs the question why do they have something to hide? That in turn has led the intelligence community to be subjected to all sorts of allegations and conspiracy theories, particularly built around Australia's alliance with the United States. Of course no one in the intelligence community or within the small category of politicians who know what the intelligence community does is going to confirm or deny all of Des Ball's assertions about their work. They do not need to. What they have to do is justify broadly the work of the intelligence community and be prepared to engage in debate about it.

Several years ago I introduced legislation to provide a legal framework for the intelligence community.[1] I worked hard to ensure it had bipartisan support. The Greens and other minor parties would not support it but then they are parties of protest, not of government. Labor had every incentive as a party of government to support the Liberal government's initiative as they themselves would one day be handed the keys to the intelligence community. They supported the Bill and it sailed smoothly through the parliament.

The Bill has been effective. Because there are now statutory parameters within which the intelligence community has to operate, with a particular emphasis on protecting the rights of Australian citizens, controversy about the work of DSD, ASIS and ASIO has faded away. At least within the mainstream of the political class it is now assumed these agencies act in a professional, non-partisan way consistent with the norm of Australian society.

What is more, these agencies are subject to oversight by a parliamentary committee. There are important limitations on what that committee can do, it must be acknowledged. In particular, the committee is denied information about operational matters. It can, however, monitor the budgets of the agencies and directly ask penetrating questions of the leaders of the intelligence community about their work. Operational matters are kept secret from committee members to avoid any untoward leaks, leaks which could jeopardise lives, reveal the names of agents and undermine other aspects of Australian diplomacy.

It is often said that every success has a thousand fathers and every failure is an orphan. In terms of bringing greater transparency to the Australian intelligence community and ensuring it operates within an acceptable framework, Des Ball is one of the fathers. There are others, of course, like Justice Hope. The role of the effective academic, though, can be decisive in helping to influence the political and bureaucratic class to act.

For me, Des Ball always made the intelligence community sound so important, exciting and even conspiratorial. His academic analysis and insights built on my enthusiasm for John le Carre and Ian Fleming. When I became foreign minister in early 1996, the mysteries were revealed. It was one of the great disappointments of my life. The world of intelligence collection is essentially prosaic. Increasingly clever use is made of sophisticated technology to collect information but human operations are limited and, in the main, weapons free. I allowed intelligence officers to be armed for the purpose of self-defence, particularly when operating with the Australian Defence Force in a hostile environment but no one in the Australian intelligence community has a licence to kill.

As part of his work on the intelligence community, Des Ball has explained much about the intelligence relationship between Australia and its traditional Anglo-Saxon partners, Britain and the United States. This is a more important part of our foreign policy than most commentators realise. We share a large proportion of relevant intelligence with each other, which means we have a level of trust that is not equalled in any of our other relationships. We also mount joint intelligence operations together. For example, Australia, Britain and the United States have worked together for some years on intelligence based counter terrorism operations in Southeast Asia. This co-operation has profound implications for our interaction with the outside world. Many commentators understandably promote Australia's engagement with Asia as a central theme of our foreign policy. Important as Indonesia, Japan and China are to Australia's long-term destiny, there will not in the foreseeable future be the level of trust between our government agencies and the comparable agencies of Asia, which exists between the United States, Britain and Australia (and to a lesser extent, Canada and New Zealand).

For a number of commentators, this is a matter of deep concern. It raises questions far beyond Australia's regional engagement though it is argued by some this intimate relationship with the Anglosphere inhibits our regional engagement. Some contend that our intelligence relationship with the Americans draws us into global controversies we would be better to avoid. For example, would there have been any implications for Australia's intelligence relationship with the Americans had we opposed the second Iraq War? I think the answer is clear. It would have caused strain in the alliance relationship and would have led to a significant diminution of trust between our respective intelligence agencies.

Just in case some may wish to extrapolate from this contention the conclusion that the reason the Howard government joined in the invasion of Iraq in 2003 was because of our intelligence relationship with the Americans: that is not the case. The Howard government supported the overthrow of the Saddam Hussein regime because it believed it was the right thing to do. But, incidentally, it did consolidate the already strong intelligence relationship between us both. Some will argue that the value of that intelligence relationship is overblown by its proponents. After all, the intelligence on Saddam Hussein's weapons of mass destruction passed to Australian agencies by their British and American counterparts turned out to be flawed.

This gets to the heart of the value of intelligence. On balance, it can be invaluable. It is a diplomatic force multiplier. Australia' negotiating capacity is enhanced by the knowledge we have of people and issues relevant to the negotiation. We get insights into issues we simply do not have the capacity through conventional means to follow in depth. For example, we have a vested interest in promoting the nuclear non-proliferation regime encapsulated in the Nuclear Non-Proliferation Treaty. We need to play our part in arresting the trafficking of illicit nuclear or nuclear related materials, particularly from or through our own region. Intelligence sharing with our partners gives us a capacity to make a contribution to that task way beyond our indigenous capacity.

Governments need to understand how to use intelligence. The value of one single slither of intelligence should not be overstated. The Blair government placed too much emphasis on the single source claim that Saddam Hussein could launch a chemical weapons attack within ninety minutes. This was uncorroborated. Yet not all intelligence can be corroborated and the one slither may be true. Intelligence, in other words, cannot replace judgement and wisdom.

Well, Des Ball was one of those who criticised the Whitlam government of not passing on intelligence to journalists in East Timor that the Indonesians were invading from the West. The journalists were subsequently killed at Balibo. It has been an enduring and often bitter debate ever since. Not even the Sherman Report initiated by Gareth Evans and pursued by me really satisfactorily solved the riddle of Balibo for many. For me the issue is not one of intelligence but of judgement on the part of the journalists. They rushed to Balibo because they believed exactly what our intelligence agencies knew; the Indonesians were invading. They were warned by other journalists on the way there from Dili to return east. They persisted because they wanted to capture the story. There is no doubt they were murdered by the Indonesians. It was a tragedy. Nothing can excuse their cold-blooded murder but they would have been better advised to take the counsel of those who fled the invasion.

Des Ball has been an academic gem. He has challenged, revealed, reviled and argued his way through the foreign policy and security debates of the modern era. Sometimes he's been right, sometimes he's been wrong. But every successful society needs people of ideas and the courage to challenge the establishment. The establishment may or may not be right. That's one thing. But they always have to be challenged.

Note

1. Commonwealth of Australia, "Intelligence Services Act 2001", *Australian Government ComLaw*, 2001, <http://www.comlaw.gov.au/Details/C2005 C00695> (accessed 12 March 2012).

9

RUMBLINGS IN REGIONAL SECURITY ARCHITECTURE

Pauline Kerr

One of the many reasons why Des loved his mother Dot was that she had a knack for capturing complexity in a few sharp words and, even when it was unpopular or controversial, speaking her mind. Certainly the local lads in the dressing room of the Timboon football club could verify the latter, especially if they were losing the game to another country town. Des either inherited or learnt Dot's knack because he applies it to his academic world of strategic studies. The title of his famous Adelphi Paper, *Can Nuclear War Be Controlled?*, captured a complicated and controversial question of the nuclear age.[1] Likewise the title for his book *A Suitable Piece of Real Estate*[2] made ordinary Australians aware that they had a dilemma in their security relationship with the United States: to support the joint United States-Australian intelligence and communications facilities in their country and risk being a target in a nuclear exchange; or play a potentially important role in deterring nuclear war by communicating early-warning information to the guardians of the United States arsenal. Getting to the essence of an issue and embracing the old adage of "speaking truth to power" seemed to be in the bones of the Ball family.

For Des, the essence of security in the Asia-Pacific region is still to be found in Dot's view on the matter: that "good neighbours have strong fences". Shifting the maxim across to the theoretical language of international relations, a move Des colourfully rejects when it came to esoteric abstractions of theory, he nonetheless understands himself as a "realist", a believer in strong (de)fences. But he is, by his own admission, "a realist with a difference". It is this depiction of Des' thinking, activism and policy advice that I believe explains his significant contribution to the study of Asia-Pacific security and architecture over the last two or more decades.[3]

In the rest of this chapter I will do four things that substantiate this claim: first, explain in more detail the logic behind Des' thinking about regional security and the resulting "realist with a difference" conceptual framework; second, demonstrate how this framework helps to explain his analytical and practical contributions over time; third, canvass some possible critiques of his approach; and finally, offer some concluding thoughts about what all of this tells us about Des' contribution to the way we ought to think about the type of security architecture that will best enhance the security of regional states and peoples.

CONCEPTUAL CONTRIBUTIONS

Des shares with the majority of his fellow strategic thinkers a profound pessimism about the behaviour of states in the international system: historically, contemporarily and in the future. The bottom line, putting aside abstract concepts such as self-help, relative and absolute gains, is that leaders of states pursue their definitions of their country's "national interests" and engage in power politics to achieve them. If economic resources allow, and often if they don't, political leaders will seek military forces to support their interests. States attempting to balance military power with others will often create action and reaction dynamics that can lead to competitive arms races, further insecurity and possibly war.

Des also shares with most of his strategic colleagues the view that when countries perceive themselves to be insecure in the international system many of them will seek alliances. The basis of insecurity may be perceptions of military threat, but, and here he may part company with some strategic studies scholars, states also form alliances to support other interests that may not pertain to their own security. The North Atlantic

Treaty Organisation (NATO), Des notes, is a military alliance of countries from North America and Europe first established through the North Atlantic Treaty of 4 April 1949 to provide collective defence to those countries during the Cold War.[4] NATO remains a military organisation with a military command but its 28 members have interests not just in protecting their own territory and population but in new types of operations, most recently the 2011 NATO 'humanitarian' intervention in Libya. Bilateral relationships, either in the form of alliances or outside of them, also remain fundamental to states' security. The more members involved in security arrangements the weaker the arrangement.

Where Des starts to part company with many of his strategic colleagues is his conviction that *because* he understands the international system of states in terms of national interests, power politics, balances of power (of which alliances can be an integral aspect) and bilateral relationships it is therefore essential that states also engage productively in multilateral institutions. Unless states try to ameliorate their in-built competitive and balancing tendencies, at least those tendencies based on perceptions of insecurity as opposed to expansionist inclinations, they will suffer the consequences of their ways: that is, become less secure and more likely to come into conflict with each other, militarily and politically. Multilateral institutions comprising states combined with multilateral "analogues" of Track 2 unofficial security experts provide a way of avoiding the security dilemma that follows from pursuing national interests through power politics and balance of power dynamics. The aim is to build confidence and reduce suspicion through routine dialogue that explains the strategic outlooks of states, makes their declarations believable through transparency of their military force structures and strategies, and negotiates regimes that set limits to or slows proliferation of particular weapons — such as, weapons of mass destruction — that destabilise relationships.

DESCRIPTIVE AND NORMATIVE CONTRIBUTIONS

Other chapters in this volume plus more than two decades of books and articles are testimony to the extraordinary contribution that Des' analysis makes to understanding of regional security and by implication the security architecture in the Asia-Pacific. In this section of the chapter the layers are explored in order to demonstrate the value of Des' analyses for understanding his views of *what is* and *what ought* to be the situation in the region: that is, the empirically observable and the normative dimensions of his contribution.

National Interests, Power Politics and Balances of Power Dynamics in the Asia-Pacific

The depth of Des' concern about the present security architecture in the Asia-Pacific is clear from his forthcoming book in the prestigious Adelphi Paper series. Northeast Asia, he argues, "is strategically the most worrisome sub-region in the world. It is wracked with inter-state tensions and disputes. The possibility of one or more of these degenerating into large-scale conflict is palpable. The consequences would be horrendous".[5] He stresses that all the countries in Northeast Asia have inter-state tensions and that each of the five main parties (Japan, China, Taiwan, North Korea and South Korea) have disputes that vary in intensity but that all are "more or less" serious.[6] All the disputes are bilateral and furthermore inter-connected, making actions by one country problematic for others. The historical issue of states making territorial claims (over sovereignty, legitimacy and borders) drive many of the tensions. Two examples of bilateral apprehensions are the following. Japan and Russia's continuing claims on the southern Kurile Islands which in recent times appear more intense following the power politics around the 2010–2011 visits to the islands for the first time by Russia's leaders and then their approval of plans to expand their military's presence.[7] And Japan and China's ongoing claims over EEZ's around islands in the East China Sea, which appeared more volatile during 2010–2011.[8] Beyond the many tense bilateral relationships, Des, like other strategic analysts, considers the major flashpoints in East Asia are the Taiwan Strait, the Korean Peninsula and the South China Sea.[9]

The essence of Des' analysis of the regional architecture and his particular contribution is his focus on the military dimensions of power politics and balances of power between the states of East Asia. Most often his analysis has several distinguishing features. First, he examines the military activities of regional states in meticulous detail. For example, he traces such events as China's intrusions into Japan's EEZ emphasising the increasing number, the escalation of 'oceanographic research' and SIGINT collection ships as well as warships, among them submarines, and reports the nature of the aggressive behaviour, which often occurs.[10] He catalogues dates, often times, the number of vessels, and the positions. And he reports the political responses of Chinese and Japanese leaders to these events. For example, the Chinese Foreign Ministry spokeswoman's statement after the September 2010 incident between a Chinese fishing trawler and two Japanese Coast Guards vessels near the Senkaku/Diaoyu islands that, "Japan's action have violated international law and rudimentary common sense in international matters", and that "they are absurd, illegal and invalid".[11] Second, his analysis reports the evolution of countries' defence expenditures. Northeast Asia, he argues, "accounts for the great bulk of the total defence expenditure and acquisitions in Asia, including most of the more disturbing new capabilities... China accounted for about 46 percent of the total Asian expenditure in 2006 and in 2010".[12] His main argument is that in Northeast Asia there is evidence of a changing acquisition process that exhibits "substantial...action-reaction dynamics [and] an emerging complex arms race...principally involving naval acquisitions".[13] He carefully documents the type, number and capabilities of the acquisitions that substantiate his argument that there is "serious maritime strategic competition" in East Asia.[14] Third, his analysis also includes examination of the proliferation of weapons of mass destruction (WMD) in Northeast Asia, which he considers to be another site for action-reaction dynamics. Again he notes the tenuous nature of many bilateral relationships and considers that "a nuclear arms race between India and China...is a real possibility".[15] Fourth, another component of Des' analysis of the regional situation is his focus on the intelligence and electronic warfare (EW) capabilities of states. Most countries in East Asia are "rapidly developing their electronic warfare capabilities" and in Northeast Asia "there is evident action-reaction with respect to naval EW capabilities".[16] Fifth, analysis of countries' information warfare (IW) assets comprise another part of Des' picture of the region and the action-reaction dynamics that he argues are so worrying. Internet monitoring and manipulation and strategic deception capabilities are just two of the developments that show there is growing interest in establishing cyber-warfare units in, for example, China, Japan, Taiwan, and North Korea.[17]

In sum, examinations of the factors listed above typically feature in Des' analyses of the regional dynamics that constitute part of the present architecture. In 2012, his view is that whereas in the past acquisition dynamics were driven by modernisation motives, today the region's increasing capabilities are spurred in many instances by serious action-reaction and this is the essence of arms racing.[18] The significance of the argument is not just its explicit and clear warning but that it is based on detailed and robust empirical research, which is extensively sourced. This combination of meticulous scholarship, analyses of pertinent factors, and strategic judgment contributes in quite unique ways to our understanding of the regional architecture. Moreover, in addition to his assessment of empirical trends, there is a normative element in his analysis evident in his critique that "there are no arms control regimes whatsoever in Asia that might constrain or constrict acquisitions".[19]

However, although he is critical of present military dynamics and supportive of measures that regulate them Des is an advocate of strong military forces to defend territory and deter expansionist intentions. As far as his own country is concerned, Des is a strong advocate of the Australian Defence Force (ADF) being equipped with the most modern weapons platforms and systems available. Furthermore, he is not opposed to a force structure that includes limited strike capabilities as part of tactically offensive operations if deterrent and defensive postures have failed.

Multilateral Institutions and Track 2 in the Asia-Pacific

Des' publications on this aspect of the regional architecture are as numerous as those on the military dimensions of competitive power politics and balance of power dynamics reviewed above. This is significant because it confirms his focus on cooperative elements of the regional architecture and this sets him apart from many of his strategic colleagues, whose pessimism about the prospects of states moving beyond competitive behaviours leads them to reject multilateral institutions as important reassurance mechanisms. Whereas Des' pessimism about the dynamics in East Asia is unambiguous he combines it with a cautious, indeed a very cautious, degree of optimism that states, out of self-interest, will engage in multilateralism, perhaps enough to make a difference. Furthermore, he is compelled to quite stridently advocate that states participate in regional institutions because he thinks it is the only way of reducing the horrendous consequences he predicts will likely follow from the present situation.

Des' advocacy is evident not just in his scholarship: in his numerous books, articles and presentations. He has been and continues to one of the region's, certainly Australia's, most energetic and dedicated activist leaders in establishing forums for security dialogue and measures for building confidence between regional states. His activism began before the end of the Cold War when he, along with his close ANU colleague, Professor Robert

O'Neill, worked with Thai associates to obtain Ford Foundation support for development of the Institute of Strategic and International Studies (ISIS) Thailand. The objective was to create a think-tank that provided robust academic strategic analyses of the regional architecture from the perspectives of smaller regional countries and informed government policy. He was an early supporter, along with another ANU colleague Professor Andrew Mack, of Tan Sri Dr Noordin Sopiee's inaugural 1987 ISIS Malaysia's Roundtable, which in 2012 held its 26th annual meeting. As discussed in depth in the following chapter, by the early 1990s, Des' zest for establishing Track 2 organisations was instrumental in setting up the first region-wide forum, the Council for Security Cooperation in the Asia-Pacific (CSCAP), and he was the first head of the Australian branch, Aus-CSCAP, a position he still holds with Professor Anthony Milner.

Des' analysis and advocacy of multilateral institutions and Track 2 in the Asia-Pacific has several dimensions that contribute to our understanding of the region's security architecture. The first is his focus on the military aspects of regional dialogue and practical measures. Whereas many other analysts, often from international relations and peace and conflict studies, usefully concentrate on political dialogue and diplomacy as means for improving security relationships — and although Des wholeheartedly supports their efforts, particularly on preventive diplomacy[20] — his emphasis is on the role that militaries play in destabilising relations through inadequate transparency about their intentions and capabilities. His warning earlier about the action-reaction dynamics in East Asia and its likely consequences gives his advocacy for a robust agenda of military cooperation within the official forums — the ASEAN Regional Forum (ARF), the various ASEAN military-to-military dialogues, and the Shangri-La Dialogue (SLD) — a sense of urgency.

For Des, the 1995 ARF *Concept Paper* provides a valuable foundation and future agenda for multilateral security cooperation processes in the Asia-Pacific region. The *Concept Paper* outlines "a gradual evolutionary approach to security cooperation" unfolding in three stages: stage one: promotion of confidence-building measures; stage two: development of preventive diplomacy mechanisms, and: stage three: development of conflict resolution mechanisms.[21] Des, like many other security analysts, considers the evolutionary approach has taken too long and that there are some successes and some (perhaps more) failures across the three stages. But it is the development of the ARF's "defence track" that is his key interest. His assessment is that since 1996–97 "several concrete steps have been taken" with regard to the participation of defence personnel (both civilian and uniformed) in the ARF's Senior Officials Meetings (SOM), the Inter-sessional Groups (ISG) and the more recent ministerial meetings.[22] Moreover, that substantial participation started when the 9th ARF Ministerial meeting in 2002 endorsed the ARF Defence Officials' Dialogues (ARF-DOD) that are to be held at least three times a year. Nonetheless, Des suggests quite forcefully that more frequent meetings are necessary.[23] Beyond dialogue, he endorses the practical cooperation among regional militaries that revolves around non-traditional security threats, including such issues as regional responses to mitigating national disasters and boosting military cooperation to cope with climate change.[24]

So far as the ASEAN military-to-military dialogue is concerned, Des reports that the second ASEAN Defence Ministers' Meeting (ADMM) in 2007 (the first was held in 2006) approved an "ADMM-Plus Concept Paper" endorsing three-yearly meetings on engagement and interactions with ASEAN's friends and dialogue partners around non-traditional security issues, such as natural disasters, pandemics, climate change and environmental problems.[25] The aim of another important forum, the Shangri-La Dialogue, is for defence ministers to 'engage in dialogue aimed at building confidence between their military establishments, whilst at the same time fostering practical security cooperation'.[26] The 2010 meeting involved defence ministers from the 10 ASEAN countries, the US Secretary of Defense, China's Minister of National Defence as well as other senior officials. Des' judgment of the SLD is that it has had "considerable policy impact".[27]

Des' overall assessment of the progress of defence cooperation efforts in the region is more circumspect and less dismissive than that offered by many of his strategic colleagues. Whereas some argue the various forums are "talkfests" and likely to remain so because states have competing national interests and cling to the principle of sovereignty, Des maintains that:

> In this region, with its immense diversity and disparate security concerns, progress with the construction of new security architecture is invariably slow, gradual and iterative, and conditional on the formation of consensus.[28]

Whereas many others claim there is little point in expending energy and resources on trying to develop meaningful military cooperation, Des advises persistence, reasonable expectations and urgency:

The challenge for the ASEAN-led processes will be to move faster, to increase the rate of their evolution and to be more adventurous with respect to the "Asian way" in order to meet emerging security issues of perhaps unprecedented scale, complexity and consequence.[29]

Integral to the heavy emphasis he puts on robust military cooperation is the second distinguishing feature of Des' analysis, namely the importance he attaches to institutionalising connections between Track 1 and Track 2 and to the development and delivery of practical policy advice from Track 2 to Track 1. The long-standing challenge of establishing links between forums for officials and forums for non-officials was eventually met with the establishment of back-to-back meetings between ARF officials involved in ISGs and ISMs and CSCAP study groups.[30] Des' activism, along with that of other regional colleagues, was instrumental in putting this connection in place. An example of a successful outcome from these types of meetings was the ARF's acceptance in July 2009 of CSCAP's recommendation that the ARF produce a Vision 2020 Statement "that would clarify the ARF's objectives and provide specific benchmarks for its progress".[31] CSCAP's recommendation exemplified its orientation towards delivering papers that were of "direct interest to the ARF"[32] and were supportive of its policy focus. Claims that the links and policy relevant nature of CSCAP papers are evidence of its loss of autonomy and intellectual rigour and its possible co-optation by Track 1 are, for Des, to be taken seriously. His concern is that although the formal Track 1/Track 2 connection is vital, unless Track 1 has the political will to address the dynamics he describes then Track 2 is stifled.

The third aspect of Des' contribution to the cooperative elements of the regional security architecture is his relentless critique combined with his reformist advocacy of the early and present structures and functions of both Track 1 and Track 2 in the region. Whereas many commentators damn the official and non-official forums for their limited outcomes and claim that in any case it is a pointless endeavour in a world of competing nation-states and interests, Des has concentrated on reforming both processes through constructive critique. A recent example is his argument that:

Track 2 organisations have been lethargic with respect to involvement in supporting or promoting Defence cooperation activities... there has been a virtually complete absence of informed dialogue concerning the identification of the most appropriate and productive sorts of cooperative activities to be accorded priority in the defence cooperative processes.[33]

His forthright assessment is combined with recommendations for how CSCAP could contribute to the defence track in the ARF: such as establishing a CSCAP study group devoted to the defence track that could "develop and refine proposals for both Map and live exercises designed to strengthen practical defence cooperation".[34] He also recommends institutionalising regular disaster relief exercises within the ARF, strengthening maritime exercises across a range of non-traditional security issues and regenerating traditional issues such as an "Avoidance of Incidents at Sea" agreement that was proposed in the original 1995 *Concept Paper*. Des' policy advice for many years has included broad defence cooperation through traditional exercises for armies, air forces and navies plus other activities that bring together senior and junior members of the different forces from different regional countries.[35] As a consequence of his analysis of the action-reaction dynamics in East Asia he is a strong advocate of the ARF acting on conflict resolution (that is, stage three in the *Concept Paper*) and suggests the first step is "to study the most likely characteristics of possible conflict in the Asia-Pacific region — in terms of their scale, intensity, naval and air dimensions, level of technology and sorts of casualties".[36]

POSSIBLE THEMATIC CRITIQUES

So far this chapter has presented a personal assessment of Des' contribution to our understanding of the regional security architecture. It suggests that his major impact is his meticulous, multifactor analyses, which are based on a conceptual framework that emphasises realist notions of national interests, power balancing, alliances and bilateralism *and* liberal institutionalist thinking about the value of multilateral forums and cooperation. His realist analyses reflect his perceptions of *what is* the situation in East Asia and his institutionalist examinations describe *what is* an embryonic form of regional security cooperation combined with his advocacy of *what ought* to be the normative objective of the regional security architecture, namely deeper defence dialogue and practical cooperation. Apart from these scholarly analyses Des' other contribution is his untiring activism in support of establishing and improving Track 1 and Track 2 forums and activities.

My next step is to raise very briefly some possible thematic critiques of Des' contribution to balance my own argument. As already indicated, Des' framework, empirical analyses and normative recommendations can be criticised. On the one hand there are realist perspectives that would in principle support his interpretation of the destabilising dynamics in East Asia but dismiss his view that the establishment of Track 1 and Track 2 multilateral arrangements have been and will be meaningful for regional order. His two logics may well appear contradictory from realist perspectives. Des' advocacy for arms control measures across the conventional and non-conventional spectrum will find both limited support and outright condemnation from realist perspectives. Des' standpoint differs from these partly in terms of his optimism (albeit cautious) that arms control regimes can regulate action-reaction dynamics and partly because he holds the conviction that there is no other option, if action-reaction dynamics are to avoid ending in conflict.

On the other hand, Des' approach can be critiqued from a host of liberal perspectives. For example, liberal institutionalist perspectives would find that the balance between Des' realist and liberal institutionalist favours the former. That is, his assessments of the dynamics in East Asia do not give sufficient weight to the ameliorating role of the growing number of regional institutions and arrangements as well as the increasing density of economic interdependence between Asia's great powers. Furthermore, his relative neglect of political and societal community building in favour of material structures for military cooperation may well be criticised from other liberal perspectives for leaving aside the role that community socialisation plays in setting the broader context for cooperation.

Interestingly, from a policy perspective Des' approach is likely to receive fewer criticisms insofar as it reflects the practical objectives of governments to have both cooperative and competitive options in the security architecture. However, Des' advocacy of the cooperative elements is clearly much stronger than that of most regional governments.

CONCLUSION

What does Des' extraordinary contribution outlined in this chapter tell us about the way we ought to think about the regional security architecture? The answers are not found entirely within this chapter's examination of Des' state-centric analysis, surprisingly. Rather they are located in another of Des' scholarly and activist contributions: namely his work on human security and in particular the human in-security of Burmese minority groups. The implication of his critique of the Burmese state and its treatment of its people is that his conception of security involves more than the state-centric focus of this chapter and that the regional security architecture ought to comprise both state and human centric dimensions. Indeed, Des' normative prescription for security, that "good" states are the key means for protecting people, further confirms that he is "a realist with a difference". Dot would be proud.

Notes

1. Desmond Ball, *Can Nuclear War be Controlled?*, Adelphi Paper no. 169 (London: International Institute for Strategic Studies, Autumn 1981).
2. Desmond Ball, *A Suitable Piece of Real Estate. American Installations in Australia* (Melbourne: Hale and Iremonger, 1980).
3. Although Des is the first to add that he does not write explicitly about architectures per se, nonetheless I believe that the conceptual framework he adopts is directly concerned with the descriptive and normative features of the regional security architecture. My arguments about Des' contribution are based mostly on past and recent conversations with him as well as two of his forthcoming publications which he kindly gave me drafts of and which I believe capture his thinking over many years (see endnotes 4 and 6 below). Nonetheless, he may disagree or agree with my arguments.
4. Desmond Ball, "Defence Security Architecture in East Asia", paper for lecture at the Sultan Hassanal Bolkiah Institute of Defence and Strategic Studies (SHHBIDSS), Brunei Darussalam, 8 March 2012. (Copy of manuscript provided by Des Ball to author.)
5. Desmond Ball, *Northeast Asia: Tensions and Action-Reaction Dynamics*, Adelphi Paper (London: International Institute of Strategic Studies, forthcoming), p. 2. (Copy of manuscript provided by Des Ball to author.)
6. Ibid., p. 2.
7. Ibid., p. 7.
8. Ibid., pp. 10–14.
9. Ibid., p. 3.
10. Ibid., p. 10.
11. Ibid., p. 12.
12. Ibid., p. 23.
13. Ibid., pp. 24–25.
14. Ibid., p. 26.
15. Ibid., p. 32.
16. Ibid., p. 31.
17. Ibid., pp. 38–39.
18. Ibid., p. 39.
19. Ibid., p. 40.

20. Desmond Ball and Amitav Acharya, eds., *The Next Stage. Preventive Diplomacy and Security Cooperation in the Asia-Pacific Region*, Canberra Papers on Strategy and Defence no. 191 (Canberra: Strategic and Defence Studies Centre, Australian National University, 1999).
21. Desmond Ball and Pauline Kerr, *Presumptive Engagement: Australia's Asia-Pacific Security Policy in the 1990s* (Sydney: Allen and Unwin, 1996), pp. 111–19.
22. Ball, "Defence Security Architecture in East Asia", p. 13.
23. Ibid., p. 13.
24. Ibid., pp. 13–14.
25. Ibid., pp. 15–16.
26. Ibid., pp. 18–19.
27. Ibid., p. 19.
28. Ibid., p. 21.
29. Ibid., p. 21.
30. Ibid., p. 22.
31. Ibid., p. 22.
32. Ibid., p. 22.
33. Ibid., p. 22.
34. Ibid., p. 23.
35. Ball and Kerr, *Presumptive Engagement*.
36. Ball, "Defence Security Architecture in East Asia", p. 27.

10

CONSTRUCTIVE CRITICISM AND TRACK 2 DIPLOMACY

Brian L. Job and Anthony Milner

INTRODUCTION

With the end of the Cold War — a period during which he had established himself as a preeminent and prolific scholar of international reputation on the primary security concerns of that era (strategic nuclear weapons, signals intelligence, missile defence) as well as on Australia's military defence — Desmond Ball's attention shifted towards the Asia-Pacific, where it has largely remained to the present. Ball was quick to realise the importance of establishing regional institutions that could promote security cooperation in the Asian region. Over the course of the last two-plus decades, Ball's efforts as a scholar, policy analyst, advisor to governments and Track 2 diplomat, have had significant impact on the shaping of the institutional architecture of the Asia-Pacific. Indeed, with his abilities to operate simultaneously across academic and policy, and official (Track 1) and unofficial (Track 2) dimensions, Ball has occupied, and continues to occupy, a near unique role in the Australian and broader regional contexts.

This chapter focuses on one aspect of Ball's efforts to advance towards a stable and peaceful Asia-Pacific security environment: that is, his work to initiate and sustain Track 2 regional, multilateral security dialogue mechanisms and institutions to facilitate security cooperation among the states of the region. Particular attention is focused on Ball's central role in the Council for Security Cooperation in the Asia-Pacific (CSCAP), which since its establishment in 1994 has been the only inclusive, region-wide Track 2 security institution with a broad agenda, productive working groups, and a relationship with its official counterpart the ASEAN Regional Forum (ARF).

We organise our reflections on Ball's contributions and achievements regarding CSCAP and its association with regional institutions across three dimensions: institution-builder on national, Track 1, and Track 2 levels; chronicler of regional institutionalisation; and innovator and critic of institutional achievement. Before addressing these dimensions, it is important first to take note of the key premises from which Ball's Asia-Pacific agenda has proceeded, in effect revealing the continuity of thought and principles that have guided his institution building and security architecture agenda.

PREMISES

In retrospect, four foundational premises have underpinned Ball's overarching efforts to enhance regional security cooperation in the post-Cold War era: a comprehensive knowledge of the security and defence policies, and deployments of Asian states; a perceptive realisation of the distinctive "security culture" of the Asia-Pacific; a conviction that multilateral mechanisms and processes were necessary to supplement existing bilateral arrangements, and that the establishment of formal institutions was required to ensure focus and continuity; and, finally, a conviction that unofficial (Track 2) institutions and processes have a critical role to play in supporting their official regional counterparts.

Any reader of Ball's work on defence and security matters, be it the United States' nuclear strategy and missile deployments, Asian states' defence build-ups, Australian defence policy, or Burmese ethnic insurgencies, is impressed with his exhaustive and complete attention to empirical detail. Given the quantity and range of his writing this in itself is a formidable achievement. Ball always has all the facts, and his facts are always correct. In this way he has established a reputation for knowledge and credibility among regional officials and militaries — an important asset when putting forward suggestions for policy change or for military-to-military cooperation across states. His empirical authoritativeness has also meant that analysts have had reason to follow closely Ball's cautions about the implications of weapons proliferation and the destabilising effects of competitive arms acquisition.[1]

Turning to the second premise, Ball differed from many other analysts steeped in the realist mindsets of bipolar, East-West nuclear strategy. With the Cold War drawing to an end, he quickly realised that the security precepts and institutional forms and practices of that era did not translate to the evolving security environment. As he put it in 1993, "understanding of the constraints and opportunities provided by three conditions: the end of the Cold War, geopolitical considerations in the Asia-Pacific region, and cultural factors — is a precondition for determining the tasks for security cooperation in the region".[2]

For Ball, by the beginning of the 1990s there were already important signals as to the drivers of regional development and security. He saw an environment of "unprecedented pace and scope of change — produced by economic dynamism, superpower drawdowns, and defence modernisation". The number of actors in the region 'would certainly increase', pointing specifically to India and China. Sounding a theme to be repeated often, he argued that the major arms acquisitions programs, particularly maritime and naval build-ups, were disturbing. For Ball, however, military concerns would "be increasingly supplemented by issues of economic and environmental security," and the demand for resources. Indeed, he argued that the most important forces to shape regional security architecture were the economic.[3]

It is interesting to contrast Ball's more immediate and nuanced grasp of the post-Cold War Asia-Pacific security environment to the more stark and simplified characterisations by other, mainly North American, analysts. Aaron Friedberg's "Ripe for Rivalry"[4] article published side-by-side with Ball's "Arms and Affluence: Military Acquisitions in the Asia-Pacific", in *International Security* is exemplary in this regard.[5]

In further distinction from many Western analysts of the era, Ball came to an early understanding that European models could not be transplanted onto Asia. Institutional agendas and modalities of interaction specific to regional conditions and security practices were called for. Ball adopted (and continues to adopt[6]) the principle that to achieve progress, proposed initiatives had to be sensitive to, and amenable to operationalisation within the security culture of the region. Always mindful of the position of analysts located on the regional periphery, Ball asserted, "sensitivity to Asian cultural dispositions will be necessary for Western participation in this dialogue".[7]

Thus, and thirdly, Ball did not see the existing bilateralised, regional security architecture as adequate to cope with emerging regional challenges. He knew, however, that strong resistance would confront any advancement of multilateral initiatives within the region in the early 1990s. Regional experience with multilateralism was not regarded as positive, as exemplified by the demise of the South East Asia Treaty Organisation (SEATO). New multilateral mechanisms were decried as 'a problem in search of a solution' by Washington, and regarded with suspicion in Tokyo, Seoul, and other capitals. This resistance — grounded in post-WWII security tradition and argued as being necessary in light of regional diversity and ongoing tensions — did not, however, prove immutable. Informal and ad hoc dialogues — largely sponsored through NGOs and national think tanks, and Asian militaries themselves — took hold and proliferated in what would appear to have been a spontaneous, natural reaction to the perceived need to come to terms with the complex issues confronting regional states and their militaries. Indeed, within several years, over two dozen confidence and security building (CSBM) initiatives were underway.[8]

Ball championed these developments, viewing them as "a significant new element of the emerging security environment".[9] He noted "a new era in confidence building", with "multilateral approaches to security, manifested in the regional confidence and security-building measures (CSBMs)" now "indubitably on the regional agenda".[10] In 1991 Ball had published a monograph, *Building Blocks for Regional Security*, which took a bottom-up approach to regional security cooperation, identifying "bilateral and limited multilateral arrangements already in place" that might act as "building blocks" for a wider regional plan. Two years later, Ball wrote a further essay examining the range of regional confidence and security-building measures (CSBMs) that were being proposed, suggesting where emphasis might best be placed and urging the adoption of criteria that could be employed in such a focusing process.[11] He was concerned to encourage security cooperation in the areas of intelligence exchange, joint defence exercises, Timor Sea issues and technology monitoring. In his writings and discussions Ball advocated a gradualist approach (one generally amenable to key regional players such as the members of the ASEAN-ISIS group). His particular audience was the Australian government, including the then Foreign Minister Gareth Evans, as much as readers in the Asian region.

Certainly, Ball's intuitive assessment of the prospects for the proliferation and scope of multilateral security dialogues proved to be on the mark. Indeed, writing shortly thereafter, Paul Evans pointed to the occurrence (in 1993) of over four such meetings per month along ten different dimensions, thus declaring the "ending [to] the allergy to multilateral discussion" within the region.[12] By 1994, the numbers of Track 1 and Track 2 activities exceeded a hundred, essentially providing the momentum for the creation of formal, multilateral institutions on both official and unofficial tracks.[13]

A primary feature, distinctive to the Asia-Pacific region, was the development of what became labelled "Track 2" multilateral security dialogue processes and institutions. Ball's recognition of the importance of these processes was the fourth of his underpinning premises. His role in helping to define and shape Track 2 has been critical. The use of the term Track 2, in contrast to Track 1 activity had an established history.[14] Within the Asia-Pacific context, "Track 2" assumed several distinctive characteristics. One was the direct involvement of governmental officials, but 'in their private capacities'. That is, officials were encouraged to be present and to participate in an environment that facilitated the exchange of ideas without these ideas being tied to government policy. At the same time, the involvement of officials would presumably anchor discussions to policy-relevant, rather than abstract academic, considerations. A second Asia-Pacific feature was a concern to foster dialogue across established lines of division on issues, to be inclusive of non-like minded parties. Finally, the precepts of the ASEAN way were to prevail: soft institutionalisation (i.e. no significant bureaucratic or regulative capacities); meetings with open agendas, operating by consensus decision making; and an overall gradualist approach within the sovereignty-protectionist comfort zones of East Asian states.

In the Asia-Pacific, Track 2 — if functioning according to these tenets — was seen to offer opportunities to advance security cooperation and resolve tensions. Thus, Ball and his colleagues referred to Track 2's possibilities as a "useful source of *advice* to governments", a "useful mechanism for *building capacity*", "a laboratory for testing and generating new ideas", and an "alternative diplomatic route when Track 1 is stalled".

The speed with which multilateral security initiatives proliferated caught Ball and other regional Track 2 entrepreneurs by surprise. Tokyo and Washington were getting on board, albeit not to the extent of their Southeast Asian counterparts, and Beijing was beginning to show interest, particularly on the economic side. When cataloguing regional CSBMs in 1994, Ball highlighted the official initiatives such as the ASEAN Post-Ministerial Consultation (PMC) process, the regular dialogue among regional militaries (particularly their navies) and the successful Track 2 workshops involving claimant states in the South China Sea. At the same time, he and others began to sense that energy was being diffused across a very broad spectrum, with duplication, lack of continuity and accumulation, and insufficient attention to ensuring that agendas concentrated on the policy-relevant needs of regional governments. Ball had initially expected that "progress with the construction of new modalities for security cooperation will be slow and painstaking, that informal, pragmatic, and evolutionary arrangements will have much better prospects than formal structures and institutions." But, his attitude and advice now changed.[15] The problem, he now said, was to "focus and institutionalize the process so as to ensure that the most significant and fecund arrangements can be effectively implemented. Otherwise, the recent efforts will remain too diffuse and will waste both intellectual and official resources; momentum will wane and opportunities will be lost".[16] Ad hoc initiatives and informal processes, Ball observed, needed to be complemented by "some degree of institutionalized dialogue mechanism".[17]

In retrospect, the first half-decade after 1989 was remarkable. Regional actors at both Track 1 and Track 2 levels moved more quickly and more successfully to mitigate tensions and to establish principles of dialogue to foster cooperative security than the experts, particularly North American and European, could have envisaged. (The regional comparisons, particularly with Europe, are striking.) Ball's judgments stand out well when reviewing the writings and reports of this period. From this point forward, Ball, along with a small coterie of officials, think tank leaders, and academics, devoted their attention and energies to building a focused and effectively functioning regional institutional architecture.

Institution Building

Building this architecture necessitated action on three fronts — motivating and supporting the Australian government's efforts to establish and shape Track 1 regional institutions, creating effective Track 2 institutions at the regional level to both lead and support Track 1 counterparts, and establishing a domestic network and forum to support Australian engagement in official and unofficial ventures at the regional level. Our discussion, in turn, is focused upon Ball's engagement in advancing the formation of a specific institution addressing each of these dimensions: the ASEAN Regional Forum (ARF), CSCAP, and the Australian CSCAP Member Committee (AusCSCAP) — consideration of AusCSCAP being taken up near the end of this chapter.

The ASEAN Regional Forum

In 1991, Ball said Australia had two broad defence needs: first, to achieve "the minimal military capabilities required for self-defence" and secondly, to promote "a network of more or less institutionalized mechanisms" for enhancing regional security.[18] This second, regional objective was very much a focus of deliberations at the Strategic and Defence Studies Centre (Ball's academic base at the ANU) in the 1987–91 period. Ball's engagement with government officials in advancing Australia's regional interests and goals concerning the ARF is a prime example of the productive relationship that he helped to foster between the academic and official communities in Canberra.

By 1991–92, planning for the creation of a region-wide institutional forum was gaining momentum. Australia looked to come on board a campaign being spearheaded by the ASEAN states (and no longer opposed by the Northeast Asian major powers and the United States). At the government level, Australian Foreign Minister Gareth Evans proposed (in 1992) a "wholly new institutional process" that would evolve "in Asia just as in Europe" — a security architecture influenced by the Conference of Security and Cooperation in Europe (CSCE), and stressing the idea of "common security".[19] Not surprisingly, this idea was not received well in many quarters of the Asian region with ASEAN-ISIS leaders communicating to Ball and others that the European experience was not relevant. (As noted above, Ball had been convinced on this matter.) Eventually, Evans himself listened to ASEAN advice,[20] and Australia became a partner in the creation of the ARF, which stressed "cooperative security" (conveying a greater respect for national sovereignty and institutional minimalism) rather than common security.

Ball and his ANU colleague Stuart Harris (previously Secretary of the Australian Department of Foreign Affairs and Trade) were in tune with ASEAN-ISIS thinking, and advocated this approach in Australia. They accepted the need to move carefully and not too ambitiously — to avoid grandiose schemes — and recognised the advantage of basing a new security institution on the Post Ministerial Conference (the annual meetings between ASEAN Foreign Ministers and the foreign Ministers of ASEAN Dialogue Partners, including Australia). These Conferences had begun in the 1970s and originally focused on economic issues. In the 1980s the Cambodian crisis became a topic, which some saw as opening up a potential for a regional security dialogue. From Japan, Yukio Satoh (later Ambassador to Australia, and then the United Nations) took a supportive and similar gradualist approach as Head of the Gaimusho planning office.

The first ARF meeting was held in Bangkok in 1993. In 1995, the ARF issued its *Concept Paper*, setting forth a three-stage process for action to move from confidence building, to preventive diplomacy, and finally to conflict resolution. The ARF, therefore, emerged very much as an "ASEAN creature in both substantive and procedural terms".[21] ASEAN principles of non-confrontational dialogue, consensus decision-making, non-interference in domestic affairs, and minimal institutionalisation prevailed. A key decision was to extend invitations to the non-like-minded states of the region, including China, thus expanding the membership and potential scope of its agenda.

Ball and colleagues remained attentive to the development of the ARF, on the Track 1 front. At the SDSC, Paul Dibb (who had been Deputy Secretary at Australia's Department of Defence) worked with Foreign Minister Evans on proposals for the ARF agenda — proposals that, in their words, "might be acceptable, both culturally and politically, to governments in the region in the years ahead".[22] This was precisely the type of approach Ball had been urging. Ball's attention, however, had now shifted to the creating of a Track 2 institution to support the fledging ARF; this was, of course, CSCAP.

CSCAP: Des Ball, Present and assisting at the creation

"The establishment of CSCAP is one of the most important milestones in the development of institutionalized dialogue, consultation and cooperation concerning security matters in the Asia-Pacific region since the end of the Cold War. It represents a major achievement in the development of multilateralism in the region."[23]

As detailed above, the rationale for creating a formal institution to provide leadership and focus to the Track 2 agenda had been building. ASEAN-ISIS, along with the Japanese Institute of International Affairs, Pacific Forum CSIS, and the Seoul Forum, set the process in motion by convening a series of meetings commencing in 1991. At this early, formative stage, no specific Australian institution was involved directly. Ball, however, was invited to join the handful of specialists that brought CSCAP into being.[24] He, along with Paul Evans — the other individual present at the table not a representative of the four institutions named — have been recognised in the region for playing a significant role in these foundational deliberations.[25] Ball engaged in the intense discussions regarding the institutional form CSCAP would take and the membership it would have. His technical knowledge helped in developing a CSCAP agenda — identifying the security issues with which CSCAP would have to grapple.

CSCAP was officially established in Lombok (Indonesia) in June 1993 with ten founding institutions, including the institutional home of Ball (the SDSC). CSCAP's structure involved Membership Committees from the then ASEAN states, Japan, South Korea, Canada, Australia, New Zealand, and the United States. It was to be directed by a Steering Committee, meeting biannually. CSCAP's functional entities were to be its Working Groups — designated to operate on their own schedules, to focus on specific issues of regional concern (e.g. the Korean Peninsula, and maritime disputes), and to produce informative reports with policy-relevant recommendations for regional governments and institutions (specifically, the ARF). A General Conference was to be held every second year.[26]

Ball has described three guiding principles as determining CSCAP's structure and mandate. The first was the engagement of officials in Working Groups and the General Conference in their *private capacities*. This was seen as essential to gain the benefit of their understanding of national interests, "to attract government resources and to ensure the value and practicability of the NGO efforts secured official appreciation".[27]

Second was the modelling of CSCAP on the experience and practice of its Track 2 counterpart on the economic front, the Pacific Economic Cooperation Council (PECC). PECC was regarded highly for engaging government, business, and academic communities; for providing advice on technical economic issues that has impact on official policy; and for providing a 'comfort zone' for officials to vet ideas freely and engage in open debate. Several of the founding leaders of CSCAP (for instance, Jusuf

Wanandi for Indonesia, Nordin Sopiee for Malaysia) saw the relationship between PECC and APEC as instructive in planning Track 1–Track 2 interaction in the security area. On the Australian side, Ball and Harris were of similar mind and solicited advice from Peter Drysdale — a central figure in both PECC and APEC. Drysdale, however, cautioned "in the political and security space it was always going to be harder to engage the central government players than in the economic space".[28]

Third, mindful of the proliferation of think tanks at the national level and multilateral Track 2 mechanisms — as well as reflecting sensitivity to the ASEAN states' desire to maintain their collective role and institutional norms of decision making — CSCAP's founders sought to build upon existing institutional arrangements in the region. At the Track 2 level, this meant maintaining close relationships with ASEAN-ISIS institutions and locating the CSCAP Secretariat with one of their members, ISIS Malaysia. At the Track 1 level, this meant establishing a relationship to the ARF. Indeed, as Ball and other key figures (such as Wanandi) argued, the ultimate test of CSCAP's relevance would be its utility to the ARF.[29]

Thus, CSCAP was launched with defined and high expectations, and with significant enthusiasm among its members. Three immediate challenges were recognised. Chief among these was negotiating membership with China, which — because of the desire by key figures in CSCAP to sustain some role for Taiwan — had refused to join. But, there was also the matter of including the non-like-minded states such as Mongolia, North Korea, and Vietnam. The second challenge was the perceived need to get CSCAP's Working Groups up and running and producing results; the third challenge was to gain notice and engagement with Track 1. Optimism was tempered by recognition of what would be "the inevitable problems of finance [and] organization" and "a legitimate worry that national committees will tend to favour particular political positions".[30] Or, as Ball put it, "there is a real concern that connections with government might be inversely related to … intellectual independence. … It is likely that the strongest Member Committees will be those that toe their official government lines most closely".[31] These were perceptive observations about what subsequently came to be termed 'the autonomy dilemma' confronted by all Track 2 institutions,[32] and what was certainly to become a continuing dilemma for CSCAP.

In the founding stages of CSCAP, and in much of its work up to the present, the role of personal diplomacy has been vital. Perhaps more so than for other regions, in Southeast Asia much stress is placed on easy and trusting relationships among government leaders and associated, unofficial elites. The term 'golf diplomacy', while often used cynically, describes the informal atmosphere operating among regional leaders (most of whom overlapped in office for long periods of time) engaged in debate and the crafting of consensus. To a significant extent, personal relationships among a subset of individuals were important in moving CSCAP forward as well, certainly in its initial decade. Here too Des proved effective. Although possessing a long-established reputation as a stern analyst willing to make a blunt, tough assessment where necessary, he also demonstrated — and continues to demonstrate — a striking capacity for establishing warm personal relations. Moving among ASEAN-ISIS leaders, Australian government officials and academic colleagues, he has offered not only strong expertise in security studies, but also a talent for sensitive diplomacy, as well as a commitment to gaining an understanding of the security and political cultures of the region.[33]

Positive personal relationships that bridged Track 1 and Track 2 were also important. When communication lines are open and information can be shared in an atmosphere of mutual respect and trust, academics and officials are able to generate considerable synergism. Ball's ability to foster such relationships over time and across communities in Australia has been remarkable. It is not an exaggeration to claim that the success achieved by Australia in advancing its official and unofficial agendas in the region owes something substantial to Ball's operating at this interface for the past several decades. Numerous generations of the Department of Foreign Affairs and Trade (DFAT) and the Department of Defence (DoD) personnel have been involved, many of whom may well have been students of Ball's before becoming officials.

CSCAP: Des Ball as Institutional Historian and Activist

Of the ten individual 'founding fathers' of CSCAP — that is, those present at the November 1992, Seoul meeting — Wanandi, Carolina Hernandez and Ball stand out as having remained consistently engaged with the Council, and as its most stalwart supporters.

A number of Ball's particular contributions deserve to be highlighted. The first is as CSCAP's historian and chronicler. He is responsible for assembling an accurate and detailed accounting of the Council's activities and achievements. Ball's hundred-plus page monograph, *The Council for Security Cooperation in the Asia-Pacific (CSCAP): Its Record and Its Prospects*, published in 2000 covers its formation and formative years. A decade later, the co-edited volume, *Assessing Track 2 Diplomacy in the Asia-Pacific Region: A CSCAP Reader*[34] provides a combination of narrative, critical assessment and recommendations for CSCAP's future. In effect, these works constitute the 'institutional memory' for CSCAP — essential reading for those studying CSCAP, or the evolution of security dialogue in the Asia-Pacific, more generally. For those engaged in efforts to reshape the region's security architecture, Ball's accounting provides valuable 'lessons learned.'

Ball, of course, was not an observer on the sidelines. He wrote as an insider. From its inception, Ball was engaged in addressing challenges facing the institution. Among the first of these was expanding CSCAP's membership to fulfil its mandate as an inclusive, region-wide forum. Four additional members were brought on board with relative ease by 1996 (Mongolia, New Zealand, Russia, and Vietnam), with another five that followed by 2001 (the European Union, North Korea, India, Cambodia, and Papua New Guinea). Gaining Chinese membership was essential to the future of CSCAP. Wanandi and Ball (working together with Harris) played important roles behind the scenes, working between Steering Committee meetings to engineer a compromise arrangement bringing China into CSCAP in 1996. The issue of Taiwanese participation in Working Groups remained fraught, coming to a head at the 2004 Steering Committee meeting in Kunming. In what was a particularly tense session that threatened to deadlock the Council, Ball played an adept role in achieving a complicated, consensus protocol as to the involvement in Study Groups (only) of individuals from "Chinese Taipei".[35]

One of CSCAP's most effective mechanisms for gaining regional attention has been its biennial General Conference. Every two years since 1997, the Council has orchestrated a gathering of several hundred persons for two-plus days, involving keynote addresses from senior officials and debate among expert analysts on the region's most pressing security issues. Ball and Australian official and Track 2 supporters were responsible for the third General Conference held in Canberra in 2001. Since then, Ball and Anthony Milner (who replaced Harris as Co-Chair of AusCSCAP in 2002) assumed a key role in assisting CSCAP Indonesia with the coordination of the four subsequent General Conferences in Jakarta (2003, 2005, 2007, 2009), and then with CSCAP Vietnam concerning the 2011 meeting in Hanoi. Arranging these major regional conferences, to include government ministers and senior officials, as well as leading specialists from member countries, involved much deliberation and planning. Ball and Milner worked with Wanandi (and Rizal Sukma and Clara Joewono at CSIS), Satoh (in Japan), Kwa Chong Guan (in Singapore) and others on the CSCAP front, as well as with Australian government ministers and officials, to secure high level representation and financial support from the Australian and other governments.[36] This collaboration — moving back and forth between CSCAP member committees, negotiating with governments, all in classic Track 2 style — met with success. The General Conference meetings in Jakarta have solidified the role of CSCAP as the key Track 2 institution in the region's security architecture.

Another example of Ball's ongoing campaign to raise the profile of CSCAP and demonstrate the breadth and relevance of its coverage of regional security issues was his push for it to publish an annual security review. In his 2000 review of CSCAP, he argued this would be "the most reliable and effective way ... to adequately stay abreast of regional security concerns".[37] Although CSCAP members at that time were not ready to embrace the idea, Ball and Wanandi were determined. In his account of CSCAP's development, Ball has reported how the proposal for publication of an annual *CSCAP Regional Security Outlook* was regenerated and how membership reluctance was overcome at the Wellington Steering Committee meeting of 2006.[38]

Ball reports this, but (as is the case regarding many other CSCAP achievements) he neglects to note his personal role in the process that led to this decision. Prior to this Steering Committee meeting, a small group, including Wanandi, Ball, and Job met to strategise. The feeling among those present was pessimistic, anticipating objections from certain Member Committees. Most everyone, except Ball, was leaning towards the option of production of the report by a subset of member committees — a second-best in that it could not claim to be a CSCAP document, per se. Ball persisted, insisting that the issue be brought to the Steering Committee, where he suspected that the chances of its approval were not that bleak. He, of course, called the play correctly.[39] Commencing in 2007, for the next five years under Job's editorship, the *CSCAP Regional Security Outlook* was produced and widely distributed at General Conferences and at the ASEAN ISIS Round Table meetings.

Ball's agitation that CSCAP sustain its viability and relevance is most apparent concerning its Study Groups (previously termed 'Working Groups'). The output of the Study/Working Groups, is the "the most straightforward measure of CSCAP's achievements is its utility to the ARF".[40] At its inception, CSCAP established four Working Groups, focused on CSBMs, maritime cooperation, security cooperation in the North Pacific, and cooperative and comprehensive security. Throughout the 1990s, these groups had more than 70 meetings and produced approximately 20 volumes of papers and proceedings.[41] However, by 2000 there was a growing sense that changes were necessary. Ball was called upon to chair a Review Committee, which in turn led to a 2003 Co-Chairs' report by Barry Desker and Job, calling for a significant reorientation to the Study Group model. In sum, the existing groups were seen to have run their course, variously having outlived their mandates, becoming too generally focused, and/or overlapping each other.[42] In order to sustain relevance, and to parallel the trend of the ARF towards focusing on "non-traditional security" threats, CSCAP would have to broaden its coverage to a greater range of the spectrum of security issues affecting the region's states and its populations.

Through the efforts of Ball and other reform-minded CSCAP figures, major changes were implemented in 2003–2004. The outcome was a move to the Study Groups, each limited to a term of one to three years, and each subject to closer scrutiny concerning its productivity. The results have been appreciable on several dimensions. In terms of numbers, commencing with six new Study Groups in 2004, more than ten additional groups were created by 2010.[43] In substantive terms, the scope of CSCAP's attention has expanded dramatically, bringing the institution more in line with the transformations of security concerns within the region itself. Noteworthy, as examples, are the Study Groups on human trafficking, energy security, climate security, the future of the ARF, security of offshore oil and gas installations, and the Responsibility to Protect (R2P).

Organisations to remain viable and relevant must change to reflect their environments. Failure to do so leads to institutional stasis and/or dissolution — the fate of many regional Track 2 initiatives over the years. Ball's efforts have been instrumental in bringing the effective changes and progressive adaptation to CSCAP that have facilitated maintaining its role as the region's primary Track 2 institution.

CSCAP: Ball as Constructive Critic

"CSCAP itself should be subject to regular review. Otherwise, it risks ossification."[44]

Ball simultaneously has been one of CSCAP's strongest supporters and one of its most consistent and vocal critics. Operating "from inside the tent" has given him a crucial vantage point from which to observe problems, but also an advantage in terms of being able to target suggestions for reform. However, Ball has taken care to temper his assessments of CSCAP with three caveats. The first, and most general, is the difficulty of establishing causality for policy change particularly in a multilateral, and multi-actor context. Beyond counting communications and meetings, there are no easy metrics that can be applied to efforts to build trust and confidence. Seldom do policy-makers acknowledge the source of their ideas or the specific factors that led to a particular decision. Assessment of CSCAP's impact, therefore, remains an imprecise undertaking.[45]

The second, as Ball[46] and others[47] have acknowledged, is that CSCAP confronts "inherent sources of tensions" — "both creative and debilitating". The dimensions of diversity that prevail within CSCAP are daunting. Disagreements prevail between members regarding procedures, agenda setting, and the relationship between Track 2, national governments and regional institutions. While CSCAP has succeeded in softening these divisions, by adopting a pragmatic and incremental approach to institutional reforms and by avoiding what certain members regard as "internal" matters, there is a limit to the extent that a multilateral institution with an inclusive membership can overcome such tensions.

Third, CSCAP is constrained by the structural parameters of its regional environment. As Ball put it over a decade ago, "CSCAP is a doubly dependent subject in the overall calculus of regional security. Its success depends on both its contributions to the second track processes ... [but] also on the extent to which the cooperative modalities are influencing regional security architecture".[48] Within this context, CSCAP is further constrained as discussed below by being tied, by default, to the ARF. Thus, "CSCAP's limitations echo the ARF's limitations".[49]

Ball characterises CSCAP's institutional life as having three phases: a formative, institutionalisation phase from 1992–93 to 1996; a period from the late 1990s to mid-2000s of CSCAP reform and ARF-alignment; and the years since the mid-2000s oriented towards institutionalisation of

CSCAP-ARF linkages. His perspective on CSCAP's progress is seen in two previously noted monographs.[50] Each reports on approximately a decade of CSCAP experience and anticipates its future. In both reviews, Ball touts the success of CSCAP, in part from an existential perspective — that is, celebrating its establishment and longevity — and in part because of what he regards, particularly in its formative years, as its "extraordinary' achievements".[51] However, concerning the ensuing years, Ball's tone has become decidedly more critical. Indeed, while acknowledging limited progress on certain fronts, mainly its relationship to the ARF, Ball in 2010 expresses some serious doubts about the ability of CSCAP to remain viable in the rapidly evolving contemporary regional security environment.

His concerns, as echoed by various others in the 2010 volume, fall into four categories. The first concerns the "autonomy dilemma," that is, the difficulty to achieve open and independent debate among Track 2 participants and across Track 1 and Track 2. In CSCAP venues, officials are often unwilling or unable to engage in their "private capacities"; unofficial participants stick to their government's positions; Member Committees are essentially government institutions and/or are financially dependent on government funding.[52]

Second, is that CSCAP's relationship to the ARF is and will remain complex. The dilemma is that it has been difficult for CSCAP to complement and support the ARF's agenda, when the ARF itself has been largely stalled on the first step of its proclaimed agenda of moving from confidence building to preventive diplomacy. In this regard, CSCAP did accomplish one notable achievement. Through the concerted energies of its CSBM Working Group in the late 1990s, a "working definition of preventive diplomacy" was crafted and subsequently accepted by the ARF.[53] Little, however, has been accomplished since then, with Ball acknowledging in 2000 and reiterating in 2010 that "progress with preventive diplomacy has been [and remains] very slow".[54]

Since then, CSCAP's efforts since the mid-2000s have focused on aligning its Study Group agendas and outputs with those of the ARF's various Intersessional Support Group (ISG) and Intersessional Support Meetings (ISM), and on producing CSCAP Memoranda to be forwarded to the ARF Senior Officials Meetings (SOMs). Initiatives advocated by Ball — including holding CSCAP Study Group meetings back-to-back with ARF ISM or ISG meetings and CSCAP Co-Chair attendance as observers to the ARF Ministerial — have been realised. The results are seen as encouraging, insofar as they coordinate with ARF activities. The larger issue, of course, remains the relevance of the ARF itself in today's evolving security architecture.[55]

The third and fourth questions centre on CSCAP's adaptability and capacity to define a role within the currently transforming regional security architecture. On the one hand, this is a matter of CSCAP's focusing its agenda on the security issues that "really matter" to the region's populations. Intrastate conflicts and the threats posed by environmental change and natural disaster are arguably more immediate and life threatening to Asia-Pacific's citizens than the traditional, interstate security preoccupations (and defence spending) of its governments. CSCAP has begun to address some of these issues through Study Groups, for example, terrorism, climate change, energy security. However, with the exception of a few tightly focused reports that have reflected substantial input from experts, either governmental or unofficial — for instance, on export-controls, or Responsibility to Protect — many others have largely repeated generalities already known and accepted.

Ball has made his opinion clear as to the necessity of CSCAP's expanding the spectrum of its attention, citing the relevance of human security, and exhorting CSCAP "to pursue an agenda which incorporates a comprehensive definition of security".[56] He has observed that the "urgency of environmental problems demands that CSCAP procrastinate no longer." In his view, "CSCAP cannot truly claim to be promoting real security in the region, unless and until the human dimension becomes a central feature of its activities".

Finally, CSCAP is faced with the challenge of defining its identity and role in the future security architecture of Asia. While it is too soon to predict any precise shape that this architecture may assume, the direction of development of new institutional forms is being debated, for example regarding the East Asia Summit (EAS). Associated Track 2 mechanisms are burgeoning (as they did in the early 1990s, another period of regional transformation), leaving the relevance of CSCAP in its current status and its tied relationship to the ARF in question. Ball's concern that CSCAP remain viable is palpable in his recent writings with colleagues. CSCAP, he says, lacks "the public profile that its capabilities and activities warrant".[57] He warns CSCAP of the danger of being the "victim of its own success." There is a "drastic need for further improvements in the relationship between Tracks 1, 2, and 3".[58] Whether CSCAP is able to adapt accordingly

— particularly in its further engagement with Asia's civil society and its security concerns — remains uncertain for Ball.

AusCSCAP: Building a Track 2 Foundation at the National Level

Ball and his AusCSCAP colleagues — specialists from academic, business, think tank, and official foreign policy and defence communities — have remained dedicated to advancing their country's role within the region, as would be expected in the regional Track 2 process. Ball and Milner have described the national Track 2 agenda as having three components:

> We have to relate to our government — build up relationships with key officials and where possible key ministers, and learn what are the issues that concern (or ought to concern) government. This has to be done at both the national and the regional level (in CSCAP's case, particularly with the ARF). Secondly, relations of trust need to be established and developed with regional Track 2 partners — relations that allow for frank and productive discussion. Thirdly, Track 2 has to reach out to other areas outside government — to academia, the media, think tanks, the business world and so forth. It needs to assume a broker role — drawing people with relevant expertise into Track 2 deliberations, making sure that topics considered to be of regional or national urgency are examined by the best specialists available. A further aspect of the broker role entails informing the wider regional and national communities about the urgent issues identified by Government and Track 2.[59]

Ball has worked in all of these directions as Co-Chair of the Australian Member Committee of CSCAP, initially with Harris and then (from 2002) Milner. Especially through the building of relations with government (as noted earlier), AusCSCAP has developed into one of the most effective Member Committees within CSCAP.

Most CSCAP Member Committees, apart from those that are simply extensions of officialdom, have relatively small, elite circles of active members, and confine their activity to a single campus or particular institute. AusCSCAP, however, is an exception. Influenced by a need to accommodate Australia's federal structure, the decision was taken to hold AusCSCAP meetings outside of Canberra, on a regular basis, in the different state capitals. The goal, which was certainly attained, was to bring Canberra-based officials and other specialists into dialogue with the concentrations of expertise in Melbourne, Sydney, Brisbane, Perth and

Adelaide — to broaden the knowledge-base, to give people in the states a better sense of thinking in Canberra.[60] In this national strategy, Ball has advanced a model of Track 2 brokering — engaging with a range of people in business, politics, the media and academia — conveying the relevance of regional security to an Australian community extending well beyond usual CSCAP circles.

AusCSCAP has been innovative on another dimension, that is, bilateral engagement with other Member Committees. The pioneering and ambitious initiative that produced the widely read *Voices of Islam in Southeast Asia*[61] volume is worth noting here. The research process involved in his project was a bilateral AusCSCAP-CSCAP Indonesia collaboration. With the assistance of Wanandi and the Singapore Islamist specialist Sharon Siddique, Ball and Milner initiated a project that brought together material from jurists, women's and youth groups, poets, activists and journalists, as well as religious scholars and political leaders. The focus of the resulting book (edited by Greg Fealy and Virginia Hooker) reflects the many facets of Islamic thinking in Southeast Asia, reaching far beyond narrow security issues to yield insights into the concerns that in some cases fostered extremism and terrorist acts.

Voices of Islam in Southeast Asia was produced at a time when both governments and wider publics in the region saw the vital importance of gaining a deeper understanding of aspirations and anxieties in Islamic community. The research itself helped to promote regional networks of trust and understanding extending beyond the normal Track 2 security community. Track 2 was reaching out, as Ball felt it always should, to people who had no previous Track 2 experience but who possessed valuable expertise and experience. CSCAP's role was as facilitator and broker. On a more personal note, Ball read diligently about Islamic social ideas, gaining genuine respect for the new points of view he encountered. He developed new friendships, and demonstrated again his flexibility and breadth of vision as a scholar and intellectual.

Bridging the Conceptual-Policy Divide

Despite the time and energy Ball has invested in building a Track 2 foundation to regional security architecture, he did not falter in his contribution to scholarship. Most individuals have difficulty in bridging what Ball and Kwa have termed the "conceptual/policy divide".[62] Within the Track 2 community, certainly as discussed within CSCAP, the tension between what is seen as abstract academic scholarship and applied policy-relevant analysis certainly exists. Academics confront the criticism that theoretical work is distant from the realities of international affairs. Policy-oriented analysts, in turn, are characterised as lacking conceptual rigor and failing to question the underlying assumptions of their work.

On regional security architecture, and particularly Track 2's role within it, Ball has sustained a dual role, contributing works that have become touchstones for his academic colleagues,[63] while also maintaining a virtually continuous output of working papers and commissioned reports providing trenchant advice to policy makers.[64] Ball remains dismissive of the notion that academic work and policy analysis are fundamentally at odds:

> Neither theoretical work nor good scholarship is incompatible with policy relevance. Indeed ... they could well have a symbiotic relationship. ... [P]olicy related activity ... should inform conceptual study. On the other hand, conceptual activity should broaden the discourse, expose fundamental linkages ... and explore possible approaches to the resolution of fundamental security issues. ... [T]hey will, of course, be judged by different criteria — excellence of analysis and policy utility — but not ones that defy optimization.[65]

Ball has, through his own work on regional security - and suggested in this chapter on Track 2 dialogues and institutions - fully met these criteria of excellence, challenging the rest of us to attain the same high standards.

Notes

1. Desmond Ball, "Arms and Affluence: Military Acquisitions in the Asia-Pacific", *International Security* 18, no. 3 (1993/94): 78–112; Desmond Ball, *The Council for Security Cooperation in the Asia-Pacific: Its Record and Its Prospects* (Canberra: Security and Defence Studies Centre, 2000) and; Desmond Ball, "Reflections on Defence Security Architecture in East Asia", *RSIS Working Paper* no. 237 (Singapore: RSIS, 2012).
2. Desmond Ball, "Tasks for Security Cooperation in Asia", in *Security Cooperation in the Asia-Pacific Region* edited by Desmond Ball, Richard Grant and Jusuf Wanandi (Washington: Center for Srategic and International Studies, 1993), p. 18.
3. Ibid., pp. 25–29.
4. Ball, "Arms and Affluence:".
5. Ibid.

6. Indeed, Ball (2012, p. 2) continues to emphasise this point today. He states "I am not persuaded that the purposes, structures, operational modalities and achievements of these organizations [NATO and the EU] are central to any consideration of a South East Asian Defence Model."
7. Desmond Ball, "Strategic Culture in the Asia-Pacific Region", *Security Studies* 3, no. 1 (1993), p. 44.
8. Desmond Ball, "A New Era in Confidence Building: The Second-Track Process in the Asia-Pacific Region", *Security Dialogue* 25, no. 2 (1994), p. 166.
9. Ball, "Tasks for Security Cooperation in Asia", p. 18 and; Ibid., p. 158.
10. Ball, "A New Era", p. 158.
11. Ball, "Tasks for Security Cooperation in Asia", p. 18.
12. Paul Evans, "Building Security: The Council for Security Cooperation in the Asia-Pacific (CSCAP)", *The Pacific Review* 7, no. 2 (1994): 127.
13. Security dialogue activity grew dramatically in the region through to the mid-1990s, dropped significantly for about five years, and escalated dramatically after 2001. For the record and analysis of trends, see: Brian Job, "Track 2 Diplomacy: Ideational Contribution to the Evolving Asian Security Order", *Assessing Track 2 Diplomacy in the Asia-Pacific Region*, edited by Desmond Ball and Kwa Chong Guan (Canberra: Strategic and Defence Studies Centre, Australian National University, 2003/2010), pp. 112–61. Original article (2003) plus research note, co-authored with Avery Poole (2010).
14. For history and definition of the terms Track 1, Track 2, and Track 3 as employed in the Asia-Pacific context, the standard reference is: David Capie, and Paul Evans, *The Asia-Pacific Security Lexicon* (Singapore: Institute of Southeast Asian Studies, 2007).
15. Ball, "Strategic Culture in the Asia-Pacific Region", p. 44.
16. Ball, "Tasks for Security Cooperation in Asia", pp. 22–23.
17. Ball, "Arms and Affluence", p. 109.
18. Desmond Ball, *Building Blocks for Regional Security: An Australian Perspective on Confidence and Security Building Measures (CSBMs) in the Asia-Pacific* (Canberra: Strategic and Defence Studies Centre, 1991), p. 89.
19. Amitav Acharya, *Whose Ideas Matter? Agency and Power in Asian Regionalism* (Ithaca: Cornell University Press, 2009), pp. 112–14 and; Jusuf Wanandi, "ASEAN ISIS and Its Regional and International Networking", in *Twenty Two Years of ASEAN ISIS: origin, evolution and challegnes of Track Two diplomacy*, edited by Hadi Soesastro, Clara Joewono and Carolina G. Hernandez (Jakarta: CSIS, 2006), p. 34.
20. Regional players and analysts appreciated Evan's "sensitivity" on this matter. See: Acharya, *Whose Ideas Matter?*, p. 116.
21. Desmond Ball, "Multilateral Security Cooperation in the Asia-Pacific Region: Prospects and Possibilities", *RSIS Working Paper* 2 (Singapore: RSIS, 1999), p. 14.

22. Gareth Evans, and Paul Dibb, *Australian Paper on Practical Proposals for Security Cooperation in the Asia-Pacific Region* (Canberra: Department of Foreign Affairs and Trade, 1993), p. 13.
23. Ball, "A New Era in Confidence Building".
24. Wanandi, "ASEAN ISIS and Its Regional and International Networking", p. 33.
25. Ball is recognised by the ASEAN editors of a history of ASEAN-ISIS — along with Paul Evans and Mely Anthony-Caballero — as a 'participant observer' who has made 'a valuable contribution' not only to CSCAP but to the development of ASEAN ISIS itself. See: Hadi Soesastro, Clara Joewono and Carolina G. Hernandez, eds., *Twenty Two Years of Asean Isis* (Jakarta: CSIS, 2006), p. 1.
26. The organisation and operation of CSCAP, details of membership, description of Study and Working Groups is set out in detail in Desmond Ball and Chong Guan Kwa, eds., *Assessing Track 2 Diplomacy in the Asia-Pacific Region: A CSCAP Reader* (Canberra: Strategic and Defence Studies Centre, Australian National University, 2010), which provides a detailed accounting of the Working Groups. Texts of the output of all CSCAP Study and Working Groups is available at www.cscap.org.
27. Desmond Ball, *The Council for Security Cooperation in the Asia-Pacific: Its Record and Its Prospects* (Canberra: Security and Defence Studies Centre, Australian National University 2000), p. 6.
28. Desmond Ball, personal communication with Anthony Milner, 18 March 2012.
29. Ball, *The Council for Security Cooperation*, p. 47.
30. Evans, "Building Security", p. 130.
31. Desmond Ball, "CSCAP: Its Future Place in the Regional Security Architecture", in *Managing Security and Peace in the Asia-Pacific*, edited by Bunn Nagara and Cheah Siew Ean (Kuala Lumpur: Institute of Strategic and International Studies, 1996), p. 306.
32. Herman Joseph S. Kraft, "The Autonomy Dilemma of Track Two Diplomacy in Southeast Asia", *Security Dialogue* 31, no. 3 (2000): 343–56.
33. Note here his contributions to the Australia-Asia Perceptions Project of the Academy of the Social Sciences in Australia (in the early 1990s) and his continuing, co-leadership of the Australian Research Council project, 'The Languages of Security in the Asia-Pacific'.
34. Ball and Kwa, *Assessing Track 2 Diplomacy in the Asia-Pacific Region*, p. 43.
35. Personal recollection of Job, who was CSCAP Co-Chair at that time.
36. Funding also came from Japan and Singapore — and ministers and senior officials from these and other regional countries also accepted invitations to attend.
37. Ball, *The Council for Security Cooperation*, p. 58.
38. Ball and Kwa, *Assessing Track 2 Diplomacy in the Asia-Pacific Region*, pp. 43–45.

39. Job's personal recollection.
40. Ball, *The Council for Security Cooperation*, pp. 58, 47.
41. Ball and Kwa, *Assessing Track 2 Diplomacy in the Asia-Pacific Region*, pp. 20–28.
42. Ibid., p. 31.
43. Ibid., pp. 33–41.
44. Ball, *The Council for Security Cooperation in the Asia-Pacific: Its Record and Its Prospects*, p. 89.
45. Ball and Kwa, *Assessing Track 2 Diplomacy in the Asia-Pacific Region*, pp. 252–54, which addresses the difficulty of assessment in more detail, as does Job, "Track 2 Diplomacy".
46. Ball, *The Council for Security Cooperation in the Asia-Pacific*, p. 1.
47. See Evans, "Building Security"; Sheldon W. Simon, "Evaluating Track II Approaches to Security Diplomacy in the Asia-Pacific: The CSCAP Experience", *The Pacific Review* 15, no. 2 (2002): 167–202 and; Brendan Taylor, and Anthony Milner, "Track 2: Developments and Prospects", in Desmond Ball and Chong Guan Kwa, eds., *Assessing Track 2 Diplomacy in the Asia-Pacific Region: A CSCAP Reader* (Canberra: Strategic and Defence Studies Centre, 2010): 179–90.
48. Ball, "Evaluating Track II Approaches to Security Diplomacy", p. 35.
49. Simon, "Evaluating Track II Approaches to Security Diplomacy", p. 170.
50. Ball, *The Council for Security Cooperation in the Asia-Pacific: Its Record and Its Prospects* and; Ball and Kwa, *Assessing Track 2 Diplomacy in the Asia-Pacific Region: A CSCAP Reader*.
51. Ball, *The Council for Security Cooperation in the Asia-Pacific*, p. 2.
52. Ball, *The Council for Security Cooperation in the Asia-Pacific: Its Record and Its Prospects*; but previously "The Autonomy Dilemma of Track Two Diplomacy in Southeast Asia".
53. See Ralph Cossa, "The ASEAN Regional Forum: Moving Towards Preventive Diplomacy," in *Assessing Track 2 Diplomacy in the Asia-Pacific Region: A CSCAP Reader,* edited by Desmond Ball and Kwa Chong Guan (Canberra: Strategic and Defence Studies Centre, 2010): 219–26.
54. Ball, *The Council for Security Cooperation in the Asia-Pacific: Its Record and Its Prospects*, pp. 40 and 82 and; Ball and Kwa, *Assessing Track 2 Diplomacy in the Asia-Pacific Region: A CSCAP Reader*.
55. Ibid.
56. Ball, *The Council for Security Cooperation in the Asia-Pacific*, pp. 64, 78, and 85.
57. Ibid., p. 252.
58. Desmond Ball, Anthony Milner, and Brendan Taylor, *Track II: Mapping Track II Institutions in New Zealand, Australia and the Asian Region* (Wellington: The Asia-New Zealand Foundation, 2005), p. 184.
59. Desmond Ball, personal communication with Anthony Milner, 18 March 2012.

60. Business-sector leaders were involved in these meetings, and in a number of cases dinner meetings have been arranged to supplement the CSCAP meeting. In some of the state capital visits AusCSCAP has held a part or all of the meeting in collaboration with high-profile local institutions — such as Asialink in Melbourne, and the Lowy Institute in Sydney.
61. Greg Fealy, and Virginia Hooker, eds., *Voices of Islam in Southeast Asia: A Contemporary Source Book* (Singapore: Institute of Southeast Asian Studies, 2006).
62. Ball and Kwa, *Assessing Track 2 Diplomacy in the Asia-Pacific Region*, p. 252.
63. See: Ball, "Arms and Affluence"; Ball, "Strategic Culture in the Asia-Pacific Region"; Ball, "Tasks for Security Cooperation in Asia"; Ball, "A New Era in Confidence Building"; Ball, Milner and Taylor, *Track 2 Diplomacy in Asia* and; Ball, Milner Taylor, "Track 2 Security Dialogue in the Asia-Pacific: Reflections and Future Directions".
64. See: Ball, "Reflections on Defence Security Architecture in East Asia"; Ball, Milner and Taylor, *Track II: Mapping Track II Institutions in New Zealand, Australia and the Asian Region*, and his numerous *Strategic and Defence Studies Centre Working Papers*.
65. Ibid., p. 255.

11

GAZING DOWN AT THE BREAKERS

Euan Graham

Maritime security, writ large, is a broad canvas enmeshing everything from high-intensity naval warfare and territorial disputes to low-end criminal acts and matters of navigational safety. Non-state and transnational issues, such as piracy, maritime terrorism and trafficking at sea, have featured prominently in the definition for much of the post-Cold War period. In recent years, however, there has been a noticeable tilt towards a more inter-state agenda, defined by such concerns as creeping jurisdiction, competition over offshore resources and a region-wide naval arms build-up. Through his Track 2 work, Des Ball has maintained a lengthy association with the full spectrum of maritime activity in the region. But it is in the context of this tilt back towards the inter-state dimensions of security that Des' earlier body of work on navies and arms control is regaining new relevance.

The maritime domain, by the same token, is also a useful thematic window on to Des' cosmopolitan interests in regional security: strategic, comprehensive, cooperative and technical. His major contributions fall within four inter-connecting themes: nuclear strategy at sea, naval arms racing, confidence building and technical intelligence gathering.

NUCLEAR STRATEGY AT SEA

Des' interest in naval affairs and the maritime domain can be traced to his doctoral research on nuclear strategy during the presidency of John F. Kennedy (1961–1963). During this still-raw phase of the Cold War — Des' intellectual point of departure for a career-spanning interest in strategic arms control — the submarine arm was first established as the most survivable prong of the nuclear triad, an attribute it maintains to this day. This did not wholly obviate the traditional concern of navies with manoeuvre and projection. But the stark mission requirement of the ballistic missile submarine (SSBN), to reliably deliver Armageddon, cast a long and strange shadow over the Cold War at sea.

The advent of the SSBN as a major focus of the superpowers' strategic competition also played to Des' abiding and somewhat double-edged fascination with nuclear strategy and military secrecy. As a young scholar exposed to the foment of the Vietnam protest movement in Australia and the United States, Des nonetheless acquired an appreciation of this esoteric subset of naval warfare, as well as the risks of escalation that he would later go on, with forceful logic, to argue were significantly under-managed. It was not until the mid-1980s that Des acquired a specific research interest in the naval domain, following the adoption of the Maritime Strategy by the US Navy. Des latched on to the emphasis on forward offensive operations within the Maritime Strategy, and the associated concept of 'horizontal escalation' in the Soviet Far East, as destabilising for several reasons:

- First, control of nuclear weapons was looser at sea given the greater autonomy of naval commanders, at least where American vessels were concerned.
- Second, the doctrines and operational procedures associated with sea-based nuclear weapons were subject to less well-defined thresholds than apply on land.
- Third, Des questioned the prevailing assumption that the use of nuclear weapons at sea could be contained more easily than on land.

Concerning the latter, he maintained that the opposite applied, since the distinction between tactical and strategic targeting at, and from, the sea had become increasingly blurred with the introduction of new technology, chiefly the Tomahawk cruise missile. *Provocative Plans*, a Canberra Paper, was published in 1991, just as the Soviet Union was unwinding.[1] Its immediate relevance, geared towards strategic competition between the superpowers, was therefore cut short. Even at the time, doubts were expressed about the operational credibility of the Maritime Strategy and its assumption that high-tempo naval conflict between the superpowers could realistically be prosecuted without triggering a strategic exchange.

Twenty years on from *Provocative Plans*, while nuclear deterrence is no longer so dominant within American naval strategy and nuclear weapons have been removed from the US Navy surface fleet, Des' late Cold War analysis still bears scrutiny. There are echoes of horizontal escalation in the emerging Air-Sea Battle concept and its presumed emphases on deep strike, stand off capabilities and the exploitation of favourable asymmetries. There is also the possibility that a variant of the Soviet 'bastion' strategy, to protect SSBNs around layered defences within adjacent waters, may emerge as a strategic option for China in the South China Sea. While Asia in other senses has moved on from the Cold War, some of the potentially destabilising strategic dynamics that Des identified in *Provocative Plans* may, in fact, be more pertinent to the early 21st century 'Indo-Pacific' maritime security environment, in which the strategic nuclear element is being re-asserted — and not only between the United States and China.

As Des has highlighted in his most recent work focusing on Asia's naval acquisitions, strategic interactions and unplanned encounters between the major maritime powers in Asia are set to increase in the coming decades. While the United States and Russia remain active players in Asia's undersea nuclear balance, China and India are both expanding their SSBN and nuclear attack submarine (SSN) fleets. For the moment, conventional power projection and 'sea denial' capabilities dominate the discourse on naval arms racing, but the nuclear strategic element has every potential to intensify in a fluid and less predictable strategic environment. Des has warned that a "nuclear arms race between India and China, which is a real possibility, would be especially disturbing".[2] He has also highlighted the need for confidence building measures specifically to address nuclear weapons at sea. In an important sense therefore, Des' formative research focus on nuclear arms control is returning full circle in Asia's maritime element.

NAVAL ARMS RACING

For the past two decades Des has closely observed trends in naval arms acquisitions and modernisation in the Asia-Pacific in a more universal sense. In the early 1990s, he was among the first academics to begin tracking the general trend towards naval arms modernisation across East Asia. At this juncture, Des was careful not to overstate the competitive acquisition dynamics in the region, which in his view fell short of the standard definitions of "arms racing". Rather, he identified economic growth and a long-term transition from internal security paradigms towards external defence as more generalised drivers.[3] However, Des' recent scholarship on this theme strikes a more concerned note about the prospects for an uncontrolled arms dynamic in the region, in particular the build-up of maritime power projection capabilities.[4] In Northeast Asia, at least, Des has tied his colours to the mast, by declaring that a naval arms race is now under way.

CONFIDENCE BUILDING AND PREVENTATIVE DIPLOMACY

One of Des' most highly valued contributions to maritime security in the Asia-Pacific has been his unstinting support and promotion of maritime confidence-building and preventive diplomacy measures on both the Track 1 and Track 2 agendas.[5] His concept paper for the second ASEAN Regional Forum (ARF) meeting, held in Brunei in 1995, was particularly influential in setting the ARF down a maritime cooperative track.[6] Des can claim a share of the credit for the ARF's later adoption of maritime security as a designated focus area for cooperation.

Des' advocacy of regional maritime confidence and security-building measures (MCSBMs) predates the foundation of the Council for Security Cooperation in the Asia-Pacific (CSCAP) in 1993.[7] Sam Bateman, who retired as a Commodore from the Royal Australian Navy (RAN) and has worked closely with Des on the maritime security agenda, recalls a meeting in Kuala Lumpur in the early 1990s at which Des launched the idea of a Regional Maritime Surveillance and Safety Regime (RMSSR), a concept which he subsequently refined and developed in collaboration with Russ Swinnerton, another retired RAN officer and well-regarded maritime analyst.[8] The RMSSR proposal was far-sighted but the concept of sharing information on such a broad level was not uncontroversial within regional navies, the RAN included. Critically, Des found a receptive ear in the then Chief of Naval Staff, the late VADM Michael Hudson (1933–2005) who considered the proposal favourably. Hudson had been instrumental in the 1988 establishment of the Western Pacific Naval Symposium (WPNS), one of the earliest and most enduring regional MCSBMs, which has since been emulated in the Indian Ocean with the establishment of an analogue naval symposium, in 2007. Other lines of influence can be drawn between the RMSSR and the onus of United States-led efforts since the 9/11 attacks on promoting regional maritime domain awareness, and other maritime information-sharing initiatives, such as Singapore's Changi-based Information Fusion Centre. Des was far ahead of the curve on this.

In the 1990s, however, such concepts were not yet mainstream; nor was Des always assured of a welcome at Russell Hill. This made Admiral Hudson's receptiveness to external, "bigger picture" thinking all the more important. Des' collaboration with Bateman on the proposed Joint Patrol Vessel project between the Royal Malaysian Navy and the RAN, was another example of their willingness to challenge the orthodoxy with creative thinking more appropriate to the evolving post-Cold War maritime security agenda, though this did not always gain acceptance within defence circles.[9]

I worked with Des on Track 2 as the Executive Officer for the Australian Member Committee for CSCAP, around 2000–01. During this time I witnessed his commitment to promoting maritime confidence-building initiatives through CSCAP and, where resistance was encountered, his ability to put together supportive constituencies at either the regional or national levels. Back in 1993, Des had been instrumental in establishing CSCAP's Maritime Cooperation Working Group.[10] Under Sam Bateman's active co-chairmanship, maritime cooperation quickly established itself as one of the most productive and influential of CSCAP's working streams and "earned a reputation as one of the most important second-track activities concerning maritime security matters in the region".[11] In all, the Working Group produced five volumes of edited papers, constituting an "excellent and well-balanced reference material on the prospects and pitfalls for Asian maritime cooperation", in addition to several CSCAP memoranda including Guidelines for Regional Maritime Cooperation, in 1997, and Memorandum No. 6, The Practice of the Law of the Sea in the Asia-Pacific, in 2002.[12]

In terms of Des' influence over my research, I first met him in 1996 as a freshly inducted Ph.D. student at the Australian National University's Strategic and Defence Studies Centre (SDSC), where (with some persuasion) he supervised my thesis on Japan's sea lane security, in the process setting me on my own maritime course. Approaching Japan's sea lane concerns — economic, military and political — comprehensively, Des' wide-angle lens was helpful for scoping out a wide range of "high" and "low" maritime security concerns, from naval strategy and alliance politics, to Japan's nuanced and quietly effective sea lane diplomacy with the littoral states of Southeast Asia. His input on the nexus between sea lane defence and United States global strategy was particularly insightful; his grasp of structure always helpful and disciplining.

Unsurprisingly, over several years at SDSC and as a tenant in the Ball household, Des' sometimes obsessive penchant for intelligence matters, signals intelligence (SIGINT) in particular, eventually insinuated itself into my research. On Japan this interest became collaborative, leading to an SDSC working paper on Japan's airborne SIGINT capabilities, while also informing my thesis and subsequent book.[13] Des' research on SIGINT in Japan continues, covering both Japan's extensive national capabilities as well as the United States' collection and processing effort mounted from bases in Japanese territory. There is a strong maritime dimension to both, focused as they are on potential sea and air-based threats emanating from the Northeast Asian littoral. The importance of Japan's role within United States strategy as an 'unsinkable aircraft carrier' became well known in the 1980s, and as a natural buffer between the western Pacific and the Sea of Japan and East China Sea. Much less widely appreciated but equally 'strategic' has been Japan's unsung function as a springboard for a vast American electronic intelligence-gathering effort to monitor the Soviet/Russian Far East, China and North Korea. Amassing a fragmented and sometimes conflicting body of evidence over several years, Des has nonetheless synthesised a detailed picture of SIGINT in Japan, which though as yet unpublished has informed his recent scholarship on naval arms racing in Northeast Asia, identifying Electronic Warfare (EW) systems, Information Warfare and cyber-warfare capabilities among the most pronounced competitive elements to recent acquisitions in the sub-region.

Des' students and intellectual collaborators come to understand that there are distinct "micro" and "macro" facets to the way he organises information and orders his thoughts, combining an intense focus on the minutiae of a problem, often technical in nature, with the ability to contextualise this at political, strategic and theoretical levels. With the added attributes of elephantine recall, a driving curiosity — for secrets especially — and a wry sense of humour, Des' eclectic intellectual toolkit gives him a well-rounded and pleasingly eccentric range. While Des' work brain is permanently engaged, out of the office I have heard him deliver impromptu lectures on subjects as diverse and compartmentalised as the life-cycle of the Murray River crayfish, the history of space-based surveillance systems, gold prospecting in the Snowy Mountains, and the Collingwood Football Club. Where the latter's fortunes and his loyalties are concerned, Des' academic detachment has been known to desert him. Des was raised in the quiet of Timboon, Victorian dairy farming country, deceptively close to Australia's most dramatic stretch of coastline near the Twelve Apostles. I once accompanied him there. Gazing down at the great breakers crashing into Loch Ard Gorge, beard and grizzled locks blowing to all four corners, he might have been taken for Neptune himself, albeit in a unique Australian incarnation.

TECHNICAL INTELLIGENCE GATHERING

Another of Des' significant research contributions in the maritime domain relates to military intelligence gathering within the 200 nautical mile Exclusive Economic Zone (EEZ). This is an activity ambiguously defined under the Law of the Sea, hence a bone of continuing international contention. On the one hand, ocean-going naval powers tend to assert maximalist freedoms of navigation and overflight. On the other, coastal states seek to maximise sovereign rights within their EEZs, while many would prefer to keep the reach of foreign powers at arm's length. United States surveillance activities within China's EEZ have been a particular trigger for tensions within Sino-American relations, but the issue is more widespread. Within the wider region India, Malaysia and Thailand have all expressed similar reservations over foreign military activities within their EEZs.

Des was among the first publicly to highlight the implications of the changing technology, predicting that the increased demand for technical intelligence collection would lead to more surface and overflight surveillance activities occurring within the EEZ, and that such activities were likely to be perceived as intrusive and provocative by coastal states. In 2004, Des published "Intelligence Collection Operations and EEZs: the Implications of New Technology" for the *Journal of Marine Policy*. The article outlined the exponential growth of SIGINT and electronic warfare (EW) activity in Asia and predicted its continuing expansion in the decade to come, including a threefold increase in the intensity of intelligence collection flights. Des correctly surmised that the increased demand for electronic intelligence gathered in offshore zones and a corresponding imperative for the targets of collection to take pre-emptive measures "will generate tensions and more frequent crises".[14] Sure enough, the issue of military surveillance activities played a significant part in souring United States-China relations in the South China Sea towards the end of the last decade, including the March 2009 incident involving the USNS *Impeccable* off Hainan, and is central to the current American diplomatic concern with upholding freedom of navigation. Des has also played a part in nudging forward Track 2 efforts in this vexed area. According to Bateman, Des' paper at the Tokyo meeting of the EEZ Group 21 had a major influence on the subsequent development of "Prospective Guidelines for Navigation and Overflight in the Exclusive Economic Zone", in September 2005.[15]

Taken across these four diverse themes, Des' contributions to the maritime security agenda in East Asia have been far-reaching, sustained and influential. It is to Des' credit that his analysis retains its relevance 25 years on. Yet it is also a salutary reminder that despite his efforts and those of like-minded collaborators to promote the maritime dimensions of cooperative security and preventive diplomacy, East Asia appears increasingly in thrall to balance of power politics and an open-ended pattern of competitive naval acquisitions, with potentially destabilising consequences.

Notes

1. Desmond Ball, "'Provocative Plans': A Critique of US Strategy for Maritime Conflict in the Pacific", *Strategic and Defence Studies Centre Working Paper 79* (Canberra: Strategic and Defence Studies Centre, Australian National University 1991).
2. Desmond Ball, "Tensions and Arms Racing in Northeast Asia", paper delivered to the IISS-Asia MacArthur Asia Security Initiative Workshop, Singapore, November 2011.
3. Desmond Ball and Andrew Mack, "The Military Build-Up in Asia-Pacific",

The Pacific Review 5, no. 3 (1992): 197–208; Desmond Ball, "Trends in Military Acquisitions in the Asia/Pacific Region: Implications for Security and Prospects for Constraints and Controls", *Strategic and Defence Studies Centre Working Paper* 273 (Canberra: Strategic and Defence Studies Centre, Australian National University,1993) and; Panitan Wattanayagorn and Desmond Ball, "A Regional Arms Race?", *The Journal of Strategic Studies* 18, no. 3 (September 1995): 147–74.

4. Desmond Ball, *Northeast Asia: Tensions and Action-Reaction Dynamics* (forthcoming 2012 Adelphi book series). (Copy of manuscript provided by Des Ball to author.)
5. Desmond Ball, "Regional Maritime Security", in *Oceans Governance and Maritime Strategy*, edited by David Wilson and Dick Sherwood (Sydney: Allen and Unwin, 2000), pp. 59–78.
6. Desmond Ball, "Maritime Cooperation, CSCAP and the ARF", in *The Seas Unite: Maritime Cooperation in the Asia-Pacific Region*, edited by Sam Bateman and Stephen Bates (Canberra: Strategic and Defence Studies Centre, 1996), pp. 1–22.
7. Desmond Ball and Sam Bateman, "An Australian Perspective on Maritime CSBMs in the Asia-Pacific Region", *Strategic and Defence Studies Centre Working Paper* 234 (Canberra: Strategic and Defence Studies Centre, Australian National University,1991); Desmond Ball and Sam Bateman, "An Australian Perspective on Maritime CSBMs in the Asia-Pacific Region", in *A Peaceful Ocean? Maritime Security in the Pacific in the Post-Cold War Era*, edited by Andrew Mack (Sydney: Allen and Unwin, 1993), pp. 158–85.
8. Desmond Ball and Russ Swinnerton, "A Regional Regime for Maritime Surveillance, Safety and Information Exchanges", *Strategic and Defence Studies Centre Working Paper* 278 (Canberra: Strategic and Defence Studies Centre, Australian National University, 1993) and; Desmond Ball and Russ Swinnerton, "A Regional Regime for Maritime Surveillance, Safety and Information Exchanges", *Maritime Studies* 78 (September/October 1994): 1–17.
9. Desmond Ball, "The Joint Patrol Vessel (JPV): A Regional Concept for Regional Cooperation", *Strategic and Defence Studies Centre Working Paper* 303 (Canberra: Strategic and Defence Studies Centre, Australian National University, 1996).
10. From 2006, succeeded by the Study Group on Capacity Building for Maritime Security, and from 2007 the Study Group on Facilitating Maritime Cooperation in the Asia-Pacific.
11. See CSCAP, "Facilitating maritime security cooperation in the Asia-Pacific", concluded working and study group, Council for Security Cooperation in the Asia-Pacific <http://www.cscap.org/index.php?page= facilitating-maritime-security-cooperation-in-the-asia-pacific> and; Desmond Ball, and Chong Guan Kwa, eds., *Assessing Track 2 Diplomacy in the Asia-Pacific Region: A CSCAP*

Reader (Canberra: Strategic and Defence Studies Centre, Australian National University, 2010), p. 22.
12. CSCAP Study Group on Facilitating Maritime Security Cooperation in the Asia-Pacific, "Memorandum 6 — The Practice of the Law of the Sea in the Asia-Pacific", Council for Security Cooperation in the Asia-Pacific, December 2002. See: CSCAP, "Facilitating maritime security cooperation in the Asia-Pacific", concluded working and study group, Council for Security Cooperation in the Asia-Pacific <http://www.cscap.org/ index.php?page=facilitating-maritime-security-cooperation-in-the-asia-pacific>.
13. Desmond Ball and Euan Graham, "Japan's Airborne SIGINT Capabilities", *Strategic and Defence Studies Centre Working Paper* 353 (Canberra: Strategic and Defence Studies Centre, Australian National University, 2000) and; Euan Graham, "Japan's Sea Lane Security, 1940–2004: A Matter of Life and Death?" (Oxon: Routledge/Nissan Institute, 2006).
14. Desmond Ball, "Intelligence Collection Operations and EEZs: The Implications of New Technology", *Journal of Marine Policy* 28, no. 1 (2004): 67–82.
15. Ball, "Intelligence Collection Operations and EEZs" and; Desmond Ball, "The Implications of New Technology" in *The Regime of the Exclusive Economic Zone: Issues and Responses. A Report of the Tokyo Meeting*, edited by Mark Valencia (Honolulu: East-West Center, 2003), pp. 62–70.

12

A REGIONAL ARMS RACE?

Tim Huxley

I first knew Des Ball at the very start of the 1980s, when I was a doctoral student in the Australian National University's Department of International Relations that then, as now, enjoyed close relations with the Strategic and Defence Studies Centre (SDSC), where Des was a Fellow. In those days the SDSC was a much smaller set-up than now, being effectively a subset of the International Relations Department: it had a handful of staff led by my supervisor Robert (Bob) O'Neill — and no students, even at postgraduate level. Des was effectively doing the bulk of the Centre's research and writing on contemporary strategic and defence issues.

The most important focus of Des' research in the early 1980s was the central strategic balance: around the time I first knew him, he had just returned from a sojourn as a Research Associate at the International Institute for Strategic Studies (IISS) in London. He was a cutting-edge expert on issues that were close to the centre of key strategic debates, and it is unsurprising that in the context of the Cold War — or 'second Cold War' as many termed it at the time — he was not taking a close interest in regional security and defence issues. As he told me in late 2011 when we met at a conference in Hanoi, with some sense of irony, Asia was in the early years of his research activity for him essentially a region that he flew over en route Europe or North America and in which he took little direct interest. In his original lack of intense interest in Asian security affairs, Des was hardly alone among Australian International Relations and Strategic Studies scholars at the time. While Australia had been closely involved militarily in Asia since the Second World War, perhaps at least partly in reaction to Canberra's commitment to the unpopular Vietnam War (against which Des had been an activist) he and many others in the field in Australia looked beyond the region to what they saw as the larger and — then at least — more important strategic game.

Des was a friendly and (importantly, from the perspective of a newly-arrived and very young postgraduate student) youngish presence in the Centre, to which I was effectively if not formally attached. Despite the differences between our areas of interest, the meticulous empirically grounded research that characterised Des' approach to Strategic Studies was an inspiration as I set out on my own research career. One important thing he taught me by example is the importance of deep background and eclectic reading: I remember once, during the 1980s, bumping into Des as he came out of the University Bookshop brandishing a newly-published paperback on Aboriginal land rights, hardly seen as a key concern by most people in defence studies at that time. The role of indigenous Australians in the Australian Defence Force (ADF) was to be a significant theme in his subsequent published work on Australian defence.[1]

Even in those days long before *Wikileaks*, some Australians showed less than complete respect for the sometimes seemingly excessive secrecy of government, and I remember the excitement of reading a book of illicitly obtained official cables and documents that Des had acquired in connection with his own research but which he lent me because it cast light on some aspects of my own investigation of the Association of Southeast Asian Nations (ASEAN) governments' responses to the communist victories in Indochina and the subsequent Vietnamese invasion of Cambodia. As it happened, one of my supervisors subsequently told me in no uncertain terms that these were sources to which I should not have had access and that the book was inadmissible as a source for my research.

At the start of the 1990s, the collapse of the Soviet Union and the end of the Cold War forced many — perhaps most — Strategic Studies scholars in the West to reassess their research focus. Some — mainly those who had made Kremlinology and the exploitation of Russian sources their life's work — collapsed almost as completely as the communist regimes they had studied — never to recover intellectually or professionally. But there was always hugely more to Des' interest in the field than the bipolar confrontation that had been his initial focus. With his interest in Australian defence concerns, by then nuclear strategy had ceased to preoccupy Des. With his research focus already broadening, the main impact of the Cold War's conclusion on Des was apparently to pose him new intellectual challenges.

Des had already been involved in Asia on a limited scale during the 1980s. In part, this was in connection with his research on the technical intelligence-gathering roles of Soviet embassies in Bangkok, Jakarta and Singapore but (as discussed earlier in this volume) with support from the Ford Foundation, Des and Bob O'Neill had played important parts in assisting the establishment of Strategic Studies centres in Southeast Asia. Des certainly showed an interest in my own work on military developments in Southeast Asia, and published several of my minor contributions in the *SDSC Working Paper* series.[2]

During the 1990s, Asian security issues became a major and enduring research priority for Des. A key area where Des has made an outstanding contribution has been in his work on the dynamics of military capability development in the region. Since the 1970s, rapid economic growth has provided numerous Asian governments with expanded resources, which they have applied to their armed forces no less than other sectors. At the same time, the end of the Cold War had thrown into sharper focus important sources of potential conflict in the region, including the dispute over Taiwan's status and tensions on the Korean peninsula and in the South China Sea. Against this backdrop, from the early 1990s through to the present, examining and assessing the nature and potential dangers of military procurement and capability development in Asia has been a main theme in Des' work.

Des' research on Asian military developments, based on persistent fieldwork throughout the region, has generated a series of important articles that capture the scale and intensity of regional states' military modernisation efforts.[3] I remember well how, at a Wilton Park conference in England on Asian security in 1994, Ric Smith — then Deputy Secretary in the Department of Defence in Canberra — mentioned to me enthusiastically Des' recent article in *International Security*, "Arms and Affluence: Military Acquisitions in the Asia-Pacific region".[4] My own long-term interest in the nature of and influences on military developments in Southeast Asia had recently expanded to include Northeast Asia, and I was increasingly aware of the dangerous combination of latent conflict, growing military resources, and the lack of arms control measures throughout the region, and this was the theme of my presentation. I remember Ric ambling over to me after my presentation and pointing me towards Des' article effectively as a corrective to the views I expressed in my presentation, which he felt, at the time, were overly pessimistic.

The main thrust of Des' important "Arms and Affluence" article was to examine what lay behind the recent 'alarmist rhetoric' in the press about a supposed Asian arms race, looking in detail at recent trends in regional states' military spending and equipment acquisitions, and to attempt to explain these developments by assessing the wide range of influences on them. Des surveyed in detail not only the diverse influences affecting the acquisition of major weapons systems, but also the major 'themes' within regional states' military procurement programmes, which he identified as: command, control and communications systems; technical intelligence systems; multi-role fighter aircraft; maritime reconnaissance aircraft; modern surface combatants; anti-ship systems; electronic warfare capabilities; and rapid deployment forces.

Des concluded that there was no arms race in the region, arguing that the two principal features characteristic of previous arms races — "a very rapid rate of acquisitions" and "some reciprocal dynamics" — were not obviously present in the region's military acquisition programmes at that time. Nevertheless, he highlighted two "disturbing" aspects that needed to be addressed if they were not to "overwhelm the more positive aspects of the emerging post-Cold War security architecture in the region". The first of these worrying features was the regional atmosphere of "uncertainty and...lack of trust" which were contributing to tensions and misunderstanding. The second disturbing element was the 'offensive' character of some of the weapons systems that regional states were acquiring: Des pointed particularly to the strike capabilities associated with maritime attack aircraft, surface ships and submarines, "all equipped with anti-ship missiles". These capabilities, along with new fighter aircraft, were "the most likely to generate counter-acquisitions". Particularly where submarines and long-range anti-ship missiles were concerned, Des pointed to worrying implications for crisis stability, and the danger of "inadvertent escalation".

Typically for Des, he was not content just to analyse the regional military build-up in depth, in terms of both its scope and its dynamics, but rather went on to make some important policy recommendations. Crucially, he noted that the region lacked "any machinery by which the processes of dialogue and cooperation could have any constraining impact", and pointed to the "critical requirement...to encourage much greater transparency with respect to major arms acquisition programs and strategic objectives". He argued that regional states should publish defence statements similar to those produced by Australia's government, and for "a public registry containing information on arms acquisitions".

Finally, Des made the case for an "institutionalized regional security dialogue" aimed at "preventing misinterpretations, misunderstandings and suspicions likely to cause tensions and even conflict". Specifically, while saying that the already increasingly frequent meetings of "defense chiefs and other high-level officers throughout the region" were "extremely important", Des argued for "regular meetings and exchanges of views" which would provide focus and continuity for security discussions among regional states. He accurately identified the ASEAN Post-Ministerial Conference (PMC) process as the "most important" development, particularly as the ASEAN Institutes of Strategic and International Studies (ISIS) had proposed to the ASEAN Ministerial Meeting in July 1991 that it could provide the basis for discussing regional security issues.

Subsequently, Des helped to translate these ideas into reality. As detailed earlier in this volume, a key area of activity for him from the early 1990s was his involvement in setting up the regional 'second-track' security organisation known as CSCAP (the Council for Security Cooperation in the Asia-Pacific) an institution in which he has remained closely involved.

Des subsequently continued his work on the regional arms dynamic. In 1996, he collaborated with Panitan Wattanayagorn, from Chulalongkorn University in Thailand, in writing a chapter titled "A regional arms race?" for the edited volume, *The Transformation of Security in the Asia/Pacific Region*.[5] This chapter was essentially a development of the "Arms and Affluence" piece, revised to include additional details on trends in regional military equipment acquisitions and defence spending and brought up to date with a brief discussion of recent measures intended to enhance military transparency such as national defence white papers (citing the example of *The Defence of Thailand 1994*) and the United Nations Register of Conventional Arms, and the institutionalisation of regional security dialogue through the ARF and CSCAP. Concluding their chapter, Panitan and Des asked whether "these and other mechanisms for enhanced regional dialogue, consultation and co-operation can be instituted to...enable the effective management of the burgeoning arms acquisition and defence modernization programmes to prevent them degenerating into a regional arms race".

Among his myriad activities during the 1990s, Des took on a responsibility closely related to his interest in promoting regional military transparency: the series editorship for Allen and Unwin's planned sequence of books on Asian armed forces. I had been working at the University of Hull in the UK since the end of the 1980s, and this new project brought me into closer contact with Des again. The ambitious project on *The Armed Forces of Asia* was the brainchild of the Sydney publisher's late dynamic co-proprietor, John Iremonger who, with Des, asked me to write the volume on Singapore's armed forces. From my point of view, this provided the ideal opportunity to bring some coherence to my work on Singapore's strategy, defence policy, and military capabilities, some of which I had already published piecemeal, including an SDSC Working Paper on the political role of Singapore's officer corps. With encouragement from Gerald Segal at the IISS, I had contributed an outline of my thinking on Singapore's defence strategy in the journal he edited, *The Pacific Review*, in 1991, and I had subsequently intended to publish a considerably expanded version in the SDSC's Canberra Papers series. But at the very end of the 1990s, with invaluable advice from Des on the structure of the book, I was able to start work on a full-length study of the Singapore Armed Forces set within the context of the city-state's threat perceptions, defence policy and national strategy, which was published at the end of 2000 as *Defending the Lion City: the Armed Forces of Singapore*.[6] Unfortunately, the extremely ambitious *Armed Forces of Asia* series — which John Iremonger and Des had expected to cover the whole region in 20 or more national volumes — was never completed, although between 1996 and 2001 Allen and Unwin did publish excellent books on the armed forces of China, Indonesia, New Zealand, Pakistan and North Korea, as well as on Russian and United States forces in the Asia-Pacific, all by leading experts.[7] Though it was never completed, this series made a significant contribution in terms of casting light on the defence policies and doctrines of states in the Asia-Pacific, as well as providing extremely detailed analyses of the structure, equipment, personnel policies and training of their armed forces, thereby contributing indirectly to Des' objective of greater transparency in regional defence matters.

Since returning to live and work in the Asian region in 2007, I have been keenly aware of Des' growing concern over military developments in the Asia-Pacific, particularly through seeing him deliver papers on the theme at workshops in Singapore, including some that the IISS has organised under the auspices of the MacArthur Foundation's Asia Security Initiative, most recently in November 2011. The state-of-the-art of Des' thinking on the issue is contained in his paper *Northeast Asia: Tensions and Arms-racing*, which the IISS will publish as one of four chapters in an Adelphi book focussing on sub-regional Asian security trends. In this latest paper on the arms dynamic in East Asia — a revised version of a paper presented at a IISS workshop in Singapore in November 2011[8] — Des presents a much more pessimistic — indeed, bleak outlook on regional military trends than he did in the early and mid-1990s.

Almost 20 years after the publication of his "Arms and Affluence" article in 1993, the situation has changed dramatically for the worse, in Des' view. He argues that Northeast Asia is now "strategically the most worrisome sub-region in the world as it is wracked with inter-state tensions and disputes". In his view, the chance of one or more of these "degenerating into large-scale conflict" with "horrendous consequences" is "palpable". After surveying the daunting range of disputes bedevilling Northeast Asia's international relations (including the existential tensions over Taiwan and North Korea, as well as acute territorial disputes involving almost every combination of states in the sub-region), he assesses defence spending trends in Northeast Asia, pointing out that China, Japan, the two Koreas and Taiwan jointly account for more than 80 per cent of total military expenditure in East Asia and Australasia. He points particularly to China's increasing defence spending (while acknowledging the difficulties inherent in estimating this). He proceeds to highlight that these substantial defence budgets are being used in part to fund a "sustained and rapid build-up of defence capabilities". In contrast to the 1990s, some "disturbing features" are now evident, notably "substantial evidence of action-reaction dynamics" and specifically "an emerging complex arms race in Northeast Asia".

In this latest paper, Des describes in detail what he sees as the three main elements of the emerging sub-regional arms race in Northeast Asia: naval capabilities (including the proliferation of major surface combatants, submarines and anti-submarine warfare capability, and large amphibious ships); electronic warfare and electronic intelligence; and nuclear weapons and missile developments, including anti-missile systems. He also analyses in detail the competitive development of Northeast Asian states' information warfare (and more specifically cyber-warfare) capabilities.

In conclusion, Des argues that because the action-reaction phenomenon "generates its own momentum" and because "there are no arms control regimes whatsoever in Asia that might constrain or restrain" future military developments, the prospect is for arms-racing to become increasingly prominent in Northeast Asia. Further, he points out that the region's future security dynamics are likely to be "much more complex" than those that characterised the Cold War, noting for example that Chinese and North Korean ballistic missile developments have led Japan and South Korea to enhance greatly their airborne intelligence collection and early warning capabilities as well as their theatre missile defences, while United States doctrine has evolved to allow the near-simultaneous employment of nuclear forces, precision conventional capabilities and information warfare operations, and "the use of nuclear weapons in otherwise non-nuclear situations". At the same time, the "distinctive categories, milestones and firebreaks that were carefully constructed during the Cold War to constrain escalatory processes and promote crisis stability" are missing. Ultimately, "in this environment, with many parties and many levels and directions of interactions, the possibilities for calamity are high".

Unlike his 1993 article in *International Security*, Des' most recent writing on regional arms dynamics does not offer policy recommendations. Perhaps this reflects his disillusionment at the failure of the institutionalised regional security dialogue to deliver tangible results in terms of arms control measures able to constrain regional military competition, not to mention the immense difficulty of imagining a way out of the present dangerous and complex security predicament in Northeast Asia. Nevertheless, in his comments at the November 2011 IISS workshop, Des spoke forthrightly about the urgent need for governments and non-government analysts alike to think constructively about developing and implementing such mechanisms. Emphasising that Northeast Asia's dangerous security dynamics should be a matter of wider Asian and global concern, he argued that it was not too late to address problems in the maritime sphere in particular and proposed 'focus groups' of experts to discuss potential military constraints. Like much that Des has written and said over the last three decades, these were inspiring words and I certainly hope that my colleagues and I in the IISS will be able in the future to contribute to new thinking about how to promote arms control in the region.

Notes

1. See Desmond Ball, ed., *Aborigines in the Defence of Australia* (Sydney: Australian National University Press, 1991) and; J. O. Langtry and Desmond Ball, eds., *The Northern Territory in the Defence of Australia: Strategic and Operational Considerations*, Canberra Papers on Strategy and Defence no. 73 (Canberra: Strategic and Defence Studies Centre, Australian National University, 1991).
2. See Tim Huxley, "The ASEAN States' Defence Policies 1975–81: Military Responses to Indochina?", *Strategic and Defence Studies Centre Working Paper* 88 (Canberra: Strategic and Defence Studies Centre, Australian National University, 1984); Tim Huxley, "The ASEAN States' Internal Security Expenditure" *Strategic and Defence Studies Centre Working Paper* 122 (Canberra: Strategic and Defence Studies Centre, Australian National University, 1987); Tim Huxley, "Brunei's Defence Policy and Military Expenditure", *Strategic and Defence Studies Centre Working Paper* 166 (Canberra: Strategic and Defence Studies Centre, Australian National University, 1988) and; Tim Huxley, "The Political Role of the Singapore Armed Forces' Officer Corps: Towards a Military-Administrative State?", *Strategic and Defence Studies Centre Working Paper* 279 (Canberra: Strategic and Defence Studies Centre, Australian National University, 1993).
3. See Desmond Ball and Andrew Mack, "The Military Build-Up in Asia-Pacific", *The Pacific Review* 5, no. 3 (1992): 197–208; Desmond Ball and Andrew Mack, "The Military Build-Up in the Asia-Pacific Region: Scope, Causes and Implications for Security", *Strategic and Defence Studies Centre Working Paper* 264 (Canberra: Strategic and Defence Studies Centre, Australian National University, 1992); Desmond Ball and Gary Klintworth, "China's Arms Buildup and Regional Security", in *China as a Great Power: Myths, Realities and Challenges in the Asia-Pacific Region*, edited by Stuart Harris and Gary Klintworth (Melbourne: Longman Australia 1995), pp. 258-283; Desmond Ball, "Arms Acquisitions in the Asia-Pacific: Scale, Positive and Negative Impacts on Security and Managing the Problem" in *The Emerging Regional Security Architecture in the Asia-Pacific Region*, edited by Thangam Ramnath (Kulala Lumpur: Institute of Strategic and International Studies, 1996), pp. 199–233; Desmond Ball, "Arms and Affluence: Military Acquisitions in the Asia-Pacific Region", *International Security* 18, no. 3 (Winter 1993/1994): 78–112; Desmond Ball, "'Trends in Military Acquisitions in the Asia/Pacific Region: Implications for Security and Prospects for Constraints and Controls', *Strategic and Defence Studies Centre Working Paper* 273 (Canberra: Strategic and Defence Studies Centre, Australian National University, 1993); Desmond Ball, "Trends in Military Acquisitions: Implications for Security and Prospects for Constraints/Controls", in *The Making of a Security Community in the Asia-Pacific: Proceedings of the Seventh Asia-Pacific Roundtable*, edited by Bunn Nagara and K.S. Balakrishnan (Kuala Lumpur: Institute of Strategic and International Studies, 1994), pp. 129–57; and Panitan Wattanayagorn and

Desmond Ball, "A Regional Arms Race?" in *The Transformation of Security in the Asia/Pacific Region*, edited by Desmond Ball (London: Frank Cass, 1996), pp. 147–74.
4. Ball, "Arms and Affluence:".
5. Wattanayagorn and Ball, "A Regional Arms Race?".
6. Tim Huxley, *Defending the Lion City: The Armed Forces of Singapore* (St Leonards: Allen & Unwin, 2000).
7. The "Armed Forces of Asia" series, see Greg Austin and Alexey D. Muraviev, *Red Star East: The Armed Forces of Russia in Asia* (St. Leonards: Allen and Unwin, 2000); Joseph S. Bermudez Jr., *Shield of the Great Leader: The Armed Forces of North Korea* (St. Leonards: Allen and Unwin, 2001); Pervaiz Iqbal Cheema, *The Armed Forces of Pakistan* (St. Leonards: Allen and Unwin, 2002); Tim Huxley, *Defending the Lion City: The Armed Forces of Singapore*; You Ji, *The Armed Forces of China* (St. Leonards: Allen and Unwin, 1999); Robert Lowry, *The Armed Forces of Indonesia* (St. Leonards; Allen and Unwin, 1996); James Rolfe, *The Armed Forces of New Zealand* (St. Leonards: Allen and Unwin, 1999); and Stanley B. Weeks and Charles A. Meconis, *The Armed Forces of the USA in the Asia-Pacific Region* (St. Leonards: Allen and Unwin, 1999).
8. Desmond Ball, "Tensions and Arms Racing in Northeast Asia", paper delivered to the IISS-Asia MacArthur Asia Security Initiative Workshop, Singapore, November 2011.

13

SECURING A NEW FRONTIER IN MAINLAND SOUTHEAST ASIA

Nicholas Farrelly

INTRODUCING A CHANGE OF DIRECTION

After devoting the first half of his academic career to the specifics of missiles, antennae and targeting protocols Professor Des Ball shifted his research in what might appear an unlikely direction. Inspired by many years as a regular traveller to Indonesia, Singapore, Malaysia and Thailand, and with a growing stable of Southeast Asia-focussed students, Des began a momentous pivot to this region. His earlier devotion to uncovering the details of sensitive strategic-level defence activities provided the analytical tools and mindset necessary for researching defence, security and political topics in mainland Southeast Asia. In this shift, which began in the early 1990s, Des de-emphasised his earlier academic interests in nuclear targeting, signals intelligence and Australian defence policy to focus, sometimes exclusively, on regional security issues. After beginning with analysis of Burmese military affairs, most notably the *Tatmadaw*'s signals intelligence capabilities, he grew to become the foremost expert on Thai security forces, especially its mind-boggling array of paramilitaries.[1] From the 1990s, the strategist, long accustomed to global-level threat analysis, became a regional tactician seeking to clarify the smallest details of deployments, configurations and tasking in a wide-ranging effort to deliver insights about what is commonly described as "human security". Increasingly he has seen his role as offering "broader perspectives on security...to try and come up with greater balance in looking at the whole spectrum of threats to human security".[2]

During these years, Des has taken the study of security in mainland Southeast Asia in new directions. His close working relationships with officials from regional military and police forces have provided access that remains, in key respects, unique. These networks are reinforced and fertilised by his dogmatic commitment to regular field research.[3] With a tempo of travel and field research that shames many other scholars, Des keeps up a heavy schedule of visits, especially to Thailand where he travels the length and breadth of the country to accumulate the obscure information that infuses the narrative of his books. Those books are packed with details not mastered by other scholars; they have become reservoirs of facts and analysis that serve to re-frame standard impressions of regional security dynamics. Lavishly illustrated with maps, photographs and tables they are encyclopaedias for interested students, scholars and journalists.[4] Even Southeast Asian security practitioners — those whose day-to-day business is regional military and law enforcement affairs — can be overwhelmed by the scope of Des' research on their specific professional concerns. There have been many occasions when Des has broken the ice with new, and sceptical, acquaintances by letting them flick through his draft manuscripts (which he habitually carries in hard copy). Even in their unfinished form these scholarly products provide ample evidence of his commitment to the task, and to his insights about tactical security issues in mainland Southeast Asia.

As other chapters in this volume indicate, Des' career has spanned at least half a dozen separate spheres of knowledge and academic enquiry in Security Studies. It is, nonetheless, only in the most recent phase that Southeast Asia has provided a distinctive locus for the fusion of his intellectual and activist adventurism.[5] To account for his work and output, this chapter begins with a general overview of Des' approach to studying security cultures in Southeast Asia, and to the challenges of understanding the sensitive tactical issues that are involved. This is followed by analyses of his research on Burma and Thailand, the countries in this region that he has come to know best. Two key examples of his work are introduced in this context — his analysis of Burma's nuclear ambitions and his exploration of Thailand's Border Patrol Police — to illustrate Des' specific approach to tactical analysis in mainland Southeast Asia. To flavour these reflections, I draw on my experiences as one of Des' recent collaborators and co-authors, and on an interview I conducted with him in May 2011.[6]

RESEARCHING SECURITY CULTURES

In his earliest research Des tackled the challenges of strategic thinking and security cultures in the shadows of the Cold War. It was an anxious, uncertain time. After choosing to pursue the serious study of nuclear policy and politics, Des developed a methodology for research on secret and sensitive topics that he has persisted with ever since. And as the characterisations of that early nuclear research contained in this volume show, Des garnered novel insights by meticulously collecting copious empirical matter to serve an unflinching analytical mission. Others have already indicated that this is a daunting style of research that requires impeccable recall, stamina and patience. It is clearly not suited to everyone but, in Des' case, it usefully blends aspects of his personal, intellectual and professional qualities to provide the foundations for an effective, and consistent, methodology. As Des told me in the 2011 interview:

> I keep very detailed files of all my overseas trips because a substantial part of my academic year is not sitting at home doing this writing: it's out in the field collecting information and collecting material. And unless I file that properly, I am going to forget it, I am going to get it confused with information that I have got on other trips. I spend quite a lot of time at the end of every overseas trip: I write up a full account of everyone that I have talked to, every place that I have been, every single person, and these trip reports now amount to many volumes of bound A4 on my bookshelves. So I can go back and check who I talked to on a trip to some part of the Thai-Burma border back in 1996 and I would have that correlated with a field file from that trip in 1996, where the scribbled notes from the meeting with that particular person would be kept. I probably over-file photocopying, I photocopy an enormous amount.[7]

For Des, this research is an idiosyncratically thorough process requiring long-term concentration and a constant awareness of how the pieces of the puzzle may fit together. In this process the weighing of evidence and the testing of hypotheses is an ordinary, everyday undertaking. I have observed over my recent years working with Des that he makes assessments of evidence almost constantly. If he can find value in a fragment of new information then it is assiduously filed away. If the information merely replicates something he already knows, or proves redundant for other reasons, then it is quickly discarded.

This method, and its associated mentality, has proved crucial to Des' ability to build an enviable mastery of security developments in mainland Southeast Asia. In tracing the genesis of his interests in this part of the world it is relevant that, beginning in the early 1990s, Des became increasingly concerned with what he called "strategic culture in the Asia-Pacific region".[8] This led to further consideration of the post-Cold War geopolitical order, the rise of new security threats, and the challenges for both government and non-government players in a rapidly changing regional context. Des' response to the collapse of the Soviet Union, and the diminution of scholarly attention to great power rivalry, was to interrogate emerging security issues in Southeast Asia with equal measures of tactical insight and humane sympathy. His enthusiasm for developing grounded, enmeshed and embedded insights about the organisations tasked with security in the region, especially in Thailand's borderlands, has come to set a new standard. At checkpoint-after-checkpoint, base-after-base, Des is a familiar face. With his hulking figure, his camera, and his briefcase of notes, maps and business cards, he tries out his modest Thai. On these trips he is often accompanied by students, colleagues, friends and family. Des' touring parties are meticulously planned and are designed to uncover new information to fill gaps in his knowledge. In June–July 2012, for example, Des travelled to the restive southernmost provinces of Thailand, he also spent time along the Thailand-Burma frontier, and in Bangkok and Chiang Mai. In each location he sought to cross-check previously acquired details with current realities, ask questions about tasking and command issues in the security units he met along the way, and endeavour to get as close as he could to the experiences of all of the police and soldiers, townsfolk and rebels, with whom he associated.

Such a method for understanding the details of security in Southeast Asia requires commitment and consistency. Piece-by-piece he has built understandings that benefit from critical readings of all the available evidence and a prevailing scepticism about the practices, if not the policies, of security organisations.[9] To sustain his active research agenda Des travels regularly, usually for 3–4 months each year, to Thailand and adjacent countries. This pattern ensures he has built up his contacts with political and social players. These range from prominent generals and intelligence supremos, to shopkeepers and sentries. Many of these contacts have also become regular correspondents, filling his in-box with tips, photographs, links and data. When he is not on the road Des currently spends each morning in his office tending to the piles of files and printouts that wash across his desk. He also calls on sources in Thailand and elsewhere to help check facts and provide responses to what can seem like an endless stream of questions. The process is an intuitive one, reliant, at all times, on Des' special ability to triangulate information from multiple source.[10] These sources often include the regional intelligence officials who remain part of his orbit. Some such figures are former students while others are long-term acquaintances met through Council for Security Cooperation in the Asia-Pacific (CSCAP) events, or other regional fora. At their request, Des is a frequent visitor to important national security installations in Bangkok, and elsewhere. He is invited for closed-door discussions and briefings, especially when there are concerns about sensitive border matters.

Along the Thailand-Burma border itself, Des has developed links with armed ethnic groups, local military and police commanders, and many journalists and activists. He has travelled frequently to Karen National Liberation Army and Karenni Army bases, and has also worked closely with Shan and Mon groups along the border. Some of Des' doctoral students, most notably Hazel Lang and David Scott Mathieson, have been influential in shaping his ideas about the borderlands. Des pays tribute to Lang in the following terms:

> Hazel Lang…is another example of how PhD students have interested me in newer areas, and indeed guided me in those newer areas. She had invited me to join her in some of her fieldwork in Mae Hong Son, Mae Sot and most particularly, Sangkhlaburi, Three Pagodas Pass, which was the subject of her doctoral research. And introduced me to some of those ethnic organisations, the New Mon State Party in particular, but also in 1999 she came with me when we were involved in meeting the leadership structure of the Karen National Union, the KNU, and the Karen National Liberation Army, the KNLA, and she came with me to Mae Hong Son and we meet the hierarchy of the Karenni political and military organisations.[11]

Mathieson has also been a key influence on Des' work. He has spent the years since 2002 living in Thailand where he has gone on to become the senior Burma researcher for Human Rights Watch. Des is particularly proud of Mathieson's human rights work; they remain regular collaborators and correspondents, and the similarities between them are, they would both accept, quite striking. Mathieson produces a steady stream of reports dealing with sensitive political and social issues inside Burma, many of which clearly take their inspiration, in method if not content, from the style of work that Des has pioneered. Other Burma watchers, including leading figures like Curt Lambrecht, Andrew Selth and Ashley South, are also key members of Des' orbit. Furthermore, he is a regular interlocutor and collaborator of important Thailand-based analysts such as Bertil Lintner, Brian McCartan, Paul Keenan and Phil Thornton (who has the next chapter in this volume). In their own ways they have all helped to shape his impressions of security in mainland Southeast Asia. For Des, research and its distribution is a collaborative, indeed social, activity.[12]

It is also an activity that requires a certain generosity of spirit. Des' sympathy for Burma's ethnic minorities, many of whom have been subjected to human rights abuses during decades of civil war, infuses his interactions. His well-known support for those ethnic minorities campaigning for justice and peace in eastern Burma gives him extra credibility in refugee camps and among hardened fighting men. In 2012, as an example, Des was honoured by the Karen National Liberation Army with a special award recognising his contributions to their struggle. He also calls the political and social situation as he sees it. In one earlier publication he noted:

> Thailand's policies for dealing with these borderland security issues are confused and poorly coordinated. Some are misdirected, especially those that require good faith on the part of the [Burmese] junta, and ultimately doomed to failure...further depreciating security for many people in the borderlands in the process.[13]

His stature in the field of Security Studies means Des can be similarly blunt on many other issues in the Southeast Asian region. Those who know him well appreciate that it is with the long-term hope of rectifying unsatisfactory situations that Des has focussed on the borderlands between Thailand and Burma.

BURMA FOR A MILITARY JUNKIE

When he first begun to wander through mainland Southeast Asia as a mature researcher, Des could not imagine how deeply enmeshed with regional security issues he would ultimately become. His first significant work in mainland Southeast Asia emerged, as it usually happens, as part of a much wider project. He was seeking to understand signals intelligence matters around the Asia-Pacific region: Burma was a relatively small part of that effort. His initial foray produced a book on Burma's military communications systems.[14] That book set the scene for a longstanding engagement to understanding Burma's armed forces and their use of many different technologies. While it is now somewhat dated, it presented a thorough, state-of-the-field overview of how Burma's armed forces communicate. As he said in the 2011 interview:

> In the mid-1990s, as I was still interested in signals intelligence, no longer in the Soviet dimension, but what Southeast Asian countries were listening to, and what that indicated about their own security priorities, I had got involved in a project to look at Burmese communications, and Burmese signals intelligence which resulted in a book called, *Burma's Military Secrets*, in the latter part of the 1990s. And to put that book together had got to know some of the ethnic insurgent organisations down the Thai-Burma border.

It is those links with groups along the border that have continued to motivate Des' interest in Burma.

Regular trips to the border indicate just how strongly he has felt about seeking to understand border dynamics, the roles of ethnic armies and the conduct of civil war in easternmost Burma. That first book was followed by a working paper, published in 2004 under the auspices of the Strategic and Defence Studies Centre (SDSC), analysing the Burmese Army's radio systems.[15] As Des has said:

> From there I got interested in not just Burmese Army communications, and the extent to which they were listening to the armed ethnic insurgents, but also the extent to which the ethnic organisations were listening to Burmese communications. And so from that very late part of the 90s and into the early 2000s, I suppose I was involved very much on the technical side of communications, communications security and, in the case of the Burmese how to break their communications security, breaking their codes, listening to their communications at the technical level.[16]

Des continues these efforts to understand communications in Burma from all angles. His technical nous and capacity to explain complicated signals intelligence topics to uninitiated audiences provides him with a set of useful skills. In this respect he has taken engagement with the study of civil conflict in Burma to another level. In that 2011 interview he suggests that:

> If I'm really such an expert in strategic and defence matters, as I am sometimes portrayed, then I think that I have an obligation to apply some of that expertise to assisting some of those ethnic armed groups which just face such overwhelming odds in terms of numerical inferiority, in terms of equipment which is battered second-hand amateurishly assembled weapons and communications gear. So where I think I have expertise that can help them, I believe that I have an obligation to apply it. And that's really what I have been doing over the last decade up there.[17]

What is intriguing about Des' relationship with Burma is that he is "not a Burma scholar". Indeed, in the 2011 interview we discussed these issues at length and he noted that:

> I'm not someone who's been intrigued by Burma's history and culture, and desperate to see the insides of Burma. I'm a military junkie who has some expertise, some ability in areas of strategy and defence for which I can, or which I can use to assist those who have decided to militarily resist the junta in Burma.[18]

For a self-confessed "military junkie" Burma has provided an incredible set of opportunities, none more so than in the analysis of Burma's potential to produce exotic weapons. This is where his early efforts to understand nuclear weapons have come in handy. Some of my earliest conversations with Ball, after he had tested my awareness of Burma's political and security scene, lurched into discussions of Burma's prospective nuclear plans. Ball had been meeting with people on the Thailand-Burma border, including defectors, who were making explosive claims about the ambitions for exotic weapons at the highest levels. In 2010 he became a prominent international advocate for the idea that Burma was developing exotic weapon systems and, in particular, a nuclear weapon.[19] Like in other cases, this academic analysis filtered out to a much wider public through journalistic write-ups. Des was, not for the first time in his long career, at the centre of an international story and his authority as a distinguished Security Studies scholar lent weight to the defectors' claims. As he pointed out in his full account of the defectors and their testimony, "the subject of Burma and nuclear-related programs is surrounded by rumours, speculation, misinformation and probably deliberate disinformation".[20] He sought to come to grips with that context. In a spirit of collegial dissent his good friend Andrew Selth responded to Des' claims.[21] The conduct of discussion on this sensitive and emotive topic drew Des to a wider audience once again.

THAILAND AND THE BORDER PATROL POLICE

On Thailand, Des has gone on to write two books about Thai security organisations, with a third, on the Border Patrol Police, to follow soon. These studies provide the baseline for substantial social and political analysis. Nobody has worked more diligently to understand Thailand's plethora of security organisations than Des. His work on what he usually describes, somewhat off-handedly, as "paramilitaries" is a testament to almost two decades of close engagement.

The first of these books analyses Thailand's para-military border guards — the *"Thahan Phran"* as they are known in Thai.[22] They are sometimes referred to, in English, as "Rangers". As Ball explains, their Thai name has an even more potent meaning: hunter-soldiers. In their black uniforms they are a presence on lonely roads and mountain passes, usually camped out in areas far beyond the ordinary patrols of Thailand's military or police. Drawn from poor villages the length and breadth of the country, recruits are generally from what could be described as different castes than the more established military units. Des was always fascinated by them and their place in Thailand's national security architecture.

This was followed by a book on another Thai paramilitary group — the *Or Sor* — authored with his protégé David Scott Mathieson in 2007. In this book, Ball and Mathieson argue that Thailand's paramilitaries require significant reform.[23] Consistent with this, in the 2011 interview Des sets out his "vision for Thai security, which is really going to be the ultimate product of this series of books". What he suggests is the need to get:

> ...rid of those paramilitaries, disbanding all of those organisations. Building up the professionalism of the army, getting the army back to the barracks and out of business and the corruption that infuses large parts of the army, and particularly in the case of the police drastic reform of the Thai police so that they can actually take responsibility for enforcement of law and order, rather than the very gross levels of corruption which infuse the Thai police today.[24]

Issues of corruption and lack of integrity among the security forces have been a long-term preoccupation for Des. As he has said:

> I think that if you had a professional army, a clean police force and a border patrol police force, which was responsible for border security. That those three organisations properly coordinated and one of the problems with these innumerable paramilitaries is that there is no coordination at

all between them. But [you need] proper coordination from the top down, then you would be able to address a large number of the security problems which currently face Thailand and allow Thailand to really fulfil many of the elements of democracy and peace and stability that we'd like to see in the future in Thailand.[25]

It is the need for peace and stability that has ultimately motivated Des in this work. For Des, the Border Patrol Police may provide some of the answer. They first caught his attention when he was researching the earlier books on *Or Sor* and *Thahan Phran*. In his many visits to Thailand he began to accumulate details on the Border Patrol Police units that he regularly encountered along the borders.

Some of my earliest significant exposure to Des' work came with his study of the Border Patrol Police. In 2008, soon after I returned to Canberra from the United Kingdom where I had been a doctoral student, we started working together on aspects of his larger study. Our attention first focussed on the nuts-and-bolts of the Border Patrol Police organisation. Des was enthused by the task of determining overall command structures, and understanding the careers of Border Patrol Police officers. We worked closely to decipher the inner workings of the organisation. He made clear that accuracy was his overwhelming priority and that he sought to explain an otherwise opaque political and social history. For Des the Border Patrol Police was, I learned, yet another system to be understood and then explained. In the service of this goal he deployed remarkable efforts of memory, intellect and astute judgement. He eagerly embraced new information and dispensed with anything redundant or irrelevant. Constantly, he sought to build a clear and presentable picture of the Border Patrol Police.

Des has gone on to become the world's preeminent authority on this subject. This research endeavour will culminate in a book simply titled *Tor Chor Dor* (the Thai acronym for this police unit) that will likely be published in 2013. The Border Patrol Police are, in Des' eyes, the most professional component of the Royal Thai Police. Their responsibilities also mean that they align closely with the activities of military forces. Des has followed the history of the Border Patrol Police right back to its earliest days, and has tracked their activities along all of Thailand's borders, and elsewhere. There is no significant English language work on this organisation and the main Thai language texts are official (and thus somewhat stilted) in character. However, with a huge array of sources Des has sought to stitch together a comprehensive narrative of the Border Patrol Police, including the only full account of the activities of its Police Aerial Reinforcement Unit (PARU). It deals in what some might consider extravagant detail with the nitty gritty of Border Patrol Police history, operations, personalities, culture, scandals and life. But, more importantly, it introduces an organisation that has, until now, been largely examined through the drama of occasional glimpses in Thai history. Des hopes to explain the broader issues that determine the centrality of this organisation.

As their name implies, Border Patrol Police are usually based in remote and otherwise inaccessible locations. He has set out to locate and visit these bases. To that end he has spent many months travelling along the borders of the country, in the southernmost provinces, in the east and in the north, and also along the border with Burma, in an effort to understand how this organisation fits into the broader security landscape. In the 2011 interview, Des told me that:

> Thailand is going through a period today where there are major splits within the political fabric and the Border Patrol Police, or at least the Border Patrol Police leadership tends to be aligned with some parts of that factionalised political structure. It's very much aligned with the Palace and hence the leadership with the yellow shirts, the PAD. It takes sides when it comes to the various political factions demonstrating, protesting in Bangkok. Though you can't say that it is consistently aligned with anyone faction because while the leadership of the Border Patrol Police may well be very strongly aligned with the yellow shirts, there are very large elements of the Border Patrol Police at the lower levels, the lower ranks who see themselves as red shirt supporters. There's no doubt about that.[26]

It is this attention to the subtleties of political and security debates that provides Des with opportunities to interrogate subject matter which tend to escape other scholars.

To illustrate this commitment to broader contextualisation, Des' attention to songs about the Border Patrol Police requires explanation. As Des has discovered there are a large number of musical tributes, pop songs and romantic ballads devoted to the Border Patrol Police. When Des first stumbled across these outputs we had no conception that there would be dozens of songs, on hundreds of albums and compilations that have been produced over decades. These songs remain popular and after each trip to Thailand Des returns with even more to add to his collection. As ever, he stores details on the finds with great attention to detail and looks to understand these quirky cultural products as part of the broader story of the Border Patrol Police as a national security institution. Links between the experiences of ordinary officers, and those they serve, help to motivate Des' interest in these organisations. He wants to know how they fit into broader political and social currents.

When asked about some of these political implications, Des offers appraisals of Thai society that go far beyond the security sector. He has suggested that:

> ...if it wasn't for the relationship which red-shirts, for example, have with former Prime Minister Thaksin Shinawatra then I would be on their side. Because I believe that the longer-term cause of justice, of fairness is on their side. The people who I am most personally friendly with are ones who I think are in a sense in the wrong. It is a great personal dilemma for me working very closely with some of these institutions in Bangkok when I've come to believe that rightness actually lays with the peasants, the rice farmers, the poor, in Isan in the northeast, and in the north, and that sooner or later if Thailand is to get through this traumatic period that it is going through now, it is only going to get through it once the demands, and not just the demands, the interests, the causes of justice are acknowledged in favour of those poorer people in those outer lying provinces. And unless that happens, and we don't see many signs of that happening at all, unless that happens Thailand is in real, real trouble.[27]

As other contributors to this volume have explained, Des embraces progressive social values and is concerned to enunciate them through his research. His obvious appreciation for those who have yet to be fully embraced by Thailand's project of national wealth creation illustrates why he has sought to deal with tactical security concerns in mainland Southeast Asia.

LESSONS FOR YOUNG PLAYERS

Future generations of scholars will learn of Des through his books, monographs and articles. His works are scattered in libraries across the world and his special contributions to different areas of research activity will resonate for many years to come. But the challenge for students seeking to digest these contributions will be to understand some of the context in which the work has developed. He has developed an impressive range of contacts with Southeast Asian security officials, including soldiers, police officers and civilians. In all cases he has been particularly drawn to special operations forces, such as the Border Patrol Police Aerial Reinforcement Unit (BPP PARU), and to the work of intelligence services. Des has continued to maintain a focus on dealing with the most sensitive, contentious and political issues. And he has also not lost sight of his moral and political responsibilities as an academic engaged in cutting-edge research on difficult, contentious topics.

As he has come to explore and explain security cultures in mainland Southeast Asia, the affection that Des enunciates for the downtrodden and forgotten has remained a prevailing theme. Des has not been shy about reporting human rights outrages and the alleged complicity of security agencies in other crimes. His rudimentary Thai is, he confesses, a handbrake on both field research and efforts to digest written sources. But he more than compensates for this deficiency by drawing on a wide range of colleagues who are only too happy to assist, and by capitalising on new technologies. Des makes very effective use of machine translation software from which he can rapidly deduce whether a particular source is worth extra scrutiny, or formal translation.[28] Ball goes about the task of understanding security in Southeast Asia in a methodical way that has much in common with his earlier research methods. The continuity from his first explorations of nuclear strategy to his more tactical assessments of security politics in Thailand and Burma are part of a story that now stretches over four decades. His inspiring work on the cultures, organisations and approaches to security in this region will be read for many years to come. It provides another plank in his scholarly fortifications, and presents us with an enduring image of the professor in the field seeking to understand the ambiguous and build knowledge where there were once only shadows.

It is from out of those shadows that his generosity and good humour marks him out as a gentlemanly presence in a tough and aggressive business. Des seeks to understand the most sensitive issues, but he is, to the puzzlement of some, prepared to share his knowledge freely to almost anybody who shows interest. In the countries of mainland Southeast Asia that Des has now seriously studied for more than two decades there are prevailing ideas of *karma* and merit. On the *karmic* balance Des has made many unheralded and meritorious contributions to mainland Southeast Asia. Such contributions would usually be considered sufficient for any single career. In Des' case the remarkable part of his academic story is that this chapter has canvassed only one phase in his life as a researcher. His major contributions to the study of security in mainland Southeast Asia will shape the field in the decades ahead. In the future it will fall to others to come to grips with the powerful legacy of a scholar who constantly sought to secure new frontiers.

Notes

1. There remains contention about the appropriate name for the country now officially known as the Republic of the Union of Myanmar. In his work Des continues his long-standing practice of calling the country Burma. This chapter mirrors that presentation.
2. Many of the statements attributed to Des in this chapter are sourced from a 5-hour interview I conducted with him in May 2011. It was produced in conjunction with Martyn Pearce and Kim Beamish from the Australian National University's Media Office. Their support with that interview is specially appreciated, as is the effort by Sheryn Lee to transcribe it. Throughout this chapter the interview is cited as, for example: Desmond Ball, interview by Nicholas Farrelly, *The Australian National University Mentor Interview Series*, transcript, 18–19 May 2011, p. 22.
3. A careful reader of Des' bibliography will note a publication from almost two decades ago: Panitan Wattanayagorn and Desmond Ball, "A regional arms race?", *Journal of Strategic Studies* 18, no. 3 (1995): 147–74. Panitan has gone on to take prominent academic and political roles in Thailand, including as spokesman for the government of Prime Minister Abhisit Vejjajiva until 2011.
4. Even a cursory examination of Des' major books on Southeast Asian security topics provides evidence of this. They often include hundreds of photos and scores of tables and maps.
5. Another of the earlier outcomes of this re-orientation to Southeast Asia dealt not with Thailand and Burma but with Indonesia and East Timor: see Desmond Ball and Hamish McDonald, *Death in Balibo, Lies in Canberra* (Sydney: Allen and Unwin, 2000).
6. For context it is worth noting that Des and I have collaborated on the following recent publications: Desmond Ball and Nicholas Farrelly, "Interpreting 10 years of violence in Thailand's deep south", *Security Challenges* 8, no. 2 (2012): 1–18; Desmond Ball and Nicholas Farrelly, "Eastern Burma: Long wars without exhaustion", in *Diminishing Conflicts in Asia and the Pacific: Why some subside and others don't*, edited by Robin Jeffrey, Edward Aspinall and Anthony Regan (London: Routledge, 2012), pp. 147–62; Desmond Ball and Nicholas Farrelly, "Burma's broken balance", *CSCAP Regional Security Outlook 2012*, edited by Brian Job (Singapore: CSCAP, 2011), pp. 18–23; Desmond Ball and Nicholas Farrelly, "Soldiers of political fortune", *East Asia Forum Quarterly* (December 2011), pp. 33–34.

7. Desmond Ball, interview with Nicholas Farrelly, 18 May 2011, p. 22.
8. Desmond Ball, "Strategic Culture in the Asia-Pacific Region", *Security Studies* 3, no. 1 (1993): 44–74.
9. For an example see: Desmond Ball, "Security developments in the Thailand-Burma borderlands" (Sydney: Australian Mekong Resource Centre, 2003).
10. While I have never asked him about this point explicitly I imagine that Des' years attempting to understand the purposes of signals intelligence infrastructure helped shape his comfort with "triangulation". Readers of Des' books and articles will know that this approach is reflected in the footnotes that pepper his text. Fragments of information are constantly compared, contrasted and interpreted to build a broader picture.
11. Desmond Ball, interview with Nicholas Farrelly, 18 May 2011, p. 42.
12. For an example of such collaboration see: Ball, Desmond and Samuel Blythe. "Radio Active" Myanmar Seeks Communications Upgrade", *Jane's Intelligence Review 1* (September 2010), pp. 22–25.
13. Ball, "Security developments in the Thailand-Burma borderlands".
14. Desmond Ball, *Burma's Military Secrets: Signals Intelligence (SIGINT) from the Second World War to Civil War and Cyber Warfare* (Bangkok: White Lotus Press, 1998).
15. Desmond Ball, *How the Tatmadaw Talks: The Burmese Army's Radio Systems* (Canberra: Australian National University, 2004).
16. Desmond Ball, interview with Nicholas Farrelly, 18 May 2011, p. 42.
17. Ibid., p. 43.
18. Ibid., p. 45.
19. Desmond Ball, "Burma's Nuclear Programs: The Defectors' Story", *Security Challenges* 5, no. 4 (2009): 119–31.
20. Ball, "Burma's Nuclear Programs: The Defectors' Story", p. 119.
21. Andrew Selth, "A Reply to Des Ball – Burma's Nuclear Programs: A Need for Caution", *Security Challenges* 5, no. 4 (2009): 133–37.
22. Desmond Ball, *The Boys in Black: The Thahan Pran (Rangers), Thailand's Paramilitary Border Guards* (Bangkok: White Lotus Press, 2004).
23. Desmond Ball and David Mathieson, *Militia Redux: Or Sor and the Revival of Paramilitarism in Thailand* (Bangkok: White Lotus Press, 2007).
24. Desmond Ball, interview with Nicholas Farrelly, 18 May 2011, p. 46.
25. Ibid., p. 46.
26. Ibid., 18 May 2011, p. 46.
27. Ibid., p. 47.
28. In 2012 the quality of some online translation software is such that Des, with his flair for the technology, can determine much valuable insight from Thai language sources. This technology, almost unimaginable when Des was a junior academic in the 1970s, suggests that we should all remain nimble with the possibilities of new academic tools.

14

"BIG BRAIN" ON THE BORDER

Phil Thornton

I first came across Des Ball's name in 2001 while interviewing Karen National Liberation Army (KNLA) soldiers at a sniper camp in eastern Burma. It seemed like an unlikely setting to bump up against an esteemed academic — the hot jungle clearing was a long way from the Australian National University professor's book-lined office in Canberra. At the time, reporting on Burma was difficult. Its isolation and a ban on international journalists made it hard to verify stories in time for news bulletins. By the time footage and witness reports were smuggled out the story had usually moved on to another international hot spot. Closed off and isolated from much of the outside world, the military regime had at the time stepped up its attacks on who it perceived as "enemies of the state" — its own citizens, ethnic minorities and the political opposition. I was in the sniper camp at the invitation of a KNLA officer and was on my way to interview Karen villagers recently displaced by the Burmese Army and now taking shelter in jungle hideouts.

A group of KNLA soldiers had just completed a series of morning drills and were making their way back to their small bamboo platforms to take rest and clean up before lunch. The hurried sound of food being readied could be heard above the soldiers' banter. Work-hardened men in singlets and shorts chopped meat and vegetables into tidy piles, their bare arms mapped with hand-etched tattoos. A blackened aluminium rice pot steamed over dull red coals. A group of young men milled around. They wore an assortment of ragged T-shirts and sarongs hiked up around their thighs. Black-ink tattoos trailed up their legs, arms and naked shoulders. Some smoked and puffed on green-leafed cheroots. The camp had about forty soldiers in it. Some of the men carried weapons, others towels and soap as they walked down the steep slope to the river to wash. Shallow foxholes dotted the edge of the camp.

I asked permission from the camp leader to interview soldiers, wanting to talk mainly about their backgrounds and motivations for fighting. I noticed a small hut built more solidly than the soldiers' basic bamboo platforms. An antenna and wires ran from the roof through a hole cut in an exterior wall. Inside the hut three KNLA soldiers were busy chatting and scribbling. On a rough-cut bench a radio set stood idle. An M16 with grenade attachment, a belt of rifle grenades and an AK47 hung from a nail hammered into one of the hut's corner supports. The midday sun began to bake the small room. The heat made it hard to ask questions of the men. Some they answered, others they left hanging in an uneasy silence. After about twenty torturous minutes, the translator indicted that the soldiers wanted to take their lunch and asked if we could continue the interview later. I agreed, as we would be in the camp for the next couple of days.

As the three men left the hut, I stayed back and cleared some space on the radio bench to check over my scribbled interview notes. To one side was an A4 pad the men had been writing in. I leafed through the stained pages until I found one that contained English writing. At the bottom, Professor Ball's name and email was printed and underlined — four or five paragraphs of text scrawled above it. The first paragraph was titled "Electronic Warfare Capabilities" followed by "The *Tatmadaw* [Burmese Army] has acquired some electronic warfare capabilities. Most of these have been provided by China, but it seems that some have also come from Singapore." The rest of the handwritten notes contained technical specifics about radio systems, frequency bands and storage capability.

The next underlined heading stated "Directorate of Defence Services Intelligence (DDSI)" and underneath "The Directorate of Defence Services Intelligence is the most powerful intelligence and security organ in Burma. All of the other agencies are firmly under its control." A number of bullet points followed and to add to their importance the writer had underlined each. I asked the colonel in charge of the sniper camp who Professor Ball was and why did they have his name. He answered that he was "a big brain…a big brain" from Australia, an expert on military strategy and a good friend to Karen soldiers. The colonel's colourful testimony of Professor Ball's worth added another dimension to my story on the KNLA. It also gave the story an Australian angle. I made it a priority to contact the professor (as I now referred to him), when next in Australia.

MEETING BIG BRAIN…

It was not hard to find background information on Professor Desmond Ball. An Internet search listed his achievements — author or editor of more than 60 publications related to defence and nuclear strategy, co-chair of the Steering Committee of the Council for Security Cooperation in Asia-Pacific, member of the Council of the International Institute for Strategic Studies, had worked for former US President Jimmy Carter and former US Secretary of State Robert McNamara. A number of the articles also indicated the professor's work and readiness to write and speak openly had butted him up at various times against the Australian intelligence and defence establishment. Others I spoke to about the professor added more detail. Senior journalists spoke of his willingness to be quoted, if he could be persuaded to talk at all, while a wide range of academics offered mixed responses.

In early 2002 I sent him an email, to tell him about finding his name in a KNLA sniper camp and he replied with a phone number and a time to call him. When we spoke, I told him about the handwritten notes and his name jotted on a writing pad in a KNLA sniper camp. He suggested we should meet. I drove down to Canberra from Sydney in what was to be the first of many visits to his home. My first knock on his door resulted in a rush of fur and furious barks as a number of dogs hit the screen, both big and small. Following the initial clatter the professor emerged from the hallway shadows to welcome me, "G'day, come in."

I followed the professor into the inner rooms of his house. The dogs skidded across the floor following him. He pointed me to a chair, a large Doberman and a much smaller fox terrier fixed on me with unfathomable eyes. We made brief small talk and began a taped interview. At one point during the discussion, he left the room to find a document. I switched off the tape recorder. The larger dog placed its head in my lap and slobbered. I tentatively patted it, expecting the professor to return shortly but up to fifteen minutes passed before he returned. By then my arm was on the verge of a repetitive strain injury from the constant patting. As the professor sat down he noticed the attention I was paying to the Doberman, "it's not the big dog you have to worry about, it's the little dog".

The professor explained that he had been visiting the Thailand-Burma border region for more than a decade and in that time had been following and documenting the Burmese Army's war against the country's ethnic people and its complicity in the illicit drug trade. His assessment of the situation in Burma was harrowing. "It's extremely bleak for the ethnic groups. The Karen has about 5,000 fighters and about 1,000 of those are full-time. The Burmese Army has overwhelming military superiority." The professor was careful not to badmouth the out-dated modes of fighting the Karen had been using until recently, as he respected many of the old soldiers. "The old methods are irrelevant to what these guys have to organise and do. The Burmese Army is shooting, torching and relocating any villages that are left. The SPDC [regime] is attempting to wipe them out. Use them for slave labour and use them to clear landmines. It is gruesome. The Karenni are a manageable population for them to try and wipe out. For the Karenni it is a fight for their survival".

The professor was keen to promote the work his colleagues at the Australian National University (ANU) had done on Burma's military regime and spread a wide range of green booklets and papers on a table for me to browse. The professor explained that for the resistance groups to be in a position to be able combat the Burma Army, they needed a political objective and strategies to achieve it.

"What are they fighting for? Why are they hitting this particular target rather than that particular target? Why kill this person and not that person — what's the point of fighting, unless you really know what you're doing it for?" The professor said the ethnic armed organisations had started to organise into small guerrilla units:

> They're now getting proper training, communication systems, not enough to beat the Burmese Army, but enough to make life very difficult if it is coordinated with a political strategy. The [ethnic] groups have to get professional, get their strategy right, ask why they want to use political force... because they want to achieve a specific political objective.

He did say there were a few bright spots for the ethnic resistance. "The loss of fixed territory has forced the Karen to go mobile and to conduct more guerrilla operations. Since about 1999 they have become more professional and have started to work with other ethnic armies and have been successful on a number of occasions." The taped interview touched on a number of topics including why the professor is prepared to speak out, especially in the current climate, when so many specialists who should have an opinion decline to do so.

"People in my position have access to a lot of information," he mused. "It is a responsibility to the people, not to the government or the various bureaucratic departments that want to control information - that is not necessarily in the interest of the Australian people. We have an obligation to be part of the critical debate on public policy." The professor talked about his love of Australia, its values, social justice and decried the politicising of the armed forces by recent governments. We talked away all of the day and well into the cold winter night. I was interested in investigating Burma's drug trade for a story I was about to propose to former editor-in-chief of Australian Associated Press, Tony Vermeer. At one point, the professor left the room and returned with a small green paper he had written, *Strategic and Defence Studies Centre, Working Paper No. 336 — Burma and Drugs: The regime's complicity in the global drug trade.*[1]

The professor said he had years of detailed research that fingered the insurgent groups protected and aligned to the Burmese military regime who were involved in the drug trade. "About 50 per cent of amphetamines and about 85 per cent of heroin used by addicts in Australia comes from Burma. The regime can't deny its involvement in the drug trade. The Burmese military and its intelligence apparatus provides security and protection for the traffickers, guards for warehouses and safe passage for the drug caravans crossing the border into Thailand". I told the professor my planned drug story would take a couple of months as I intended to try to track the drugs from an Australian user back to drug refineries in Burma. The professor said he would photocopy a number of documents and official military maps that would help my research. We made plans to meet in the Thai border town of Mae Sot in April or May 2002.

KAREN STATE

When I returned to Thailand I visited a KNLA camp and spoke to a colonel known to the professor. The colonel was quietly putting the finishing touches to a plan to attack a Burmese government military outpost that was about to receive reinforcements. He said that even though the Karen were hopelessly outnumbered by the better-equipped Burmese military, his men compensated by using specialist guerrilla skills.

"The Karen have to win so all of Burma can have freedom, but we can't afford to fight head-on anymore," he said echoing the professor's words. "It's now more effective to attack specific targets, take equipment and move out. We don't take fixed positions — it's too costly. Now we hit those who are causing our people the most pain". The soldier operating the radio interrupted the colonel who allowed a small smile to crack his tight face. "We're listening to the SPDC radio commands and when they send reinforcements, we'll ambush them". Without warning mortar shells boomed overhead, announcing the KNLA found their target.

BORDERLINE STORIES

By the end of March, the heat on the northwest border area of Thailand turns the fertile rice and cornfields to dust. Farmers torch dried out rice and corn plants and burn large tracts of forest in preparation for planting when the monsoon season arrives at the end of April. Haze from the forest fires blankets the region, blocking out the view of the distant, but usually visible, Dawna Mountains.

I agreed to meet the professor at Mae Sot's *Porn Thip* Hotel. The hotel is a couple of streets away from the town's main market. The professor was working at the time on a book on 'human security' in and around the Thailand-Burma borderlands. He was particularly interested in studying the *Thahan Phran* [Rangers] — Thailand's paramilitary border guards — an organisation the professor pointed out was founded by the Royal Thai Army in 1978 to combat Thailand's communists. He noted that the *Thahan Phran,* or as he preferred to call them, "the boys in black", were now the first line of defence on Thailand's border with Burma.

We left the air-conditioned cool of the *Porn Thip* Hotel and walked to the market. I wanted to introduce the professor to a Burmese activist friend, Arkar, who ran the *Morning Flower* teahouse, a health clinic and a library for factory workers. The teahouse was located in an unsavoury covered section of the market known to locals as *Burma Alley*. The professor was interested in what Arkar could tell him about the various groups operating in the market. Mae Sot was renowned as the unofficial headquarters for the Burmese opposition organisations and activists. Armed groups used the town and its markets to resupply their soldiers and border camps.

Well-founded rumours also placed Burma government spies in the local cafes, gem market, guesthouses and hotels.

An article in *The Bangkok Post*, on 10 June 2001 reported that, "Over 1,000 Burmese Military Intelligence Service agents have infiltrated Thai border towns, spying on and sometimes assassinating anti-Rangoon elements, reporting on Thai military movements and, inevitably, supplementing their meagre incomes with drug money". Special Branch Police Commissioner Pol Lt-Gen Yothin Mattayomnan was also quoted, saying that Thailand was flooded with Burmese military intelligence agents. "Some of them sneak into the country as illegal immigrants or as job seekers or enter legally as businessmen. But their main objective is the same: spy work". Thai security officials were also quoted, saying they had evidence a number of Burmese secret agents were involved in illegal businesses, including drug trafficking. According to the newspaper's military intelligence source, Burmese agents operating in Thailand belong to the Military Intelligence Service's (MIS) Unit 5 and Unit 19, also known as MIS-5 and MIS-19. "There are perhaps 1,000 or more, mostly spying along the western border".

We made our way through the hot, chaotic and cluttered streets that sold bales of fabric, clothing, fresh cut flowers, live fish, fruit and vegetables and tables piled high with bloodied slabs of meat. I wrote at the time that 'to the casual tourist Burma Alley is a shadowy walk on the wild side. Smells, colours and whispers add an exotic spark to an otherwise dull day".

Mae Sot can also be dangerous. Loan shark enforcers used their spare time to sing along with teahouse *karaoke*. Illegal migrants were at risk from job brokers eager to take their savings and in return transport them to the highest bidder irrespective of the danger or health risks attached to the work. Drug deals were carried out in Burma Alley's murky shadows. Rumours circulated among market shoppers about the various teahouses — which ones were frequented by government informers, Democratic Karen Buddhist Army (DKBA) drug runners, the locally-run mafia or off-duty soldiers, and which ones arranged for the smuggling of illegal workers to big city destinations.

Arkar sat us at an outside table and ordered condensed milk sweetened tea and coffee and plates of deep fried dough sticks. As we sat and made small talk, Arkar would nod his head towards passing *cyclos* and say, 'drug seller' and indicated a distant teahouse where the men staring at our table from behind fake designer sunglasses were government spies. Sipping on his hot tea, the professor leaned into me and said with a huge grin, "this is my sort of café". Arkar was able to detail for the professor alleged incidents where factory workers had been abused as they passed through military or police checkpoints on their way to work, back to refugee camps or on their way to health clinics. I noticed that the professor, when meeting people, always carried a writing pad, in which he dated each page and named each conversation.

From then on, the professor's regular trips to the Thai-Burma border involved a rigorous schedule that he kept to religiously. The trips took in a huge loop covering many thousands-of-kilometres through Chiang Mai, Bangkok, Mae Sot and most of the remote villages in the northwest Thai border with Burma. On these trips, everything was of interest — antennas, checkpoints, installations, troop movements, changes in personnel, rosters, documents, eye-witnesses to events, militia, shops selling insignia of the various paramilitary groups, border trade routes, smuggling crossing points, river sand dredgers, army deserters, security personnel and ethnic and Burmese Army communication installations.

The professor photographed a large electricity pylon that stretched cable across the River Moei from Thailand to Burma. An electricity grid in that part of Burma does not exist. It was obvious the local DKBA battalion had arranged either officially or under the counter to buy electricity from somebody in Thailand. We then drove twenty kilometres north from Mae Sot to a restaurant at the Moei River crossing point at Ban Wang Kaew, which lies diagonally opposite the Burmese Town of Ko Ko, home to the DKBA's 999 battalion. Over lunch we discussed why the DKBA was prepared to fight against its own Karen people and its alignment with the Burmese Army. "There are more than 600,000 people forced from their villages and living in jungle camps. The murder, torture, rape are well documented but mostly ignored. I have been documenting for a long time".

The professor admitted that he was prepared to advise, where he could, the various ethnic armies up against the Burmese Army if it would help in any way to stop the abuse of civilians. "There have been incidents where the Burmese Army and their allies, the DKBA, would go into villages and take 20 or 30 young women and rape them for days and then kill them". The professor explained that having this information made it difficult for him to go back to Australia and do nothing. "I have communication knowledge that could be useful to the groups in helping to track down the perpetrators of the abuses. I have had an association with those ethnic armies that are now using guerrilla strategies of ambushes and sniping Burmese Army officers who are responsible for ordering the abuse of villagers".

As we parked the car we passed a group of Karen men preparing two roosters for a fight on the riverbank. The men crouched on their haunches as the two birds circled. One of the roosters launched a two-foot attack and the other was bloodied. The fight was over in minutes. Money changes hands between the men. The bloodied bird's neck was quickly cut and the blood drained into a tin cup. The rest of the fowl's carcass was plucked, cut into sections and dropped into a pot simmering over a charcoal brazier. The rooster went from fight to curry in less than 15 minutes.

THE GOOD SOURCE

The professor and I shared a number of sources of information. They ranged from easy-to-find documents such as stories in local newspapers, reports from community-based organisations and international humanitarian groups to the harder-to-come-by confidential documents leaked from military sources, government agencies or direct testimony from soldiers, deserters, victims of abuse and ethnic armed groups.

Much of the professor's work on the border involved a lot of travelling, taking a huge number of photographs and asking many questions. He knew the territory well. The professor's research and the collection of data and materials on his trips are legendary. For some it may border on obsessive. But he told me he does it to nail the issue and to make sure his analyses is complete. His attention to even the most minute detail, his willingness to travel tough and meet militia, army soldiers, rebel fighters and ethnic villagers on their home ground gains the professor's work respect from many regional defence establishments. One day, the professor countered my claim when I accused him of "getting a little obsessive" over his latest stack of music CD's related to his research on Thailand's *Tor Chor Dor* (Border Patrol Police). The professor had collected well over 100. "I try to collect everything there is on a subject, like I have with these *Tor Chor Dor* CD's. It is not enough to rely only on newspaper items or websites. You have to spend time getting first hand testimony, make frequent field trips, official reports and when you can obtain '[leaked] materials' from inside sources. Then you are in a position to analyse your research and form an opinion".

Over the years I have witnessed the professor revisiting the same small roadside soup kitchens, paramilitary units, ethnic army camps, refugee camps, internally displaced people's camps and smuggling points for both people and goods over and over again. Year after year the professor has visited many of these sites and is known and mainly made welcome at each. He has made these trips in the notorious monsoon seasons when whole slabs of road are swept away (during the 2011 wet season I counted 22 landslides on the 88-kilometre stretch of road linking the towns of Mae Sot and Tak in a single trip) and during the March-April hot season when temperatures can reach as high as 45 degrees.

It was on one of those hot season days that the professor and I were down on the edge of the River Moei that separates Thailand from Burma. The professor was complaining of the heat and the two-kilometre trudge along a dust track to the river's edge. Our shirts were stained with large patches of sweat. He pointed across the river towards a green-glassed building and said, "that's where the *Wa* [an ethnic minority] are warehousing their drugs". In 2002, the Rim Moei market and shops were vastly different than they are today. It was rough. Market stalls were small humpies perched on a mud floor. There were no concrete footpaths along the riverbank, only small dirt tracks leading down to the river. A number of rubber inner tubes served as ferries floating customers back and forth, with shirtless inner tube drivers kicking both ways. The drug story for Australia Associated Press (AAP) involved a number of interviews with DKBA soldiers, drug users and dealers, Australian and Thai police commissioners, KNLA leaders and soldiers. The professor added an official map that detailed the number of drug refineries on the Burma side. AAP syndicated the story in January and February 2003.

CEASEFIRES

In late 2003, a group of KNLA officers under the guidance of General Bo Mya entered secret ceasefire discussions with the Burmese military regime. Many within the Karen movement were concerned the ailing Bo Mya was not up to the task of negotiating a lasting peace. To many observers the regime's ceasefire talks with the Karen faction looked like a ploy to create division among the political opposition groups. In May 2003, regime-sponsored thugs attacked Daw Aung San Suu Kyi while she was in Depayin, wounding her and killing at least 70 of her entourage and injuring hundreds more. Between the attacks on Aung San Suu Kyi and the Karen ceasefire talks, the regime jailed hundreds of its political opposition. By mid 2004, reports of attacks by the DKBA on Karen villagers were swirling around Mae Sot. Radio transcripts confirmed the Burma Army was involved, clearly spelling out the Burmese Army's Strategy Commander's 773 intentions: "...all battalions under my control to attack KNLA positions along the Moei River and clean them out" (27 August 2004). Other transcripts logged one month later stated that Major Mya Min Aung's 59 Battalion Column 2 would combine with Battalion 106, commanded by Myint Khaing, to attack the KNLA's 202 Battalion.

I was inside Karen State when the attack on the KNLA's 202 Battalion by a large contingent of Burmese Army and DKBA soldiers was launched and I heard how a mother and son from the village of Hti Per were wounded by DKBA shelling. The professor said such tactics are common. The professor agreed with the fears and frustration a KNLA officer expressed to me about the ceasefire having no rules. "The officer's right. Ceasefire rules need to be spelled out for all sides and strictly adhered to. Otherwise you get what has happened here, the Burmese Army taking advantage to wander around mapping Karen positions and noting where the displaced people hiding sites are".

By 2006 the KNLA's ceasefire fears were realised. International human rights groups described the Burmese Army's concentrated attacks on Karen villagers as the worst since 1997. I was in a position to cover the attacks for a number of regional and international publications. I interviewed displaced villagers, KNU leaders, Burmese Army deserters and the professor. In June 2006, the professor said the Burmese Army attacks were part of a long-term strategy to wipe out the Karen resistance. "The regime has an army of occupation in eastern Burma — generals who want the country locked down under military control — and it has 400,000 troops to achieve it. This is an army against its own people".

By July 2006, humanitarian aid groups had estimated that as many as 76,000 Karen people had been displaced. Around 700 had made the arduous journey to a temporary camp, Ei Tu Hta, on the Burma side of the Salween River. Naw Sha Paw, 60, was one of the people who made the long trek to Ei Tu Hta. When I spoke to her at the time she was bruised, tired and fed up. She was frail and in need of more medical help than the young Karen medic could offer. "I walked more than one month to get here. My whole body aches. I only had my two legs to get me here. I've got chest pains, leg pains and I've had dizzy spells for more than a week".

Naw Sha Paw was angry. Just over a month before we talked she had her six grown-up children around her and her betel nut garden to enjoy. "I had a small piece of land. I could grow what I needed. The Burmese soldiers came and cut down my fruit and nut trees. They were more than 12 years old and in five minutes they were all gone".

It was not the first time Naw Sha Paw had felt the brutality of the Burmese regime. In 2001 they came for her husband. Remembering made her thin body shake. She stopped talking, swallowed hard and fingered strands of grey hair strands off her face. Her face was a map of pain. It was not easy telling a stranger how soldiers took her husband. "They tortured him. They tied a log to his back and put him in the river until he died. I cried for seven days, I still do. I miss him, but what can I do. These men are not brave." Naw Sha Paw says the soldiers smashed her home and thrashed her land. "We grew fruit trees, mango, banana, jackfruit and betel nuts. We caused no harm, we're villagers. I don't know why they hate us, but they do. We stayed in our village, but still they kill us". By the years end the numbers of the displaced people finding their way Ei Tu Hta had increased to over 6,000. When discussing the ongoing abuse in Karen State, the professor becomes visibly upset. "For many of these people, it's a fight for survival. You literally have more than 600,000 people on the run, hiding in jungles and the mountains. The murder, rapes, beatings and gross abuses by the Burmese Army soldiers are quite sickening — there's no way I could return to Australia and pretend I can't do something about it".

UNNATURAL ALLIES

It is not hard to find human rights reports on the Burmese regime's abuses against its own people. Groups such as *Human Rights Watch*, *Amnesty International* and the *Karen Human Rights Group* have produced many credible and verified reports dating and documenting the abuses.[2] But finding people who have committed such abuse and getting them to talk was more difficult. I had a number of sources in and around Mae Sot who had started to have contact with Burmese Army deserters. I started to interview these deserters and agreed with the professor that I would ask questions related to his interests — SIGINT, intelligence, cables, antennas, radio and troop movement. Myo Zaw was a soldier in the Burmese Army for 23 years until he was court marshalled for battering his officer with a farm hoe. In spite of breaking the officer's ribs and putting him in hospital, Myo Zaw says he respected the orders he was given from his superiors. While he was in the army he said he never worried what villagers thought of him and that he only respected his orders. "I try to rationalise what I've done in my military career. To ease my conscience I say I was obeying orders. If an officer tells you to destroy a village, soldiers do it without question. They just get on with it and do it. I feel sad and sorry, I know if my family was among those attacked villagers I would feel terrible".

The professor agreed with Myo Zaw's assessment that Burmese Army professionalism has been deteriorating for years. "There's enough evidence to suggest that. Soldiers have been acting with impunity, they know they will not be punished and this legitimises their crimes…the rapes…the killing and the torture."

NUCLEAR TALES

I was still working on stories about displacement in eastern Burma when the opportunity came up to talk to a young officer who had recently deserted the Burmese Army. The deserter, now given the alias, Moe Jo, would meet me in a safe house on the outskirts of Mae Sot. Moe Jo reluctantly agreed to let me tape the interview as long as I assured him his voice would be disguised. I had told him I wanted to use it for a radio feature. It was a slow and complicated process. Moe Jo had reasonable English, but not good enough for a radio broadcast. I asked the questions in English through a translator who then asked Moe Jo in Burmese, Moe Jo replied in Burmese and the translator gave the answer in English. Soon it became apparent Moe Jo wanted to talk about more than the Burmese Army's strategy on displacement and its human rights abuses. He said he had been involved in Burma's nuclear program and had studied in Moscow. The importance of what he was trying to tell me did not sink in at the time and I said we would finish the taped interview first and then he could tell me about the nuclear project. I took notes, more for the professor than for my own use. My interest in nuclear issues was low. The professor was in Mae Sot at the time, but it was impossible to locate him by phone and get him to come to the meeting. I was scheduled to meet with him later that evening, but getting Moe Jo back for another meeting would be difficult as he was living in a refugee camp and needed to sneak out.

When I later took the professor aside to brief him about my interview with Moe Jo, his initial reaction was sceptical and dismissive. I convinced him he should at least meet with Moe Jo and set up an interview for lunchtime the next day. It was June 2007, the monsoon season. The midday sky was bleak and dark. Rain battered against tin awnings. Humidity was high, as were the mouldy patches of damp climbing the concrete walls in the small, hot airless room we were using. Moe Jo had recently deserted, had crossed the border into Thailand and was still in the initial stage of fright brought on by his flight from the army and loss of community support. His hands shook and he worried about what price his family would have to pay for his actions and disclosure. Before rejecting his country's nuclear plans, Moe Jo was an officer with 10 years exemplary army service. A former graduate of Burma's prestigious Defense Services Academy, he specialised in computer science and in 2003 had been selected by the regime to spend two years studying at Moscow's Engineering Physics Institute in the Faculty of Experimental and Theoretical Physics.

The professor's expertise in the subject matter resulted in Moe Jo talking animatedly about Burma's nuclear program and it was late into the afternoon before we stopped. The professor was visibly moved and impressed by Moe Jo and fondly shook his hand, asking him if he needed anything. The interview with Moe Jo would be the first in a series of many clandestine meetings in dingy rooms and safe houses that would continue until early July 2009.

Later, in the parallel worlds that exist on the border, the professor and I sat in a fan-cooled café and over an iced banana shake and soda we discussed what the professor now thought about Burma's nuclear plans. "Initially I thought it was all bullshit. I still think 90 per cent is bullshit, but now I know 10 per cent is fact and that gives me something to work on".

Talking to regional security authorities or their embassy staff about Burma having a nuclear program usually generated two responses: total disbelief or horror. There is good reason why regional intelligence sources are sceptical of the Burmese military regime's nuclear capacity. Verifying stories coming out of Burma has been hard. Defectors may inflate their own importance in the hope of getting themselves resettled to a third country and exiled Burmese political activists need to keep the international spotlight on the regime's negative activities. It is not unknown for the regime to also put out misinformation to cover what it is really doing. In recent years the United States government voiced concerns over North Korea, Syrian and Iranian plans to build weapons of mass destruction, but at the time had kept silent about Burma. In May 2007, in a press release announcing the deal to build a nuclear research reactor in Burma, Russia's atomic energy agency, Rosatom, said it would be under the control of the International Atomic Energy Agency (IAEA). Burma is already a signatory to the Non-Proliferation Treaty, established under the responsibility of the IAEA, and it is required to allow inspections of its nuclear facilities but so far has failed to do so. Sceptical regional security agents and embassy insiders are willing to concede that the Burmese regime cannot be trusted. And for good reason - Burma lies near the top of the world's worst lists: child soldiers, landmines, forced displacement and labour, suppression of political opponents, disease control, illicit narcotics, trafficking of people and corruption. A recent number of high profile interventions by the international community involving both Burma and North Korea added to the distrust. A North Korean freighter the *Nam Kam 1* had been shadowed by United States warships (sanctioned by the United Nations) as it headed to Burma with an unknown cargo, but believed to be arms. On 1 July 2007, the global edition of *The New York Times* reported that Japanese police arrested a North Korean and two Japanese nationals for allegedly trying to illegally export to Burma a magnetic measuring device that could be used to develop missiles. The interviews and research we did on the issue led the professor to believe Burma did have a nuclear program, but he was uncertain as to the extent of it.

The professor and I subsequently co-wrote an article on the subject, which was published by *The Sydney Morning Herald* and *The Age* newspapers and then picked up by the international media. Judging by the number of briefings we heard of, regional security authorities started to apply closer scrutiny to Burma's nuclear plans.

HE'S A DECENT BLOKE

The professor cares. He is switched on to who is getting killed and who is doing the killing, and more importantly he is prepared to make a stand by speaking out or offering advice to the downtrodden. Over the 10 years I've known him he's been prepared to leave the comfort of his university and mix with people on the ground — soldiers, militia, border guards, smugglers and the displaced. He hates tropical heat. He might grumble his way up hills, cross rivers, sit in tin shacks and eat warmed up soup dotted with animal innards if it takes him one more fact closer to his research objectives. He is a decent man. He makes time for students, hotel staff and journalists. He maintains a level of decency as he navigates his way around and through a complicated maze dotted with self-serving politicians, career-driven academics, regional security agencies, soldiers, humanitarian agencies, students, journalists and others while trying to make his research and writing meaningful and beneficial for a wider purpose. I have seen him lose his cool over the inaction of United Nations agencies to provide security for the displaced and I have seen him take principled stances over issues he genuinely cares about.

He is frustrated that the world does not focus its attention on the killing and displacement in Burma, for long enough to do something to end the suffering. As he says, "It's not a little issue. The civil war in eastern Burma has now been running for more than 60 years. Burma is a problem for the region. Most security analysts turn a blind eye to it. I have a real understanding of the extent of human rights abuses being committed by the Burmese Army against civilians. These are not armed groups, but villagers…civilians. I have over the years got to know many of these ethnic people and that has encouraged me to set aside my objectivity and become sympathetic to their political causes. I think I have an obligation to help".

Notes

1. See Desmond Ball, "Burma and Drugs: The Regime's Complicity in the Global Drug Trade", *Strategic and Defence Studies Centre Working Paper* 336 (Canberra: Strategic and Defence Studies Centre, Australian National University, 1999).
2. See reports from Human Rights Group, available at <http://www.hrw.org/burma>; Amnesty International, available at <http://www.amnestyusa.org/our-work/countries/asia-and-the-pacific/myanmar> and; Karen Human Rights Group available at <http://www.khrg.org/reports/reportsbyyear/index.php?rep_year=all>.

Australian Strategic and Defence Policy

15

A NATIONAL ASSET

Kim Beazley

In 1986 when I was Defence Minister, I wrote to the Australian National University and said, "To appoint Dr. Ball to this position as a Special Professor at the Australian National University would do the nation a substantial service." At that point of time, Des Ball's research output would have constituted a lifetime's work for most academicians. My recommendation was not about volume. Nor was it about quality, substantial though that was. I wrote because the work that Des did from the academy was a critical part of the foundation of core elements of Australian national security policy. To see him leave Canberra for Harvard or elsewhere would have diminished our capacity to ground and round out some important directions in planning for the defence of Australia.

At that point, when Des, then head of the Strategic and Defence Studies Centre (SDSC) at the Australian National University (ANU), was appointed to a personal chair, the government was about to launch a seminal white paper on the defence of Australia, and about to complete a substantial renegotiation of the agreements controlling the major joint facilities Australia hosted for the United States. The new agreements were to see a major incorporation of Australians in the workforce of the facilities and a cementing of the government's purpose to secure "full knowledge and consent" with regard to their operations.

Much of the change reflected the product of an intellectual interaction between the political leadership of the then government and the academy of almost two decades' standing and during a period of considerable fluidity in Australian strategic thinking. Des Ball was not alone in this creative interchange. One thinks of figures such as Robert O'Neill, Hedley Bull, Coral Bell, J. D. B. Miller, T. B. Millar, Geoffrey Jukes, Paul Dibb (when out of government), Ross Babbage, Jim Richardson and a few others. However it was only about a cricket team's worth and in that context Des as often as not opened the batting.

Across the globe, in the nations of the Western Alliance, the academy played a significant role in framing the debate not simply about national security but civilisation's survival. The development of nuclear weapons changed the whole character of defence debate, dragging it out of the bowels of the bureaucracy into the broader political environment. There was too much at stake for ordinary citizens to allow it to remain arcane. The awesome destructiveness of the weapons required a deep understanding of the psychological and political underpinnings of the minds of decision-makers. Classic military thought had to be massively broadened. Calculations had to be made with minimal value in historical test cases. No one wanted a nuclear war as a test bed for theory. The character of it all elevated the academy as exemplified in an exchange between one early theoretician, Herman Khan, out of the United States Air Force sponsored think tank, the RAND Corporation, and a senior military officer who criticised his lack of military experience. "How many nuclear wars have you fought recently?" asked Khan. When silence was the response: "OK, we start out even".[1]

In the Australian academy, though by no means alone, the SDSC was at the core of intellectual influence on government decision-making. For most of the latter half of the 1970s, Des was the Deputy Director. For most of the 1980s, he was the Director. I would argue that he and his colleagues have never been so influential as they were then. This does not diminish the work done later or now. Des and his colleagues in the 1990s were largely responsible for the creation of the Council for Security Cooperation in the Asia-Pacific (CSCAP), an important part of the Southeast Asian security dialogue. This initiative in second-track diplomacy was important in the development of the ASEAN Regional Forum (ARF) in 1994, the most significant institution of first track strategic discussion in the region. The SDSC model has been a useful example for the creation of a multiplicity of think tanks in the region.

Des was to be found again in discussion with the then Minister for Defence in the Rudd Government, Joel Fitzgibbon, prior to the 2009 defence white paper, among those arguing for a cyber warfare centre. On the other side of politics, Des successfully engaged Liberal migration ministers on the case for refugee status for persecuted minority tribes, particularly from Burma. His interests have ranged far and wide and outside military-related prospects for human catastrophe to the more likely health and environmental.

As I can attest, the results of his and his colleagues' research are read avidly by the foreign policy interested political class. However, though quality is sustained and enhanced, its influence has become more diffuse. There are two main reasons for this. Firstly the 1980s role of Des and his immediate colleagues is now much more broadly replicated in the academic and think tank community both within Canberra and around Australia, many of those participating are graduates of the ANU process.

Secondly, foreign policy issues and national security issues, while important, have lost the saliency they had when the world was ruled by the fear of a massive nuclear exchange and for Australia, in Australia's region, seventy years of tradition in defence thinking seemed to have been trashed by the outcome of the Vietnam War. National security in the 1970s and 1980s was at the heart of political debate. Factions were organised around positions. Parties had to be demonstrably reliable as a prior condition of electoral success. I have argued elsewhere that the most important policy debates in Australia when Labor was in government took place at the National Conference of the Australian Labor Party (ALP). In those debates, on all sides of the issue, Des' work informed the participants. Des, the self-confessed "military junkie", was at his most influential.

Des Ball's immensely productive academic life is arguably, in publication terms, the most productive in our history. It is a celebration of a man who values the universal qualities of a life of the mind. It would be more appropriate for an introduction to this part of the volume dealing with Australian strategic and defence policy to highlight all facets of the progress of his thinking to be elaborated on later by other contributors. However, beyond what I have already identified, I am not going to do that. I am going to focus on his contribution in the 1970s and 1980s because I was on hand then to witness directly his influence on key developments at the heart of Australian strategic thinking, which was in turn at the core then of Australian politics.

The two key questions in strategic policy around which Australian debate evolved were: what should Australia contribute in the American alliance, and what should our national defence posture be? Though only at the onset of his academic career, Des was a major contributor to the answers devised at the time to both these questions. These were matters of importance to both sides of Australian politics (and to minority parties as well) and Des' work was influential for all. However, he was particularly influential with the Australian Labour Party. He was and is essentially a man of the left. But he also transcended the left. His intellectual curiosity compelled him to seek a deep understanding of the global military distribution of power.

He was not simply going to find fault and danger in the American position, he was going to delve into the attributes of Soviet capacity and direction as well. He was no Muscovite agent of disinformation. On the issues of national defence strategy, President Nixon's 1969 "Guam doctrine" gave him (and all of us) political space to think outside the hitherto electorally popular and basically conservative comfort zone of "forward defence" towards a strategy of self-reliance. The Nixon doctrine, devised as the United States withdrawal from Vietnam began, assigned to areas such as Southeast Asia secondary status in the hierarchy of global United States-Soviet Union competition. Essentially American friends and allies in such a zone were to prepare their own defences in the first instance, relying on the United States for intelligence and enabling technologies but only *in extremis*, United States forces. As a man of the left, not only intellectually but in lifestyle and demeanour, almost alone among key Australian strategic thinkers at the time, his views were accessible to all factions in the ALP at the time and to left minority influences outside it. His work however, involving as it did much field work in the United States, access to some of the arcane reaches of the United States military/intelligence community and involvement with think tanks like RAND, was also read as authoritative by the conservative side of politics, even as it annoyed some in the Australian defence bureaucracy.

The Whitlam Government, particularly its defence ministers Lance Barnard and Bill Morrison, set Australia's national strategy as defence self-reliance. I used to say Lance was the father of self-reliance when I was defence minister. It was an interesting start to the Whitlam Government when Whitlam and Barnard formed a two-man government. Whitlam was fond of pointing out that when the two did so it was the only government consisting of 100 per cent members of the RSL! I realise now that argument around an Australian defence force structure, founded on self-reliant principles, pre-dated both Whitlam and the Guam doctrine within the Australian bureaucracy and briefly under Menzies when in 1963–64 uncertainty as to long-term British and American intentions in our region prevailed. In opposition, prior to government in 1972, Labor speakers in parliamentary debates were beginning to show evidence of reading work done at the ANU both on joint facilities and Australian defence. Barnard tipped his hat to that work by providing funding for two places at the SDSC. As O'Neill details in an earlier chapter, one of the awardees of those places was Des Ball.

The Whitlam Government concluded with Labor in a state of confusion and indecision about where it should be both in terms of Australia's relationship with the United States and on the context of self-reliance. On the latter, the ALP's defence ministers had been heavily preoccupied with the restructuring of the defence department, amalgamating the separate service and supply departments. There had not been time to think through implications for military strategy and force structure. On the former, Labor had been immensely proud of the Whitlam Government foreign policy initiatives in the region but experience with the joint facilities left a bitter taste.

Whitlam had been surprised by the use of North West Cape in the October War (1973).[2] A subsequent agreement resolved some of the issues of forewarning but placed no constraint on American use. Whitlam extended the agreement covering Pine Gap. However he did this seemingly against his own view. This he outlined as: "The Australian Government takes the attitude that there should not be foreign military bases, stations, installations in Australia. We honour agreements covering existing stations. We do not favour the extension or prolongation of any of those existing ones".[3] Extrapolating from evidence of American discomfort with the Whitlam Government, some in the ALP believed the hand of the CIA was in the mix with the ultimate dismissal of the government in 1975. Labor was left with the understanding that a struggle with the United States over the presence of the joint facilities would see it electorally devastated. But how could acceptance of the facilities be incorporated with consistency within a policy, which sought to pursue idealistic aims on arms control and outreach to a variety of concerns and causes in the Third World? More particularly, how could the United States alliance be fitted in this framework?

Through the latter half of the 1970s and in the prelude to government in 1983, Labor in Opposition incorporated the three major facilities into a logic which ran roughly as follows: North West Cape communicating with ballistic missile submarines (SSBN) assisted an invulnerable American second strike capacity and therefore aided deterrence; Nurrungar's early warning function was essential for crisis stability as it enabled correction of false alarms elsewhere in the system and gave a US President time to think in the event of a Soviet attack; Pine Gap was crucial for arms control verification and any hope of arms reductions. Whatever other purposes the facilities served, particularly in the context of nuclear war fighting, these purposes were robust enough to sustain an argument for their presence.

This logic was important to Labor broadly, though not acceptable to a minority, for whom an American presence was an anathema. It was also a logic increasingly incorporated within Liberal Party discussion of the issue though they mocked Labor difficulties with alliance commitments. It was a logic however based on a highly sophisticated understanding of the structure of the global balance, the character of both sides' nuclear forces and the scenarios within which a nuclear confrontation was contemplated.

WHERE DID THIS COME FROM?

Well, in no small measure from Des. One of the most influential books produced in Australian debate on our connection with the United States deterrent was *A Suitable Piece of Real Estate*, published in 1980.[4] It had of course been preceded by a mountain of writing around the same subject. Influential were his contribution (and those of others) in a compendium edited by O'Neill, *The strategic nuclear balance: An Australian perspective*, in 1975.[5] Des' views and data were drawn on by both sides of the argument on whether or not the joint facilities should be retained. Those of us who have been briefed (like myself) cannot comment on the accuracy of his data. However, the strategic perspectives he outlined had to be engaged. As far as the Labor party was concerned, what Des had to say was going to be significant.

The main argument against the installations was the prospect they would involve Australia in a nuclear war. I do not know if my Liberal colleagues realised it but all these issues were wrapped up at the time by the Joint Parliamentary Committee on Foreign Affairs and Defence in a report, *Threats to Australia's Security: Their Nature and Probability*.[6] On the Labor side, our purpose was to reinforce with our colleagues the arguments for the joint facilities outlined above. To conclude the debate, we quoted Des' evidence at length:

> I have no doubt in my mind whatsoever that those three installations would be targeted by the Soviet Union. However, that should not be the whole point of the question. At least three other issues should be addressed. One is that whilst they would be targets in the event of a nuclear war, I do not see a nuclear war as very likely. One could argue that the existence of these installations deters the outbreak of war. But one still has to come to the conclusion that if a nuclear war does come, those stations are to be targeted. A second point is that the consequences of them being targets are really not very great. I do not like the idea of nuclear bombs falling on Australia, but the vision that some people have of what it would involve seems to be quite exaggerated. I cannot imagine any scenarios involving nuclear bombs falling on Australian cities. It seems that one draws the lines at those three installations.

The point for us was not so much what was said but the fact Des said it. Gradually his data was incorporated in Labor's debate on the side of the facilities' retention. However there were important consequences of doing so. Having said arms control was an important thing, it had to be pursued. The Hawke Government did this with a range of global and regional initiatives. Des having argued that Australian ministers were in ignorance of the functions, we needed to be able to put hands on heart and say we had full knowledge of their operations and consented to them. With adjustments to covering agreements and much deeper involvement of personnel, that could be said. It also meant that we began to get from the facilities much more that was of value directly to Australian defence. A final irony, given where the debate began, and just about my final act as Defence Minister, was the start of a negotiation with the US Secretary of Defense for an Australian take-over of North West Cape.

The upshot of the intensification of the discussion in the 1980s, and the fact that so much information courtesy of Des was out there, transformed the facilities' significance to the United States-Australia relationship overall. Senior American policy makers like the Secretaries of State and Defense had them brought by us to the forefront of their thinking. As they came to understand how significant they were, they began to tolerate space to the Australian Government to pursue its policy objectives. The Reagan Administration was very tight with its allies on nuclear burden sharing (think cruise and Pershing missiles). However, mindful of the importance of the joint facilities, they let the Hawke Government off the hook on assisting

MX missile tests; were prepared to concede publicly the non-involvement of the facilities in planning around the United States Strategic Defence Initiative (SDI); tolerated Hawke initiatives on potentially difficult arms control agreements like the South Pacific Nuclear Weapons Free Zone; did not inhibit continued close Australian defence relations with New Zealand; and put more on the public record about the facilities themselves.

This is not to say that Des was involved in all of this but his research had been fundamental to the debate, which produced it. The same could be said about the other great discussion of the 1970s and 1980s, "defence self-reliance". Here those who were engaged for and against forward commitment with allies met at the same point. In a sense the Nixon Doctrine foreshadowed no other outcome. Des was firmly on the side of reticence in engaging in expeditionary activities yet he recognised one dilemma in planning for a self-reliant Australian defence. As he said in a recent interview: "One of the ironies of our defence posture is that it is almost impossible to build an independent posture without access to the intelligence and high technology we get from the United States".[7]

In the 1970s and 1980s when he was not writing about issues of nuclear strategy, he was writing about the defence of Australia. During the late 1970s, he wrote a contribution in another enormously influential compendium, again edited by O'Neill, *The Defence of Australia — Fundamental New Aspects*.[8] He discussed equipment issues. Over a decade and a half, he wrote on mobilisation, warning time, tactical fighters, over-the-horizon radar, the prospects of exotics like fuel air explosives and seminally on the character of Australia's north and the defence value to the nation of our indigenous people.

The thing about Des' writing was the fieldwork on which it was based. He was famous for accessing American technical journals and the Congressional Record. But he went to look at things. He used, for example, his technical knowledge to understand what the antennae meant at a Soviet SIGINT site. He walked the ground that might be fought over in defending Australia's north. He directly examined aspects of Australia's civil infrastructure that could be incorporated into a military effort. His work, which reflected his military fascination and his intellectual curiosity, when combined with that of his colleagues, provided a blueprint on which the government could build a public consensus around approaches emanating from the defence bureaucracy, which shifted 70 years of mainstream views on how Australia should be defended.

Des summed up his approach in the interview cited above:

> The answer to that [the defence of Australia] was really to take advantage of that ocean moat that surrounds Australia that anyone who wanted to commit aggression against us had to cross, and although we have small resources in terms of population, relatively small in terms of defence budget, given the enormity of the continental land mass and the exclusive economic maritime zone around us, it turns out that a defence posture which is focused on maritime strike capabilities to stop someone crossing that ocean moat can be quite successful. In fact, there is no country against whom we could not defend even with our limited resources with a proper mix of strike aircraft and submarines and surface combatants sealing off that ocean moat to our north and north-eastern and north west.[9]

Des once called the 1980s "the golden age" of Australian defence policy. In government national and military strategy, force structure and resources, the framework of Australian defence came most to resemble the perspectives that Des and his colleagues had argued. Though his interests in recent times have focused heavily on his concerns for minority peoples in South and Southeast Asia, where he brings the value of his military knowledge to communities in difficult circumstances, the old commitments are there.

The end of the Cold War diminished both the saliency of national security issues in Australian political debate and the disciplined thinking it necessitated. Recent times have seen events begin to pull elements of that old discipline back onto the agenda. The United States is focusing on our immediate region as it winds down aspects of its Middle East engagement. As it does, it is becoming interested in how Australia defends Australia utilising Australia's territory. Growing economies and defence capabilities in our region are compelling us to look again at vulnerabilities in our north. Nuclear weapons proliferation is putting the issue back in play with a much more complex task for deterrence. All this is grist to Des' mill. This collection of writings in Des Ball's honour promises to do for the contemporary defence debate much of what those compendiums and individually authored works Des has been associated with over the years. All contributors to a degree stand in his shadow.

Notes

1. See Sharon Ghamari-Tabrizi, *The World of Herman Kahn* (Cambridge: Harvard University Press, 2005), p. 49.

2. See Desmond Ball, *A Suitable Piece of Real Estate* (Sydney: Hale and Iremonger, 1980), pp. 50–57.
3. Gough Whitlam, speech to the Parliament of Australia, Canberra, 4 April 1974.
4. Ball, *A Suitable Piece of Real Estate*.
5. Desmond Ball, "United States Strategic Doctrine and Policy with Some Implications for Australia", in *The Strategic Nuclear Balance: An Australian Perspective*, edited by Robert O'Neill (Canberra: Australian National University, 1975), pp. 36–57.
6. Joint Committee on Foreign Affairs and Defence, *Threats to Australia's Security: Their Nature and Probability* (Canberra: Parliament of Australia, 1982).
7. Desmond Ball, interview with Nicholas Farrelly, *The Australian National University Mentor Interview Series*, transcript, 18 May 2011.
8. "Equipment Policy for the Defence of Australia", in *The Defence of Australia — Fundamental New Aspects*, edited by Robert O'Neill (Canberra: Australian National University, 1977), pp. 97–124.
9. Desmond Ball, interview with Nicholas Farrelly, *The Australian National University Mentor Interview Series*, transcript, 18 May 2011.

16

THE DEFENCE OF AUSTRALIA

Ross Babbage and J. O. Langtry

THE NEED FOR ORIGINAL RESEARCH

Desmond Ball's interest in the challenges of planning for the defence of Australia was triggered by the unusual circumstances of the early 1970s. Australian and American forces were completing their withdrawal from Vietnam, Washington was abandoning its military presence elsewhere in Southeast Asia and the principles of the Guam Doctrine made clear that United States involvement in Southeast Asia was undergoing fundamental change. The long-standing foundations of 'forward defence' strategy in Australian defence policy were crumbling and there was a need to develop a well-thought-out new approach that was robust and sustainable.

Des Ball was familiar with the academic writings on Australian defence policy and planning from the previous decade authored by T.B. Millar, Max Teichman, Harry Gelber and others. However he realised that these earlier works did not address the fundamental challenges now confronting Australian defence policy. Des was also broadly aware, largely from ministerial statements and informal discussions with politicians and officials, that the Department of Defence was starting to give serious thought to the demands of focussing more strongly on what might be required for the direct defence of Australia with a higher level of self-reliance.

He realised that the core foundations of Australia's future security would be determined during the next few years and that they were deserving of a great deal of deep analytical thought.

When Des Ball was appointed as a research fellow in the Strategic and Defence Studies Centre (SDSC) in 1974, he found himself working alongside a kindred and energetic spirit in the Head of the Centre, Robert O'Neill. Unlike Ball, O'Neill brought a broader background to the defence of Australia agenda. He was a former Army officer who had served with distinction in Vietnam and who retained strong links into the Defence Force and the Defence Department. O'Neill also recognised the need for serious research into Australia's future defence and broader security options and so together they started to conduct research in the field, stimulate discussion on relevant topics and build a small team that could work on key issues in a sustained manner.

The emergence of a strong and energetic research team at the ANU working on many of the key issues then facing the senior leadership of the Defence Organisation received a mixed reception initially. Some senior officials were suspicious about academics researching the principles and options for defence policy. While they were used to academics debating the more general and conceptual dimensions of foreign relations, and describing defence issues in general terms, some felt that academics were simply ill-equipped to contribute to the practical issues of detailed defence planning and that they might confuse or mislead the public. There were also some concerns about potential breaches of national security. Above these concerns was a sense amongst a few senior officials that defence policy and planning was their prerogative and should not be shared with academics or with members of the public.

These defensive bureaucratic responses were not, however, shared by the majority of those serving in the Defence Organisation. From early stages, senior military and some senior civilian officials were happy to engage in discussions on a wide range of contemporary issues. They clearly enjoyed and valued these interactions and, in particular, the opportunity to test aspects of new thinking and planning with informed outsiders. Des' early work on the Defence of Australia soon attracted the attention of ministers and other politicians. In consequence, Ball and O'Neill were invited to brief senior politicians and parliamentary committees on a variety of topics. They also soon became regular presenters at the Defence Force's Staff Colleges.

MODES OF OPERATION

Des realised from the outset that the scale and complexity of the research that was needed on Defence of Australia issues would require much more than his own time and energies. In consequence he worked closely with O'Neill to build a strong team to work on these issues at the SDSC.

An opportunity arose early in 1975 to invite a young civilian Defence official, Ross Babbage, to join the Centre to work on strategy and planning options for the defence of Australia. Des had first met Babbage at the University of Sydney in 1973 when he helped supervise Babbage's master's thesis, which had examined the challenges of attempting to defend Australia against a range of future threats. Babbage joined the Centre as a Ph.D. student in April 1975 although, as the Centre was not entitled to supervise students at that stage, he was formally enrolled in the Department of International Relations.

In 1976 another opportunity arose to strengthen the SDSC team. For some time O'Neill had been aware of the innovative and energetic career of Colonel J. O. (Jol) Langtry. Langtry had performed demanding and important work in Defence intelligence assessment as well as in operations and policy planning. He had most recently been Director of Army Combat Development. Fortuitously, O'Neill had convinced Wang Gungwu, the Director of the Research School of Pacific and Asian Studies, that resources should be provided to appoint a suitable person to assist in organising seminars and conferences and in managing the Centre's growing publications program. Langtry was encouraged to respond to the newspaper advertisement for the position and, following an interview with O'Neill and Ball, he was duly appointed.

Ball and O'Neill appreciated that in order to make rapid progress on the many priority Defence of Australia issues they needed to involve a much wider circle of experts. Some senior academics were prepared to assist. They included Hedley Bull and J. D. B. Millar in the Department of International Relations, as well as Ron May from the Department of Political and Social Change. Indeed, during this era there developed a strong cooperative and collegiate culture in SDSC, the Department of International Relations and elsewhere in ANU. There was a tangible sense that they were working on important security issues and it was best to work on them together in a cooperative spirit.

A special contribution was made at this time by Peter Hastings, who was employed as a senior journalist at *The Sydney Morning Herald* but who participated actively in the SDSC as a Visiting Fellow. Peter's primary research focus was Papua New Guinea and the Southwest Pacific, but he also assisted the staff of SDSC in some of their early visits to northern Australia, most notably by drawing on *Sydney Morning Herald* funds to charter light aircraft to fly into some remote locations. Hastings was also willing to use his established relationships with senior officials in Defence to reassure them that expanding ANU research efforts in this field were healthy and non-threatening.

As the momentum in the Defence of Australia work developed opportunities arose to involve many recently retired military officers, some business people (particularly from defence industry), some state and local government officials and a diverse range of others. Des Ball encouraged this much larger team by personally inviting many of them to seminars and conferences and encouraging a diverse selection to write discussion and research papers on relevant topics.

Particularly notable early conferences on Defence of Australia issues were those conducted in October and November 1976. The first was entitled *The Defence of Australia — Fundamental New Aspects*. About 120 officials, military officers, academics and others participated in what proved to be a path-breaking set of discussions on many of the new security challenges. Des was intimately involved in planning this conference and in delivering one of the primary papers, on 'Equipment Policy for the Defence of Australia.'[1]

The second of these landmark SDSC conferences was entitled: *The Future of Tactical Airpower in the Defence of Australia*. Des led this project and edited the subsequent volume of papers.[2] For this project he drew on his extensive understanding of advanced military technologies that was developed largely through his voracious appetite for aviation and technical defence magazines. In his own conference paper he described and discussed at some length the logic for selecting a multi-role strike-fighter for the Royal Australian Air Force's (RAAF) developing tactical fighter force. The strength of these arguments was felt across the defence and broader national security community and was subsequently credited as influencing strongly Defence's selection of the F/A-18 *Hornet* over the F-16A *Fighting Falcon*.

By late 1976 Des Ball and his colleagues were clearly making a substantial contribution to developing thinking on Defence of Australia issues and SDSC was viewed as the primary source of independent advice on these issues.

KEY THEMES IN BALL'S THINKING ON THE DEFENCE OF AUSTRALIA

Des appreciated at an early stage that one of the key challenges following the demise of forward defence was the need to adopt a more self-reliant defence posture. This thinking was well accepted by the government of the day and was a feature of the landmark 1976 Defence White Paper.[3] However, in the mid-1970s Des was concerned that the concept of enhanced self-reliance be accorded more than lip service in Australian defence planning. He realised that in the new strategic environment the Australian Defence Force would need to change many things. One important shift was the requirement to instinctively operate as a joint force — rather than as single service attachments to the forces of allies in forward theatres. Another important change was the need for much stronger independent intelligence capabilities, especially for strategic and operational assessment. Des emphasised, in addition, the critical requirement for Australia to develop its own capabilities to devise and manage campaign strategies, rather than relying on those of major power allies, as in the past.

The challenge of devising and implementing a coherent and workable strategy for the defence of Australia was a strong recurring theme in the work of Des' team. The 1976 Defence White Paper talked in general terms about Australia's need for defensive and deterrent capabilities. It also discussed briefly the need to select and acquire capabilities suitable for a 'core force' that could be expanded appropriately were a more challenging threat to emerge.

Des and Jol felt that these general concepts lacked rigour and clarity and provided an inappropriate basis for Australian defence decision-making, particularly for capability development. In a major research report published in 1979, they argued convincingly that the approach described in the 1976 White Paper was inadequate:

> The existence within the Defence establishment of many disparate Service and civilian groups with vested interests and quasi-autonomous sources of power means that the types of forces in the 'core' are likely to include more than that warranted by the theory. There is an inevitable tendency, as exemplified perfectly in the current force structure, to buy 'little bits of lots' of equipments. The inefficiency of this, in sheer cost-effectiveness terms, should by itself tend towards a movement away from the core force approach. Moreover, 'follow-on' or replacement equipments, rather

than equipments decided on a more objective requirements basis, also figure more prominently in a force structure 'decided' on the basis of this approach. In fact, the core force concept in practice becomes little more than a rationalisation for the extant capabilities and force structure.[4]

Des and Jol also argued that the core force concept relied for its effectiveness on the Australian Government not only receiving many years' advance notice of a major security threat but that it would decide to act decisively to expand defence capabilities four to eight years before a substantial attack on Australia could be launched. They argued that even a cursory review of history showed that these assumptions lacked credibility.

Des and Jol considered in depth a range of strategic concepts that might be a better fit for Australia's new security challenges. Des was able to draw on his extensive prior research into aspects of global nuclear deterrence but, nevertheless, he and Jol decided to review closely the thinking of the classical masters of strategy. Their key conclusion was that Australia needed to develop its own approach by combining aspects of deterrence and defensive logic. In short, they argued that Australia should acquire and exercise capabilities, which have powerful deterrence effects; that can dissuade and redirect any aggressive opponent that seeks to attack Australia. However, because of the inherent imprecision of seeking to redirect an opponent's intentions, they argued that Australia's capabilities also needed to possess powerful defensive force.

Des and Jol felt strongly that the Australian Defence Organisation needed very clear guidance for force structure design because the country would never be able to afford every type of defence capability. They considered, in consequence, that Australia should aim to control her threat environment by investing selectively in capabilities that would force any opponent to invest disproportionately in much more expensive capabilities if they wished to attack Australia with any hope of success. By forcing any opponent to spend far more money, materiel, personnel, time and other resources in attempting to overcome Australia's defences, they argued that almost any opponent could be effectively deterred:

> Because Australia, for the foreseeable future, will restrict itself to relatively small standing forces backed up by relatively small reserve forces, in a military crisis it will depend on the large-scale mobilisation of untrained manpower. This makes time available for defence preparation critical. A posture of progressive deterrence, based on the concept of disproportionate response, would assist Australia to control her threat environment,

particularly in terms of forcing upon a potential aggressor lengthy lead-times for the acquisition and development of essential capabilities. To illustrate, it is conceivable that the purchase by Australia of a further ten relatively cheap submarines might cause a potential enemy to offset this with anti-submarine capabilities costing, say, ten times as much. But in addition to cost, he will need to extend his force preparation time greatly, since these capabilities require complex command and control facilities and procedures, logistic support, trained crews etc. The mere extension of our submarine force might well cause a potential enemy to defer for years, if not altogether, any ideas of a large-scale sea-borne assault on Australia.[5]

Des and Jol considered that advanced surveillance and knowledge systems, electronic warfare capabilities, sea mines and long-range stand-off precision air strike capabilities offered similar strong disproportionate response and deterrence effects as well as contributing cost-effective defensive power. They argued that these were the types of capabilities that should be given priority in Australian force structure development:

> Because Australia currently has the military advantage within the region it is possible through the proper application of the theory and practice of deterrence and the concept of disproportionate response to 'control her threat environment' rather than to react to it. It demonstrates that it is possible to develop a relatively 'threat insensitive' defence posture — a posture designed around 'contingencies to be deterred'.[6]

A notable feature of Des' approach to these challenging defence strategy, policy and planning issues was his remarkable openness to alternative approaches. For instance, he was prepared to consider the potential contribution not only of conventional military forces but also of 'territorial' or irregular forces. He debated at length whether it was always wise for Australia to press for the most advanced and expensive systems and whether it may not be more sensible in some fields to trade-off the last five percent of quality and performance, which was usually exceptionally expensive, for much larger numbers of systems.

Des also spent considerable time discussing with colleagues and Defence Force officers the validity of many operational and strategic assumptions. What were the essential pre-conditions for an Australian submarine force to successfully impose a disproportionate response on an opponent? How much effort should be put into trying to protect the Royal Australian Navy's (RAN) surface combatants in a range of demanding contingencies? Were not the costs of attempting to protect RAN warships rising steeply because of the increasingly sophisticated threats from anti-shipping missiles, long-range torpedoes, advanced sea mines and other new-generation systems? Even if warships could potentially be protected, would this not require extraordinary efforts and costs? Was there not a risk that by following this route the ADF could itself be driven into a serious disproportionate response and waste a substantial proportion of its scarce defence resources? While some of these debates resulted in reasonably clear conclusions others did not. Nevertheless all parties valued the discussions and appreciated anew the need for ongoing and rigorous analyses of these types of key questions.

Des recognised that many of the demands of the Defence of Australia would pose new challenges for defence personnel and may take them beyond their comfort zones. There was a need, in consequence, to review the country's approach to training and developing Defence Force officers and other personnel in order to prepare them for the more demanding and wide-ranging tasks required. Des and his colleagues concluded an extended discussion of these key issues with the following paragraph:

> The main task then for the system of regular officer development in the Australian Army will be to enable as many people as possible to stay abreast of and probing beyond the moving frontier of knowledge, requiring the acceptance within the Army of a more mobile or dynamic approach to professional activity than ever before. The institution of this approach will require the concerted utilization of the whole of an officer's service, both in formal education and in practical experience.[7]

Another recurring theme in the thinking of the SDSC team about the requirements of the Defence of Australia was the need for new approaches to joint operations and command and control. Whereas during the forward defence era Australian defence units were routinely attached to the relevant single service elements of their sister services from the United States or the United Kingdom, the very different demands of the Defence of Australia meant that Australian defence units would almost always need to operate independently as joint (that is, comprising more than one Australian service) forces under unified Australian command. Effective joint operations required new joint doctrine, extensive new training and many other things besides. Des and his colleagues realised early that a development of this joint culture, combined with a flexible approach to mission-oriented directive control would be essential for the Australian Defence Force to adapt successfully.[8]

Des' team was also mindful of the fact that in any serious Defence of Australia crisis the country's civilian resources would have an extremely important role to play and that it made sense to plan creatively for the mobilisation of these civilian resources in any integrated defence planning process. Des and Jol argued:

> The capabilities of a nation's armed forces are a direct product of the resources that can be mobilised in support of those forces. Hence, unless a nation is already fully mobilised, its war-fighting potential will generally be much greater than the strengths of its forces-in-being. On the other hand, it will never reach its full potential unless its total human, technical and natural resources can be efficiently brought to bear. Countries with relatively large populations or munificent natural resources do not necessarily have high military capabilities. Military capability is very much a function of resourceful mobilisation.
>
> But mobilisation contributes to far more than war-fighting capability. The ability to bring particular diplomatic, political and military resources to bear against an adversary, so as to deny any potential fruits of success to that adversary, or at least to ensure that the costs of that success are greater than the benefits, would be a powerful deterrent.[9]

In thinking through the practicalities of implementing such concepts, Des realised that if Australia's natural advantages were fully exploited the country's real deterrence and defensive capacities could be expanded markedly. A particularly important positive to flow from the shift to the Defence of Australia was that the primary location of future large-scale military operations was now more certain — they would most probably be conducted on or from northern and offshore Australia. Des' team felt that if Australian defence planners and military personnel became intimately familiar with the operating environment in northern and offshore Australia, they would be operating on their "home turf", could carefully tailor their operations to exploit local conditions and facilities and that this would confer enormous advantages. However, in order to convert this "home game" advantage into a real operational edge, the Defence Force needed to do a great deal of work in partnership with local communities. The imperative to get this detailed work done led to establishment of a new joint force headquarters in Darwin in 1988 called Northern Command (NORCOM).

Jol soon convinced Des that it would not be enough for SDSC to simply argue the importance of knowing Northern Australia. The team felt that, in order to properly understand the dimensions of defence operations in the north, they needed to travel there and visit all key civil and defence installations and consult many government, industry, community and Defence Force personnel who were living there. Des took to this challenge with considerable energy. He cut large slices of time from his busy diary as 'holidays' and travelled with other members of the team across Northern Australia, including to some very remote locations. The team soon appreciated that there were at least six distinct regions across the north and several markedly different seasons, meaning that defence planners needed to be very careful about making generalised judgements about operations in the north.

As they travelled across the north, Des and his colleagues discussed the enduring strategic significance of various parts of northern Australia. A key conclusion was that the strategic heartland of the north was the transport and logistic 'spine' running south from Darwin to the RAAF base at Tindal near the town of Katherine.[10] These centres contain the most critical defence facilities, skilled populations and transport nodes in northern Australia. It was appreciated that if a future enemy was able to seize the Darwin-Tindal axis, it would be exceedingly difficult to recapture this region quickly and it may well prove to be impossible if this region was lost during the wet season.

Australian defence planning had previously assumed that sufficient warning would be received of such an enemy operation to permit the timely deployment of relevant elements of the Defence Force from the south. However, Des, Jol and their colleagues concluded that northern Australia was rather more vulnerable than had hitherto been assumed and that a far superior approach would be to base a brigade group in Darwin to operate together with the growing RAAF presence at Tindal and the RAN vessels operating from Darwin Harbour. This substantial pre-emptive deployment, they argued, would alter fundamentally the calculations of any future aggressor. The proposed strengthening of defence capabilities in the 'top end' would force any potential aggressor to plan on assembling and transporting a force of at least a full army division, and more likely two-to-three divisions, across a wide and hazardous sea-air gap just to seize an initial bridgehead. This would be a completely different and far larger type of military operation to that which an opponent might contemplate in the absence of the proposed Australian build-up. The concentration of such a large assault force by an opponent would be detected at an early stage and it would potentially be very vulnerable in its launching bases, during its air-sea crossing and also once elements landed. Des' team argued that the costs and risks to an opponent would be so high that the opposing command may well be deterred from seriously considering such an attack. They further concluded that if an opponent decided to attack elsewhere across northern Australia the ADF would be well placed to respond so long as it continued to hold the Darwin-Tindal axis as a viable base for expanded operations.

This innovative strategic logic was supported by then Defence Minister Beazley and its key themes were taken up by Paul Dibb in his Review of Australia's Defence Capabilities[11] and in the subsequent 1987 Defence White Paper.[12] Planning was soon put in train to deploy the 2nd Cavalry Regiment to Darwin with the force being further expanded soon thereafter to a full brigade group. Australia's strategic deterrent was thereby strengthened greatly in the north, but so was the ADF's capability to respond rapidly and effectively to the crisis in East Timor in 1999 and the Tsunami crisis in Sumatra in 2004.

During the Northern Australian expeditions by Des and his colleagues they would periodically set up temporary offices in a motel to reflect on the significance of what they were seeing and record key conclusions. Sometime later he reflected on these visits as follows:

> The field trips we made around northern Australia during the 1980s, using Coastwatch or RAAF aircraft, 4-wheel drive vehicles and river barges, mapping the local infrastructure and vital installations, proffering novel operational concepts for northern defence, and seeing these being tested in large-scale defence exercises, were exhilarating affairs. In addition to my first trip across northern Australia, from Cape York to the Kimberley region of Western Australia, in July-August 1984, I still have vivid memories of trips through the East Kimberley in October 1986, and around the Torres Strait with Babbage, Langtry and Dr Cathy Downes in May-June 1987. My daughter Katherine, born in 1984, was named in part after the township 320km south of Darwin, which we had identified as the focal point for the defence of the Top End, and where the first squadron of the new F/A-18 fighters would soon be based. One of the particular northern infrastructure projects for which we became leading proponents was construction of an Alice Springs to Darwin railway connection, and it was very pleasing to be invited to Darwin in October 2003 to see the first train come up the line.[13]

Another key lesson Des and Jol drew from these expeditions was the inter-dependence of civil and military developments across northern Australia. They argued cogently that civilian developments in northern and offshore Australia were of critical importance to the region's defence. Conversely, they argued that whatever Defence did in Northern Australia needed to be undertaken in a manner that would also support broader civilian development there.

In 1982 Des and Jol decided to explore these themes in some detail by drawing on the expertise of a wide range of federal, state and local government officials as well as business and community leaders and others. Papers were commissioned from these people over a 15-month period and then in November 1983 more than 200 experts gathered to consider the potential for more effective civil-military interaction across the north. The collegiate discussion at this conference was path-breaking. The subsequent 649 page volume of papers featured a foreword by Prime Minister Robert Hawke and substantive papers from both then Minister for Defence, Gordon Scholes, and the then Minister for Aviation and Minister Assisting the Minister for Defence, Kim Beazley.[14] This program, more than any other, demonstrated that Des and his colleagues were playing a key role in agenda-setting and policy development in the defence of Australia.

During this period Des had the chance to frequently discuss his insights with ministers, senior Defence Force officers and leading officials. The Minister for Defence during the mid-1980s, Kim Beazley, was particularly interested in Des' thinking about how to best progress planning and preparations for the Defence of Australia. When Beazley and Ball talked over these issues, one concern they shared was the challenge of accurately recording and having readily available for defence purposes the vast mass of information on terrain, weather, infrastructure and human assets across northern and offshore Australia. Des had become fascinated by the rapidly-emerging Geographic Information Systems (GIS) that were starting to record, organise and display electronically huge quantities of geographic and infrastructure information for the Lands Departments of state governments, for some corporations and other organisations. He felt that although parts of the Australian Defence Organisation were working with similar systems, there might be scope for doing much more by developing a comprehensive approach. Beazley readily agreed and asked Des if he would be prepared to organise a small conference to explore the potential applications of Geographic Information Systems for the Defence of Australia. Des quickly contacted fifteen leaders in the field and persuaded them to prepare and deliver papers at a major workshop in Canberra in August 1987. Not only was this workshop a success, but it facilitated the development of an informal network of experts across the country and helped accelerate progress within the Department of Defence. This project, and the volume of papers Des subsequently co-edited,[15] contributed to developing the logic for establishing the Defence Imagery and Geospatial Organisation (DIGO) within the Department of Defence in 2000.

Des and his colleagues realised that if effective operations in the defence of Australia required the active involvement of many other federal and state government agencies and numerous parts of the civilian community, effective policy development and planning could not be confined to the Department of Defence alone. For some twenty years Des argued that the real decision-making challenges were those of national security, rather than just defence, and that there was a need for a special committee of the federal cabinet, that he generally termed a 'national security council', to be formed with its own advisory staff.[16] Many senior officials and even some ministers came to appreciate the logic and some worked actively to institute this reform. Eventually in 1999, Prime Minister John Howard announced the creation of the National Security Committee of Cabinet and the development of a new National Security Division within the Department of Prime Minister and Cabinet. In 2008 a National Security Advisor was appointed to oversee national security coordination with direct access to the prime minister. The championing of this broader concept of security by Des and others was so successful that by 2010 it had become conventional wisdom in Canberra.

PERSONAL STYLE AS DEFENCE OF AUSTRALIA TEAM LEADER

Des Ball brought a very particular style to the challenges of researching the Defence of Australia. While he was certainly capable of conducting independent work in this field of a very advanced nature, his preference was always to involve colleagues and to listen intently to their thoughts. His style was almost always informal. There was a sense that he was still a boy from Timboon — his childhood hometown in rural Victoria. There were frequent informal discussions over coffee or a lunch, there were informal seminars and there was the periodic circulation of draft papers — or short draft ideas — in order to test concepts and facilitate discussion.

Des almost always worked with his door open. He encouraged his colleagues, postgraduate students and others to drop in and, indeed, he frequently went out of his way to invite them to do so. He was generous with his time and also with his intellect. He never claimed ownership of his cutting-edge ideas. Indeed, it is a notable feature of his publications on defence of Australia issues that nearly every major paper and book is co-authored or co-edited with one or more of his colleagues.

When Des needed to write a paper or even a larger piece of work, he had the remarkable capability to hand-write a text with double spacing in a matter of hours. When he was in production mode his floor would often be strewn with relevant files and he became very focussed. The amazing aspect of this pre-computer mode of operation was that he was almost always able to produce a text from scratch that required virtually no amendment prior to publication.

Desmond Ball brought an exceptionally rigorous approach to his Defence of Australia work. While he certainly listened to those who described to him the features of a particular airfield, port installation or mine in northern Australia, he was rarely satisfied until he had visited personally, measured key installations, counted vehicles and recorded many other features. His forensic approach certainly enmeshed him in extraordinary detail but he felt that only by immersing himself in the facts on the ground could he be sure that he could weigh up the pluses and minuses of alternative security approaches.

During the course of his extensive travels in the north Des made hundreds of friends. This meant that when he saw the need to undertake a new project (such as the book on *Aboriginals in the Defence of Australia*[17]) or when he needed to check on the capabilities of a new installation or some other northern development, he had a strong personal network on which he could draw. All of his associates seemed to welcome the opportunity to share in his work.

Des saw many potential benefits flowing from his work on the Defence of Australia. But perhaps the most important was the opportunity it provided to give the Australian public a stronger sense of security. He often lamented that Australians lacked confidence in their ability to defend themselves. He sometimes referred to the 'siege mentality' that had driven deep popular anxieties since the days of first white settlement. He saw the potential for well thought-out national security planning and preparations to engage the Australian public more effectively. With the new focus on defence operations on and from Australian territory, he felt that there were greater opportunities for the civilian community to be fully briefed, to become involved and to participate in exercises and operations. In contemplating this prospect, he remarked in 1986 that:

> Such exercises, backed up by continuous planning and civil-military interaction at the regional level, together with the development of a large informed and attentive public, will do much to relieve the state of insecurity, which is widespread in our remoter areas. In so doing, it will strengthen the greatest asset which the Australian Defence Force can possibly have in executing its responsibility for the defence of the country — that is the confident and informed support of the Australian people.[18]

Coming from his internationally acclaimed work on global nuclear strategy, Des never saw his diversion to research options for a more self-reliant defence of Australia as additional workload. It was rather a set of challenges that needed to be addressed well and promptly. He viewed it as a vital national, professional and personal priority. He didn't hesitate to apply his full intellect as a true patriot. His contributions are numerous, substantial and enduring.

Notes

1. Robert O'Neill, ed., *The Defence of Australia – Fundamental New Aspects* (Canberra: Strategic and Defence Studies Centre, Australia National University, 1976), pp. 97–125.
2. Desmond Ball, ed., *The Future of Tactical Airpower in the Defence of Australia* (Canberra: Strategic and Defence Studies Centre, Australian National University, 1976).
3. See *Australian Defence,* A White Paper presented to Parliament by the Minister for Defence, the Hon. D.J. Killen (Canberra: Australian Government Publishing Service, 1976), pp. 10–11.
4. J. O. Langtry and Desmond Ball, *Controlling Australia's Threat Environment: A Methodology for Planning Australia's Defence Force Development* (Canberra, Strategic and Defence Studies Centre, Australian National University, 1979), p. 4.
5. Langtry and Ball, *Controlling Australia's Threat Environment*, p. 22.
6. Ibid., p. 60.
7. Ross Babbage, Desmond Ball, J.O. Langtry and Robert O'Neill *The Development of Australian Army Officers for the 1980s,* Canberra Papers on Strategy and

Defence, no. 17 (Canberra: Strategic and Defence Studies Centre, Australian National University, 1978), p. 66.
8. Babbage, Ball, Langtry and O'Neill *The Development of Australian Army Officers for the 1980s*, p. 34.
9. Desmond Ball, "Conclusion" in Desmond Ball and J.O. Langtry's *Problems of Mobilisation in the Defence of Australia* (Manuka: Phoenix Defence Publications, 1980), p. 139.
10. See the argument made in: J. O. Langtry "Geostrategic Imperatives" in *The Northern Territory in the Defence of Australia: Strategic and Operational Considerations*, edited by J. O. Langtry and Desmond Ball (Canberra: Strategic and Defence Studies Centre, 1991), pp. 120–21.
11. Paul Dibb *Review of Australia's Defence Capabilities: Report to the Minister for Defence* (Canberra: Australian Government Publishing Service, 1986) p. 80.
12. Kim C. Beazley, *The Defence of Australia 1987* (Canberra: Australian Government Publishing Service, 1987), p. ix.
13. Thatcher and Ball, *A National Asset: Essays Commemorating the 40th Anniversary of the Strategic and Defence Studies Centre*, p. 66.
14. See J. O. Langtry and Desmond Ball, eds., *A Vulnerable Country: Civil Resources in the Defence of Australia* (Canberra: Strategic and Defence Studies Centre, Australian National University, 1986).
15. See Desmond Ball and Ross Babbage *Geographic Information Systems: Defence Applications* (Brassey's Australia, Rushcutters Bay, 1989).
16. See this case made, for instance in Desmond Ball and J. O. Langtry "Conclusions: National Development and National Security", in *A Vulnerable Country: Civil Resources in the Defence of Australia*, edited by J. O. Langtry and Desmond Ball (Canberra: Strategic and Defence Studies Centre, 1986), pp. 603–604.
17. Desmond Ball, ed., *Aborigines in the Defence of Australia* (Canberra: Australian National University Press, 1991).
18. Desmond Ball and J.O. Langtry "Conclusions: National Development and National Security", in *A Vulnerable Country: Civil Resources in the Defence of Australia*, edited by J. O. Langtry and Desmond Ball (Canberra: Strategic and Defence Studies Centre, 1986), pp. 608–609.

17

AMERICAN BASES IN AUSTRALIA REVISITED

Richard Tanter

TEMPER DEMOCRATIC, BIAS HUMAN[1]

Desmond Ball's labours through four decades to elucidate the character of United States defence and intelligence facilities in Australia, to document the evidence, test the balance of benefits and dangers to both national security and human security, and then tell the story to his fellow Australians is unparalleled in Australian intellectual and political life, and I suspect on an international scale. The dedication, often neglected, to the most famous and influential part of this work, *A Suitable Piece of Real Estate: American Installations in Australia*, was the call "for a sovereign Australia". We might best sum up the character of Ball's work of a lifetime — or more precisely, this one, brightly coloured, thread of a multi-stranded body of work — by recalling the enduring watchwords of an earlier Australian nationalist, Joseph Furphy: "temper democratic, bias Australian". Both elements are keys to understanding the animating force behind Ball's work on the American installations in Australia — the concern for a fully and properly informed public as a prerequisite to democratic debate about the American bases, and the concern that Australians identify their country's specific interests concerning the bases, citing Malcolm Fraser's prescient but often ignored 1976 warning that the interests of the United States and the interests of Australia are not necessarily identical".[2]

And yet, this is not enough, on either count. One might more properly say of Ball on the bases that the work is characterised by "temper offensively democratic, bias human". Ball's anger is clear for those Australian officials and politicians who would hide the true nature of these military and intelligence bases behind unwarranted secrecy, unjustified discounting of risk, and willingness to traduce the fundamental civil rights of citizens in a democracy. At root, Ball was not only sure that truths hidden or obfuscated by government would always be revealed in the end, but he was confident that a properly informed Australian public would be able to make judicious assessments on the merits of a case that a reasonable government committed to both genuine national security and a viable democratic polity could live with.[3]

Moreover, while retrieving national sovereignty has always been central to Ball's critique of particular American facilities (or particular aspects of some or all of them), from the beginning of his career Ball has often gone beyond questions of national interest to identify the ways in which the outcome of misconstrued or inadequate conceptions of national interest have implications for the wider human interest — or indeed, a planetary interest — albeit in a distinctively Australian accent.[4]

PURPOSE AND METHOD

Tellingly, Ball's published work on the American bases begins in 1975 with a 14-page article titled "American bases in Australia: the strategic implications" in the venerable Australian adult education magazine the *Current Affairs Bulletin*.[5] Over the next decade and a half Ball published two major works, four monographs and a series of research and policy papers documenting, analysing, and assessing the implications of these American installations. Of these, Ball's 1980 book *A Suitable Piece of Real Estate: American Installations in Australia* became the best known of all of Ball's dozens of books. The book has an iconic status for many Australians, in part because it is often assumed to be principally about the Joint Defence Facility Pine Gap.

In fact only 24 pages of the book are devoted specifically to that base, but the apparent error of fact is a slip of the mind that reflects the profound significance Pine Gap has acquired in Australian culture, as well as in practical political life, in both cases largely due to Ball's work. Among all the many American (and Australian) military installations past and present in Australia, Pine Gap occupies a literally iconic place in the Australian imagination. Through Ball's work, the base has acquired a sense of specialness — a place of difference, and a place of manifold potency, not least politically.[6] In the minds of many Australians, American concern about a threat to the future of Pine Gap was enough to bring down the elected government in 1975. Its association with uncontrollable foreign powers, extraordinarily sophisticated technology, the exotic and necessarily fantasy-laden realm of space, and its associations with the use of nuclear weapons (including being a target of them) all contributed to the mystique. Physically located just a short way from Alice Springs, a town that most Australians never visit, Pine Gap vies with Uluru for primacy as the symbolic centre of the country. The physiognomy of the base, with its faceless white domes jumping out of the browns and greens of the McDonnell Ranges behind it, quietly captured in an often reproduced still from Gill Scrine's 1981 documentary *Home On The Range* contributes much to this sense of mystery and potency, and its ongoing capacity to act as a container of powerful projections of promise and threat.

For many Australians of a certain generation, *A Suitable Piece of Real Estate: American Installations in Australia* was profoundly shocking. Never before had any researcher provided a list of even half of the "more than twenty" American military, intelligence, scientific and space facilities in Australia that Ball documented.[7] Never before had the major bases been documented in such detail. Never before had the nature and activities at these facilities been documented primarily from mainstream United States military, congressional, technical and corporate sources, leaving no doubt about the credibility of Ball's claims about their strategic implications. Never before had a writer — and in particular one from the country's premier research university — so comprehensively, systematically and so elegantly spelled out a framework for the assessment of the advantages and risks associated with each of these facilities within a framework that drew on strategic studies, defence policy, and democratic understandings of the national interest. And, once the misleading, artful, and incompetent official Australian government explanations and justifications for the bases were exposed and found laughably wanting, never again did Australian public consciousness of the bases' double-edged and complex blending of benefit, violation and dread ever completely evaporate.

Seven years later, in the more closely argued *A Base for Debate: The US Satellite Station at Nurrungar*, Ball exemplified his argument on the need to understand the precise nature and function of each particular facility in order to assess its desirability, strategically and politically. Ball prefaced his study of the Australian ground station for the US Defense Support Program by setting out a precise list of differences between the three major American bases of the day: Nurrungar, the US naval communications station at North West Cape, and the Pine Gap signals intelligence ground station. These differences, Ball wrote, "are in terms of:

1. Their respective functions and missions;
2. The nature of their relationships to the US strategic nuclear posture and their role in US deterrence and war-fighting postures;
3. Their implications for the global strategic balance;
4. Their role (if any) in the promotion of arms control;
5. The consequences to surrounding areas of nuclear attacks on them; and
6. The extent to which their location in Australia is simply a matter of convenience."[8]

Examination of these dimensions of American facilities then enabled Ball to make grounded strategic and political assessments of each of the major bases — rejecting North West Cape as "simply incompatible with Australian sovereignty";[9] recommending either prompt closure of Nurrungar or maintenance for a limited time subject to stringent (and politically improbable) conditions on its nuclear war-fighting role; and finding, regarding Pine Gap, that despite its essentially American character and purpose, its role in nuclear warfighting plans, and its status as a likely nuclear target, on balance "it is simply not possible to seriously support arms control and disarmament and at the same time argue for the closure of the Pine Gap station".[10] This stress in Ball's work on an understanding of the technical and physical characteristics of defence and intelligence facilities as a prerequisite to comprehending their strategic and policy significance in democratic polities has often led to two unwarranted conclusions.

The first is a criticism of Ball's intelligence studies as "merely technical" or "empiricist", implying an inappropriate attention to matters outside the domain of more important questions of strategy and politics. In fact, Ball's analysis of the technical functions and physical characteristics of particular facilities provided him with the solid ground from which to make keen and subtle distinctions as to the relative balance of benefits and risks in each case — most famously in the case of Pine Gap, which is, as he explained with some anguish in 1999:

> the one which I have had to force myself to come out and support... simply because I regard the intelligence which is collected there as critically important and collectable in no other way.[11]

The second conclusion drawn from this link between technical understanding and capacity to assess strategic and democratic policy implications is not so much a criticism as a muttered excuse for avoidance of the research field. This is the belief that Ball's achievement is too difficult to match — the sense that the technical issues are so complex for those not technically trained and the materials so difficult to obtain for people outside a certain charmed circle of "respectable" insiders that the ordinary researcher in academia or civil society can neither continue the work in its contemporary setting, nor critically assess Ball's work from a comparable foundation.

Lack of information is certainly not true: Australian and foreign media have reported many developments related to the bases prominently, if not in depth. A great deal of informative and detailed background material is readily found by anyone who looks — especially in government and industry circles in the United States.[12] In fact the problem is often a matter of being swamped by data and analysis. Understanding the broad technical characteristics of particular systems may not be easy, but neither is it overwhelmingly difficult.

Given the actual possibilities of emulating, extending, and critiquing Ball's work, and the research facilities and time available to Australian university-based researchers, more powerful explanations are needed to explain this comparative silence. These include academic researchers' belief in risks — imagined or real — of damage to career prospects of inquiring too closely into certain questions, or aversion to "technology matters", and among those employed in fields of politics, international relations and social inquiry, preoccupation with downstream theoretical questions and distaste for unfashionable technically and historically grounded empirical work.

FOUNDATIONS

In two respects, Ball's work on the American bases rests on foundations, which, if not unique, are certainly not common. Speaking to members of a parliamentary committee frustrated with the refusal of the Department of Defence to provide any substantial explanation of the role of Pine Gap, Ball hinted at one foundation of his own work:

> It really depends on the relationship which this committee has with people in the Department of Defence, the personal levels of connections which have been built up and the trust in the end which exists between members of this committee and the Department of Defence as to the extent to which they might be a little bit more forthcoming with you.[13]

Ball's work on other matters has brought him into close contact with defence and intelligence officials in Australia and the United States over four decades. While often officially close to *persona non grata* to Australian senior officials at particular times, equally Ball has held the respect of other senior officials and political leaders, and is clearly trusted as an informed but discreet dialogue partner by at least some of those in a position to know. Trust built slowly over many years brings a certain level of access impossible for almost anyone else outside authorised circles. At the Strategic and Defence Studies Centre, former Defence Department officials such as Paul Dibb and Ron Huisken, while careful to observe the severe limitations on what they could say flowing from their security commitments in their previous careers, played an important part in Ball's thinking at certain times.

One striking product of those relationships was the detailed testimony that Ball and Dibb gave to the Joint Standing Committee on Treaties in August 1999 on the subject of Pine Gap. Ball spoke first in a prepared statement followed by question and answer, for 18 pages of transcript. Dibb followed, making clear the limitations on what he could tell the Committee. The sequencing was intentional and significant, with Dibb listening to Ball's presentation. Not only did Dibb not dissent from any of Ball's analysis, but he went on to give it his overt, if partial, imprimatur: "Professor Ball can go somewhat further than I can. He and I would have significant areas of agreement".[14]

Ball acknowledged the fine line the maintenance of this trust required him to walk:

One draws the line with regard to the technical operational secrets of how this intercept technology parked up in space actually works, and how some of the more sensitive intelligence collected through that technology works, but we do not talk about that. If you look carefully at my various writings, you will see where I draw the line and simply will not go any further, regardless of whether I know about it or not.[15]

That fine line was invisible to government critics of Ball's work on the bases in the United States and in Australia.

Yet despite perennial official criticism, Ball established and maintained good relations with many senior United States military leaders, Defense Department officials, politicians (including Jimmy Carter), and leading researchers at institutions such as the RAND Corporation. This was a source of deep concern to senior Australian Defence Department officials, including its secretary, Sir Arthur Tange. Dismayed that a radical (and long-haired!) critic of the department could have such access that he could enter any building at the RAND Corporation, the department pressured RAND relentlessly over more than a year to dismiss Ball. Senior RAND officials supported Ball for a long period against demands conveyed through the military and Defense Department, and only relented when Australia raised the matter at official diplomatic level with the State Department.[16]

While the fraternity of writers on the United States electronic intelligence facilities in Australia and other countries is a small one, Ball's work on the American bases has not been a solitary endeavour. Indeed, much of its success derives from his partnerships and collaborative exchanges with a coterie of researchers, journalists, publishers, and activists around the world, as well as, *sotto voce*, government officials. The most sustained of the work on the bases, *The Ties That Bind* (1985) on the UKUSA countries' security and intelligence bureaucracies, was a joint effort with an American intelligence researcher, Jeffrey T. Richelson. Richelson's own 1999 *America's Space Sentinels*, a full-length study of the Defense Support Program, built on Ball's Nurrungar study a decade earlier.[17]

The pioneering New Zealand peace researcher and activist Owen Wilkes was an early and longstanding collaborator with Ball in research on American bases in Australia and the Pacific, nuclear targeting, and signals intelligence in a number of countries, including Japan. Ball's work on the American bases involved extensive collaboration with the British activist and journalist Duncan Campbell, the New Zealand activist researcher Nicky Hager, the Maoist activist Albert Langer, the American military analyst William Arkin, the Canadian signals intelligence specialist Bill Robinson, and the Australian journalists Brian Toohey, Bill Pinwill and George Munster.

Ball has also always been aware of the need to take the results of academic research into the public sphere. Relationships with journalists and publishers, as well as with politicians, are a key part of Ball's working method. In a small country like Australia, book publishing is a tender and sensitive plant. In 1980, Ball began a decade-long collaboration with the entrepreneurial publisher John Iremonger, who brought out *A Suitable Piece of Real Estate* under the Hale and Iremonger imprint. Probably the best selling and best known of Ball's books, *A Suitable Piece of Real Estate* was distinctive and well-designed, memorable for its cover photograph, and successfully marketed commercially by Iremonger, finding eager readers in a then burgeoning peace movement animated by apparent Australian enthusiasm for the Reagan administration's ramping up of the Cold War. After Iremonger moved to Allen and Unwin, he and Ball went on to publish *The Ties that Bind*, *A Base for Debate*, and *Pine Gap*.

The second unique foundation of Ball's work on the American facilities in Australia in the intense decade and a half from 1975–1990 is the fact that Ball was simultaneously engaged in three other streams of work: nuclear war-fighting doctrine and planning; cooperation among the global intelligence community centred on the UKUSA agreement; and a reorientation of Australian defence towards what came to be called the Defence of Australia outlook. Each of these buttressed the American bases work, and provided insights unlikely to spring to mind from more restricted concerns.

ASYMMETRICAL COOPERATION AND THE "JOINT FACILITIES" TODAY

It is now more than three decades since Ball began his work on the American bases in Australia. In that time there have been profound changes in the number, character and role of the many that he catalogued in *A Suitable Piece of Real Estate*. Many of the minor facilities had already disappeared by the end of the 1980s, when only North West Cape, Nurrungar, and Pine Gap remained of the major facilities. Today, Nurrungar has gone after being rendered redundant by technological change, leaving only a Remote Ground Station at Pine Gap to link to the DSP satellite network and its successors.[18] As a result of similar technical change, as well as shifting strategic concerns, North West Cape has gone from being a major and vital United States communications base to an Australian-run base with only minor American interest, to once again being not only an important United States communications base operated with Australia, but a new and vital element in American space war-fighting capacities.[19]

Pine Gap's growth in capacities is evident externally, and whereas the facility had 26 satellite antennas in 2002, it now has 34 satellite antennas, 20 in radomes and 14 without.[20] Pine Gap has not only greatly expanded its principal signals intelligence function of monitoring missile testing, but has expanded its secondary SIGINT functions to include collection of signals intelligence vital for American conventional war-fighting in the wars in Iraq and Afghanistan, and in American-led global counter-terrorism activities. Moreover, the remote ground station facility at Pine Gap for the DSP/SBIRS thermal imaging satellites now has an expanded role beyond detecting missile launches, and is capable of detecting jet fighters using afterburners, and major explosions in war zones like Afghanistan. These satellites provide the United States with early warning of missile attack, but they also provide the United States with nuclear targeting data. Without the crucial "cueing" information on the trajectories of incoming ballistic missiles provided by these geostationary thermal-imaging satellites to American and Japanese missile defence systems, missile defence would be impossible.

In the past decade, a new set of Australian facilities have been opened to the United States, a shift emblematic of much deeper and broader cooperation between Australian and American military forces, with plans for considerably more to come. Overall there may be fewer military and intelligence facilities in Australia to which the United States has significant access than in the 1970s, but their number has risen again after diminishing in the 1980s–1990s. Those that remain and those that have been added have considerably increased the importance of the Australian connection for the United States, and bring both renewed versions of old concerns, and new ones.

It is true that there is a much higher level of Australian involvement in the operation of Pine Gap than in the past, and Australia directly receives and utilizes considerable intelligence data and product from the facility.[21] However, "American" is how Ball refers to all of the titles of the works from 1975 to 1999 under discussion here. Successive Australian governments in recent decades have referred to Pine Gap and other bases as "joint facilities", and insisted that there are no US bases in Australia.[22] However, the cooperation involved is fundamentally and inherently asymmetrical. Pine Gap, as well as North West Cape and other current "joint facilities" are best understood as American bases to which Australia has access. They were built by the United States, the core facilities are paid for and maintained by the United States, and the facilities only function in concert with the huge American investment in military and intelligence satellite and communications systems. Take the last away, and nothing of significance is left. The bases do involve cooperation, and indeed increasing levels of cooperation and integration with US systems, but the consequences of the asymmetries of that cooperation need continual reassessment of benefits and risks, in light of questions of sovereignty.

Inevitably, any consideration of Ball's work on the American bases in Australia circles back to Pine Gap. For Australians there are two vital conclusions Ball reached a quarter of a century ago that must be re-tested by each generation. The first concerns Ball's conclusion, since confirmed by senior Australian officials such as Paul Dibb, that Pine Gap was a high priority nuclear target for the Soviet Union.[23] The second is his substantial, if reluctant, two-part conclusion to the question of whether the retention of Pine Gap is in the Australian national interest and the wider human interest. That is, that on the basis of the contribution Pine Gap makes to arms control and disarmament, and because for technical reasons there is no possibility of relocating it elsewhere, whoever speaks for arms control must speak for Pine Gap.

While many in the Australian peace movement who admired and drew on Ball's work were dismayed by the second conclusion, few were more aware of the ghastly tensions between these two conclusions than Ball. Ball's investigation of the question *Can Nuclear War Be Controlled?* concluded that the pursuit of the "chimera of controlled nuclear war" would best be replaced by "greater attention to the conditions of conventional deterrence".[24] Equally, his concern for accuracy and precision was not a mere matter of the sometimes chilling edges of realism, but a strongly moral position, as when he chided Carl Sagan and his colleagues for overstating the nuclear winter case, saying:

> I thought that it was just as wrong to overestimate the possible consequences of nuclear war, and to raise the spectre of extermination of human life as a serious likelihood, as to underestimate them (e.g., by omitting fallout casualties).[25]

Pine Gap as Nuclear Target

With the publication of *A Suitable Piece of Real Estate* in 1980, Australians had good reason to believe that Pine Gap would be a target of nuclear attack in the event of global war. Ball drew that particularly Australian conclusion from his parallel work at the time on the global question "*Can Nuclear War Be Controlled?*"[26] Ball's answer was that, amongst other clearly significant factors, the "enormous" vulnerability of even hardened command and control systems (and accompanying communications links) is such that control of nuclear forces is likely to be lost early in even a limited nuclear exchange.[27] With such a loss of control, an uncontrolled paroxysm of all-out attack was a likely outcome. The vulnerability of facilities such as North West Cape, Pine Gap, and Nurrungar was not only a matter of great danger to Australia,[28] but also pointed to an endemic and fearful weakness in current American and Soviet planning for nuclear warfighting in the guise of the latest phase of "stable deterrence". This dense, deeply informed technical work on one key aspect of what Judith Wright once called "the contained argument of the bomb"[29] provided Ball with the technical sources to contribute to informed national debate on the question.

When it came to the risks Pine Gap's target status brought to the population of Alice Springs, or possibly Adelaide, and the abject failure of Australian authorities to approach the question of civil defence protection for those populations, Ball's anger was clear. While in fact Ball was a defender of the grand bargain at the heart of the alliance — Pine Gap is the price Australia pays for the global nuclear balance, and access to American technology to sustain the "knowledge edge"[30] — he could never have adopted the unapologetic tone that Paul Dibb did in 2005, looking back at the calculus of mass death the defence establishment ensured was never presented for democratic debate:

> US intelligence also helped us to assess the risk of Soviet nuclear strikes on Australia in the event of global nuclear war. We were able to identify the locations in Australia that were targeted by Moscow and assess likely casualties. We judged, for example, that the SS-11 ICBM site at Svobodny in Siberia was capable of inflicting one million instant deaths and 750,000 radiation deaths on Sydney. And you would not have wanted to live in Alice Springs, Woomera or Exmouth — or even Adelaide.[31]

The first question today is whether Pine Gap remains a likely high priority nuclear target. Clearly, the threat of all-out nuclear war between the United States and Russia is much less than at any time in the Cold War. Moreover, China, the country that the United States and Australian defence establishments do consider a serious nuclear threat,[32] has a very much smaller nuclear arsenal than the United States or Russia under its policy of the "minimal means of reprisal", and there must be more serious uncertainties about how that limited number of weapons will be deployed than in the case of the overkill paradigm cases of the United States or Russia. With that caveat, the question remains of whether Pine Gap, today, is still a tempting and potentially high priority target for a country with the will and means to engage in nuclear war with the United States.

The question can be asked of the two distinct roles of Pine Gap: the DSP/SBIRS remote ground station uplinking and downlinking command, control and data from infrared imaging satellites; and the far larger complete onsite command, control, data down-link, and data processing functions for the geo-stationary signals intelligence satellites. The DSP/SBIRS satellite constellation and its ground-stations at Buckley in the United States, and Pine Gap continue to provide both early warning of missile launches (and aircraft and explosions with a detectable thermal signature) and assist in attack preparation and targeting. Destroying or significantly degrading the DSP/SBIRS system — the thermal signature monitoring "eyes in space" of the United States targeting system — would undoubtedly be a priority objective. Yet destroying the Pine Gap Remote Ground Station would not greatly impair these capacities of the DSP/SBIRS system, because there are reportedly functionally adequate, multiple robust communications redundancies, which would allow continued communications from the Buckley control station to the satellite previously controlled via the Pine Gap RGS. In Ball's words, these communications redundancies render the Pine Gap and other Remote Ground Stations "really quite marginal elements", and hence unlikely nuclear targets.[33]

The situation concerning Pine Gap's principal, signals intelligence, function has some similarities, but also differences that almost certainly lead to a more pessimistic conclusion. The increase in sensitivity, coverage, targets and global systemic intelligence integration further increases the already high Cold War priority for targeting the American system of space-based electronic intelligence, particularly the geo-stationary satellite elements. Unlike Pine Gap's limited role as a Remote Ground Station for the early warning DSP/SBIRS system, Pine Gap's signals intelligence role is very different, with a very direct and substantial responsibility for

American Bases in Australia Revisited

satellite station-keeping, controlling satellite house-keeping and monitoring activities, commanding satellite surveillance operations, and receiving and processing downlinked data. In itself, this renders Pine Gap a lucrative and reasonably high priority target.

While Ball provided a detailed account of the communications capacities of the early SIGINT geostationary satellites, little is known of the communications architecture of the current constellation of ADVANCED ORION satellites. There have been attempts to establish redundancies for communications systems for the SIGINT geostationary satellites, but these do not appear to have reached the point where satellite crosslinks are viable replacements for the vital uplink and downlink communications through Pine Gap. The satellite-satellite crosslinks that are in place for the ADVANCED ORION signals intelligence satellites are unlikely to have the capacity to process huge amounts of SIGINT data onboard to transmit in secure encrypted form via a satellite crosslink.[34] Consequently, attacking Pine Gap almost certainly remains a plausible and lucrative way of degrading or destroying the United States' geostationary signals intelligence capability — the "ears" of its nuclear war-fighting capacity.[35]

Pine Gap: Is There Any Alternative?

If it is reasonable to conclude that Pine Gap is still a priority nuclear target, then the contemporary adequacy of Ball's calculus of the grand bargain calls for assessment: on the balance of benefits and disadvantages, Pine Gap should be retained because its arms control role is irreplaceable, and so whoever speaks of arms control has no alternative but to speak for Pine Gap. Leaving aside for this purpose Ball's accounting of the negatives and the positives, the vital task is to focus on the claim of the unavoidable necessity of Pine Gap for arms control and disarmament, especially at a time when an American president's statement of a goal of an ultimately nuclear-free world has reinvigorated calls for both disarmament and abolition. For both of these goals, reliable, robust and trusted means of verification are essential.

Ball spelled out his reluctant conclusion from two separate directions, one about the role of signals intelligence and the arms control process, and the other concerning the lack of any viable alternative location for the Pine Gap station outside the Australian continent. The first draws on a two-part argument advanced by Richelson to the effect that United States willingness to engage in arms control and disarmament is dependent on technical intelligence from space-based systems. Firstly, Richelson argued, "distinctions between arms control monitoring and military intelligence are often arbitrary and misleading" because not only are these National Technical Means of Intelligence (NTMI) required to monitor weapons systems under arms control agreements for verification purposes, but they are also necessary for the United States to know enough about weapons systems not covered by the agreements to know that the arms control agreements will not lead to a damaging outcome, and to judge what might safely be put on the table for the next round of discussions. Secondly, he argued, technical intelligence systems are not developed for verification purposes, but for military intelligence on a range of specific matters which may then, on the basis of utility and experience, be applied to the arms control process:

> "Verification technology" is not developed after an agreement; rather, technical capabilities to some extent dictate the type of provisions that can be included in a treaty. Today's espionage is tomorrow's verification.[36]

Ball's second argument derives from technical reasons why the Pine Gap facility was located in Central Australia, and why no location outside Australia was acceptable to the United States. This concerns the security requirements needed to ensure that the massive amounts of data downlinked from the signals intelligence satellites in geo-stationary orbit to a ground receiving station are not intercepted by adversaries. For satellites positioned over the Indian Ocean or Southeast Asia, the downlink station needs to be located somewhere between about 50 degrees longitude (the western Indian Ocean) to 180 degrees (mid-Pacific). The size of the area that needs to be secured against adversary interception is, Ball wrote, a function of the transmission frequency and the diameter of the downlink antenna on the satellite. When the geo-stationary SIGINT satellite constellation was planned in the mid-1960s, these were about 24GHz and 2.5 metres respectively, yielding a requirement of a secure area of about 160 kilometres in diameter. Accordingly, downlinking to small islands such as Diego Garcia or Guam would have been too vulnerable to interception by Soviet SIGINT-equipped ships or aircraft, and crowded land areas in the Philippines or Japan unable to be protected against covert interception system in nearby areas.

Taking the technical argument first, Ball ruled out the obvious line of inquiry immediately: larger antenna size and higher frequencies "were simply not technical options".[37] Unfortunately Ball gave no information as to exactly what these excluding technical factors were, so it is difficult to know the nature of the limits on frequency and antenna size he was including. Leaving the frequency band issue aside, there are in fact a range of electrical and physical issues affecting choice of antenna size and characteristics for downlink antennas from geostationary orbits, such as the accommodation constraints deriving from configuration of the satellite platform (especially when adjacent to receiving antennas more than 100m. in diameter, as well as antennas for the telemetry, tracking and command subsystems, and optical crosslink to other satellites), radiated power and cross polarisation discrimination requirements, and accommodation and deployment mechanism constraints from the fairing of the satellite launch vehicle, and others. Moreover, there have been considerable advances in downlink antenna design for communications satellites in geostationary orbits in order to more precisely shape the size and configuration of the downlink footprint, including the use of mathematically adjusted surface profile shaping of the antenna. Certainly the payload size of signals intelligence satellites has increased considerably, as have the capacities of the launch vehicles. Yet until more is known about the actual characteristics of the current constellation of American signals intelligence satellites — concerning the variables Ball raised as definitive, as well as others — it is not possible to say more than that there are a wider range of technical issues that must be assessed, and that there is considerable urgency to do so. If there is a technically viable alternative location for the Pine Gap downlink facility, then that offers the Australian government and its people an alternative conclusion to Ball's painful acceptance of the balance of benefits and costs of hosting the facility. But it is still not possible to determine the answer to that question.

The arguments Ball adopted from Richelson have in certain respects become stronger over time, while in others less compelling. The primary verification function performed through Pine Gap's signals intelligence capacity has always been its original purpose: intercepting telemetry from advanced missile testing in order to determine the characteristics and capacities of the missiles. As ballistic missile technology has progressed and proliferated — well beyond the nuclear armed states — then so too has the need for telemetry interception, both for basic military intelligence purposes and for any serious attempt to regulate horizontal and vertical missile proliferation.

The quantitative and qualitative development of both the thermal signature detection and signals intelligence functions carried out through Pine Gap — and the wider systems into which they are more closely integrated — undoubtedly bring greater space-based capabilities to the potential service of arms control and disarmament verification.[38]

Yet, the fundamental flaw in the argument remains reliance, or acceptance, of the unilateral character of the verification capacities offered through these technical intelligence systems. At a very general level, put simply but not necessarily simplistically, technical systems and capacities that give one side the confidence that measures of disarmament will not be disabling or worse should be available to the other side. In a fundamental sense, the sum of a situation where both sides have such capacities for assurance is greater than the parts. As Ushioda put it:

> Verification is today largely unilateral and non-cooperative. Each state makes its own evaluations; it reacts to any breach of an agreement to which it is a party on the basis of its own interests. As a result, in the absence of a collective process, verification appears to be not a guarantee that the agreement will be implemented but a guarantee of the individual security of the parties.[39]

At the height of the Cold War there were proposals, originally from France, for the United Nations to develop an International Satellite Monitoring Agency (ISMA), resulting in a UN expert study, focusing on space-based imaging.[40] While that proposal died under the disdainful gorgon stare of the nuclear superpowers, it has returned in a number of different forms in the past two decades.[41] In some respects, the idea of an ISMA-like body with a dedicated space-based imaging capacity has been rendered at least partially redundant by advances in commercial space-based imaging, though this is not the case in relation to either real-time thermal signature detecting of missile launches and detonations or electronic intelligence (or space security verification issues).[42]

Moreover, while such ideas were originally cautiously proposed in the hostile and indeed Manichean bipolarising world of the Cold War, logically the argument for multilateral verification structures is a great deal stronger in the nuclear multipolar world of today, where the majority of the nine nuclear armed states have nuclear-armed intercontinental or medium-range ballistic missiles at their disposal. And from the wider view of space security where more than 50 countries have launched over a thousand satellites and other space assets, only a very small number of countries have the capacities to ascertain what is happening with these satellites, and many of these countries would have little reason to be confident their interests would be pursued by the major-powers with impartiality and diligence.

The facilities at Pine Gap (and in the future at North West Cape) and the systems, of which they are an integrated part, are tasked exactly to address such a situation. The question arises, then, if Pine Gap is uniquely required for unilateral American arms control and disarmament verification purposes, and if another location is at present technically not viable, are there ways in which particular, partial functions of the facility can be utilised for collective, multilateral arms control verification purposes, without diminishing genuine (as opposed to knee-jerk) claims of American national security? What forms of provision of data could be considered, in relation to both real-time thermal signature detection of missile launches and detonations or electronic intelligence? Under what institutional, legal, and security conditions? With the current rapid pace of nuclear weapon proliferation, long range ballistic and cruise missile proliferation, and the competitive militarisation of space, serious assertion of collective rights to verification assurance capacities is necessary, and must engage closely and imaginatively on an informed basis with national interest-based, unilateral national technical means of verification. An Australian government committed to the goal of a nuclear-free world articulated by its ally should be considering the ways in which the American facilities it embraces so willingly could be enlisted in such a process.

Richelson and Ball specified that one condition for the maintenance of the UKUSA arrangements, in addition to "firm, effective and responsible governmental oversight and control":

> is that the citizens of the five democracies be officially and fully apprised of the nature and operations of these agencies, and of the consequences (both beneficial and disadvantageous) of the international cooperative arrangements among them — to the extent permitted by the genuine requirements of national security.[43]

There has been a little progress. In 2008 the NRO acknowledged Pine Gap as a Mission Control Station, and subsequently the existence of the US SIGINT satellite systems. In 2010 the US and UK governments released redacted versions of a series of UKUSA agreements for the period 1940–1955.[44] Yet fundamentally we remain even further from the democratic condition Richelson and Ball sought than when it was suggested, even as the task becomes more urgent. Moreover, what is true for the civil rights of citizens of the five UKUSA countries also holds true for citizens of the rest of world in a situation of globalised threat from the nuclear weapons systems to which Pine Gap contributes. The task is to discover ways in which these national technical means of verification can be brought, however partially, haltingly, and unwillingly, into the service of universal human security.

Notes

1. My thanks to Peter Hayes, and to Jeffrey Richelson and Bill Robinson for providing important material for this chapter. However my greatest debt is to Desmond Ball for three decades of friendship and teaching.
2. Hansard (House of Representatives), 1 June 1976, p. 2738, cited in Jeffrey T. Richelson and Desmond Ball, *The Ties That Bind: Intelligence Cooperation Between the UKUSA Countries – the United Kingdom, the United States of America, Canada, Australia and New Zealand* (Sydney: Allen and Unwin, 1985), p. 303. For Fraser's more recent extended critique see "Politics, Independence and the National Interest: the legacy of power and how to achieve a peaceful Western Pacific", 2012 Gough Whitlam Oration, Sydney, 6 June 2012; and Malcolm Fraser, "Our star spangled manner", *The Age*, 7 June 2012.
3. Referring to the limitations and obfuscations in the 1988 statement to parliament by then-Prime Minister Bob Hawke on the rationale for the major "joint facilities", Ball concluded by saying "The irony is that if the 'unwarranted mystique' surrounding Pine Gap was removed, the Australian public would overwhelmingly endorse the continued maintenance of the station." See Desmond Ball, *Pine Gap: Australia and the US Geostationary Signals Intelligence Satellite Program* (Sydney: Allen and Unwin Australia, 1988), p. 95.
4. See Desmond Ball, "The Probabilities of *On the Beach*: Assessing 'Armageddon Scenarios' in the 21st Century", *Strategic and Defence Studies Centre Working Paper* 401 (Canberra: Strategic and Defence Studies Centre, Australian National University, 2006).
5. Desmond Ball, "American Bases in Australia: The Strategic Implications", *Current Affairs Bulletin* 51, no. 10 (March 1975): 4–17.
6. To Ball's chagrin, these qualities are sensed by large numbers of UFO enthusiasts who importune him with requests for the still hidden truths of the facility.
7. See Desmond Ball, *A Suitable Piece of Real Estate: American Installations in Australia* (Sydney: Hale and Iremonger, 1980), p. 19.
8. Desmond Ball, *A Base for Debate: The US Satellite Station at Nurrungar* (Sydney: Allen and Unwin, 1987), p. xii.

9. Ibid., p. 86.
10. Ball, *Pine Gap*, p. 94.
11. Commonwealth of Australia. "Testimony of Professor Desmond Ball to the Joint Standing Committee On Treaties, Reference: Pine Gap", Official Committee Hansard, Parliament of the Commonwealth of Australia, Parliament of the Commonwealth of Australia (9 August 1999), p. 3.
12. Recall that all of the works about the bases under discussion were written prior to the internet.
13. Commonwealth of Australia. "Testimony of Professor Desmond Ball", p. 14.
14. Commonwealth of Australia. "Testimony of Professor Paul Dibb to the Joint Standing Committee On Treaties, Reference: Pine Gap", Official Committee Hansard, Parliament of the Commonwealth of Australia, Parliament of the Commonwealth of Australia (9 August 1999).
15. Commonwealth of Australia. "Testimony of Professor Desmond Ball", p. 9.
16. Desmond Ball, interview by Stewart Harris, National Library of Australia, 26 October 1994.
17. Richelson and Ball. *The Ties That Bind* and; Jeffrey T. Richelson, *America's Space Sentinels: DSP Satellites and National Security* (Lawrence: University Press of Kansas, 1999).
18. The DSP Overseas Ground Station — the Joint Defence Facility Nurrungar closed on 12 October 1999. There is also a Relay Ground Station — Europe at Menwith Hill in Britain.
19. For a brief discussion, see: Richard Tanter, "After Obama — The New Joint Facilities", *Arena Magazine*, May 2012.
20. See *Satellite antennas/radomes at Pine Gap, 1967–2011*, Table produced by Desmond Ball and Bill Robinson, 2007; updated by Richard Tanter and Bill Robinson, 2012.
21. See Ball, "The strategic essence"; and Commonwealth of Australia. "Testimony of Professor Desmond Ball".
22. See Judith Ireland, "US marines not a 'US base' on Australian soil: Smith", *The Age*, 4 April 2012.
23. Paul Dibb. "America has always kept us in the loop", *The Australian*, 10 September 2005.
24. Desmond Ball, *Can Nuclear War be Controlled?*, Adelphi Paper No. 169 (London: The International Institute for Strategic Studies, Autumn 1981), p. 38.
25. Desmond Ball, "The Probabilities of *On the Beach*: Assessing "Armageddon Scenarios" in the 21st Century", *Strategic and Defence Studies Centre Working Paper* 401 (Canberra: Strategic and Defence Studies Centre, Australian National University 2006), pp. 4–5.
26. Desmond Ball, "Can Nuclear War be Controlled?", p. 38.
27. The vulnerability of C3 systems is discussed at pp. 9–26. US facilities identified

as likely targets include, amongst others, Pine Gap, North West Cape and Nurrungar.
28. Desmond Ball, "Limiting damage from Nuclear Attack", in Desmond Ball and J.O. Langtry eds., *Civil Defence and Australia's Security in the Nuclear Age* (Sydney: George Allen and Unwin, 1983), pp. 143–81.
29. Judith Wright, "The precipice", *The Two Fires* (Sydney: Angus and Robertson, 1955).
30. Desmond Ball, "The strategic essence", *Australian Journal of International Affairs* 55, no. 2 (2001): 238–39.
31. Paul Dibb, "America has always kept us in the loop", *The Australian*, 10 September 2005.
32. Commonwealth of Australia, *Defending Australia in the Asia-Pacific Century: Force 2030, Defence White Paper 2009* (Canberra; Department of Defence) p. 39.
33. Ball, "The strategic essence", p. 242.
34. In *Pine Gap* Ball briefly discussed the issue of limitations on then feasible satellite crosslinks of the Nd:YAG (neodymium-doped yttrium aluminum garnet) laser types on the DSP satellites, reporting that the CIA had concluded that requirements for volume, security and quality were then "beyond current and foreseeable technological developments". See Ball, *Pine Gap*, p. 92.
35. In *The Kingdom and the Quarry: China, Australia, Fear and Greed* (Black Inc., 2012, p. 128) David Uren reported that in a "secret appendix" to the 2009 Defence white paper "defence thinking is that in the event of a conflict with the United States, China would attempt to destroy Pine Gap." The document concerned was the classified Force Posture Review (Uren, private communication).
36. Jeffrey Richelson, "Technical Collection and Arms Control", in *Verification and Arms Control*, edited by William C. Potter (Lexington: Lexington Books, 1985), p. 205.
37. Ball, *Pine Gap*, p. 90.
38. Richard A. Bruneau and Scott G. Lofquist-Morgan. "Verification Models for Space Weapons Treaties: A Flexible, Layered Approach as a Negotiating Tool", in *Building the Architecture for Sustainable Space Security* (Geneva: United Nations Institute for Disarmament Research 2006).
39. Setsuko Ushioda. *Satellite-Based Multilateral Arms Control Verification Schemes and International Law* (Ph.D. Dissertation, Institute of Air and Space Law, McGill University, Montreal, 1992), pp. 303–304.
40. United Nations. "Report of the Secretary-General, The Implications of Establishing an International Satellite Monitoring Agency" (New York: United Nations Department for Disarmament Affairs, 1983).
41. Ushioda, *Satellite-Based Multilateral Arms Control Verification Schemes and International Law*; Bhupendra Jasani. "International Satellite Monitoring Agency — Has the time come for its establishment?", Proceedings of Workshop on

Safeguards Perspectives for a Future Nuclear Environment, Cernobbio Villa Erba, Italy, 14–16 October 2003; Trevor Findlay. *A standing United Nations verification body: necessary and feasible*. Compliance Chronicles 1 (December 2005); Walter A. Dorn. *The Case for a United Nations Verification Agency: Disarmament Under Effective International Control* (working paper 26, Canadian Institute for International Peace and Security, July 1990); and United Nations Office for Disarmament Affairs, *Verification in all its Aspects, including the role of the United Nations in the field of verification* (New York: United Nations Department for Disarmament Affairs, 2008).
42. See Walter A. Dorn. *Tools of the Trade? Monitoring and Surveillance Technologies in UN Peacekeeping* (New York: United Nations Department of Peacekeeping Operations, September 2007).
43. Richelson and Ball. *The Ties That Bind*, p. 309.
44. See "NRO Mission Ground Station Declassification "Questions and Answers", National Reconnaissance Office, <http://www.fas.org/irp/nro/declass101508.pdf>; Jeffrey T. Richelson, "Out of the Black: The Declassification of the NRO", National Security Archive Electronic Briefing Book No. 257, 18 September 2008, <http://www.gwu.edu/~nsarchiv/NSAEBB/NSAEBB257/index.htm>; and UKUSA Agreement Release 1940-1956, National Security Agency, 24 June 2010, <http://www.nsa.gov/public_info/declass/ukusa.shtml>.

18

CYBER SECURITY AND THE ONLINE CHALLENGE

Gary Waters

I first met Des Ball in 1986 when I was on the Directing Staff of the Royal Australian Air Force (RAAF) Staff College and he delivered several lectures on strategic and defence topics. That relationship continued for a couple of years but was substantially reinforced in 1990 when I became the RAAF's first visiting fellow to the Strategic and Defence Studies Centre (SDSC), where I was privileged to work closely with Des. He already had a substantial list of publications to his name, including a major air power contribution from 1988 in which he outlined global developments and Australian perspectives on air power, and he was also Head of SDSC at the time I joined the Centre.

So, one can imagine my excitement at having someone like Des around to provide the direction, mentoring, and other support as I settled down to research and write on air power. There was also a sense of trepidation as he was the Head of the Centre and my respect for authority had been ingrained in me through some two decades of military service. I was to learn a lot during my 18 months with Des — and not just about how to put together a compelling argument in a book.

The contrast between us was striking. Here was Des Ball — something of a radical — renowned for climbing on a statue of George V[1] to demonstrate against the Vietnam War and well known for his many exploits in exposing signals intelligence; and here was I, the very first RAAF officer — by definition not a radical — entrusted to his care. And from there, a lifelong friendship and professional relationship grew. While I was at SDSC, the Gulf War broke out in 1991 and Des encouraged me to focus on how the air war played out, which led to a book published in 1992 that analysed Australian air power doctrine in the context of how allied air power contributed to the liberation of Kuwait, while Des concentrated on the intelligence war in the Gulf that resulted in his monograph in 1991.[2] I learnt from Des that when the opportunity presents itself to write, you need to get on with it and write. So, my time with Des was very productive and he guided me through getting three books published. I could not have done that without him.

It was during my time with Des at SDSC that he introduced me to two people who would figure in my life further down track. One was Robert (Bob) O'Neill, who was then at Oxford University as the Chichele Professor of the History of War and was visiting Australia at the time, and the other was Kim Beazley, the then Australian Minister for Defence. My task was to pick up Bob from Canberra airport and escort him to Parliament House for a meeting with Kim, which I was able to attend as well. It was a most rewarding experience for a mid-ranked military officer. Some years later I was to catch up with Bob at Oxford during my time in London and again when we had both returned to Australia around 2004. Kim Beazley would, a few years later on, write a foreword in a book that Des and I worked on together. You cannot help but meet interesting people when you are around Des Ball.

While the topic of this chapter is relatively new, the significance of Des' contribution to cyber security does build on his extensive work and considerable influence in SIGINT, as discussed earlier in this volume. Indeed, one need simply refer to Hansard for insights into what the Joint Standing Committee on Treaties thought after Des' testimony on Pine Gap on 9 August 1999.[3] The terms of reference for the inquiry, chaired by Mr. A. Thomson, were to review the Agreement between the Australian and United States Governments to further extend the December 1966 Agreement for the Joint Defence Facility at Pine Gap. Des was even then regarded as an expert and was well prepared for his testimony, having published separate books on Nurrungar and Pine Gap in 1987 and 1988 respectively.

During Des' testimony in 1999, one of the committee members, Mr Hardgrave, asked Des whether he had any suggestions about how the committee could find out what was going on there — a clear indication that Des knew how to get to the bottom of things. Later, Mr Hardgrave said, "I must say it is a pity that it is the professor who has to tell us these things — although I agree with what he said — and not the departmental officials".

Senator Coonan, the deputy chair, also seemed to hold great respect for Des' opinion and judgment when she asked "I am really interested to know if you have any constructive suggestions about how we might better inform ourselves about the consequential classified agreement". There is no question in my mind that this kind of respect for Des from members of parliament continues to this day. Indeed, I remember being invited by Des to join him and the then shadow Defence Minister Joel Fitzgibbon for a conversation about cyber issues just prior to the 2007 federal election. Fitzgibbon went on to become the Defence Minister in the Rudd Government.

It was during a discussion with Des in 2004 that we decided to write a book that brought together Des' interest in intelligence and information superiority and my interest in network centric warfare. This led to the 2005 publication *Transforming the Australian Defence Force (ADF) for Information Superiority*.[4] In this book, we examined the key issues involved in ensuring that the ADF could obtain information superiority in future contingencies. We looked at force posture, associated command and control systems, information support systems, operational concepts and doctrine. We examined the ADF's approach to Network Centric Warfare (NCW) and outlined some of the principal challenges. Through Des' efforts, we were able to present a number of hypothetical Information Operations scenarios, in which the Australian Defence Force was able to defeat an enemy's air assault by cyber attack; immobilise their naval fleet by electronic warfare attack; jam and deceive their air defences; destroy or incapacitate their command, control and communications systems; and corrupt their networks. Again, through Des' efforts we were able to sketch out an Information Warfare architecture for Australia.

It was clear in 2005 that reliance on information networks would mean enhancing the capability and survivability of networked infrastructures to ensure sustained and protected flows of information. And this would become increasingly problematic as reliance on commercial technologies increased. There was very little public discussion about cyber issues at this time, and it was Des who was pushing the pace on greater transparency and public debate.

In 2007, Des delivered a paper as part of a series of lectures at the Australian War Memorial, in which he advocated the need for an Australian cyber warfare centre. We met up just after that and discussed how we might combine that piece with work I was doing on defending information and communications technology networks. This time we included Ian Dudgeon, who brought to the team a wealth of knowledge and experience on information infrastructures at the global and national levels. This led to the 2008 publication of *Australia and Cyber-Warfare*.[5]

It was clear to Des that over the three years since our first book, national security planners, including in the Department of Defence, were being challenged by an increasing and sustained tempo of operations; these planners were also becoming more involved in coalition and regional matters; and there were real concerns emerging around cyber vulnerabilities spilling over into the physical world. It became evident that much needed to be done to ensure Australia would have the necessary capabilities for achieving the level of information superiority that we had talked about previously and that a re-think was required on the implications of cyber security issues for Australia.

These developments also led us to conclude that our earlier work had been incomplete, which had essentially ignored the offensive opportunities and challenges of Network Centric Warfare and the offensive role of information warfare and cyber warfare more generally. Indeed, it was clear that the 'war on terror', while stimulating some aspects of information operations, was distracting planners from the longer-term construction of an all-embracing architecture that addressed the offensive and defensive aspects of information warfare. Our conclusion was that recent achievements had been essentially defensive, involving investigative and forensic activities, rather than exploiting cyberspace for offensive information operations.

We seized on Australia's 2007 Defence Update, which stated that: "there is an emerging need to focus on 'cyber-warfare', particularly capabilities to protect national networks to deny information".[6] Yet, we could also see a myriad of complex issues that would require resolution before more appropriate command and control arrangements could be adopted, new technical capabilities acquired, and different operational concepts tested and codified. Time was of the essence as these sorts of issues would take many years to resolve and even longer, in some cases at least a decade, for the ensuing decisions to be fully implemented.

And so it was that Des extended his argument in *Australia and Cyber-Warfare* that a critical deficiency in Australia's cyber posture was the lack of a cyber warfare centre. He recognised that there were many organisations, within and outside Defence, concerned with some aspects of cyber warfare (including network security), but they were poorly coordinated and were not committed to the full exploitation of cyberspace for either military operations or information warfare more generally. Nor were they coordinated enough to significantly improve the nation's cyber-defensive posture.

As Des argued, a dedicated cyber warfare centre was fundamental to the planning and conduct of both defensive and offensive information operations. It would be responsible for exploring the full possibilities of future cyber warfare, and developing the doctrine and operational concepts for information operations. It would study all viruses, denial of service programs, 'Trojan horses' and 'trap-door' systems, not only for defensive purposes but also to discern offensive applications. It would study the firewalls around computer systems in military high commands and headquarters in the Asia-Pacific region, in avionics and other weapons systems, and in telecommunications centres, banks and stock exchanges, ready to penetrate a command centre, a flight deck or ship's bridge, a telephone or data exchange node, or a central bank at a moment's notice, and be able to insert confounding orders and to manipulate data without the adversary's knowledge.

Such a Centre would identify new capability requirements that would reach across the national security community. As to its location and reporting hierarchy, Des was clear that it should be located in a building in the Russell Hill complex, close to the Defence Signals Directorate (to draw on that organisation's expertise) and be run by the Department of Prime Minister and Cabinet. It was in his discussion about a cyber warfare centre that Des raised the issues of the conflation of electronic warfare and cyber warfare as the electro-magnetic environment and cyberspace merged. This was subsequently picked up by others who have examined in great detail the commonality between the two when it comes to military operations. But it was Des who was one of the first to argue that cyber techniques would be increasingly used to penetrate the electronic components of weapons systems and collect electronic intelligence for later use, whether as a support measure, a counter measure or a counter-counter measure.

Des' thoroughness gets to the technical heart that allows him to comment knowledgeably on a raft of complex issues — such as telecommunications architectures (including terrestrial microwave relay networks, satellite communications, and fibre-optic cables); firewall penetration, including of avionics systems and use of wireless application protocols to insert 'Trojan horses'; the insertion of viruses and worms; and the ability to control networks undetected by the hosts and thus covertly corrupt databases, deceive sensors, and manipulate information and data.

His perceptiveness comes through in his analysis of pre-war activities and Australia's willingness and capacity to engage in such activities, especially in terms of penetrating networks and implanting technical devices. He argues that information operations and cyber operations, more broadly, place a premium on carrying out preparatory activities that encompass covert actions in peacetime. This is far more than operational and logistics planning for contingencies. As Des points out, to gain information supremacy, one must have intimate familiarity with the adversary's command and control structure, public media, defence communications systems, sensor systems, and cyber networks. The electronic order of battle must be known, including electronic warfare systems, antenna systems and electronic equipment in platforms and command centres. Offensive capabilities are needed for developing software that can penetrate firewalls of targeted networks; for developing worms, viruses and Trojan horses; for disabling or corrupting websites and databases; and for installing 'back-door' programs in designated networks that allow data to be copied undetected or that allow control of infected computers.

Eventually, in 2009, the Australian Government established the Cyber Security Operations Centre (CSOC) in the Defence Signals Directorate. Its task is to provide all-source cyber situational awareness and an enhanced ability to facilitate operational responses to cyber security events of national importance. Thus, Des had his cyber centre but with probably a broader and more encompassing remit than he had originally envisaged, even if public disclosure of the full extent of its capabilities remains less than hoped for. And while the Centre is run from the Defence Signals Directorate, the Department of the Prime Minister and Cabinet did establish a National Security Chief Information Officer in the Office of the National Security

Adviser in 2009 and late the following year assigned responsibility for cyber policy coordination to that position. So, while Des may not have got exactly what he was after, the current arrangement does go a long way towards addressing his concerns. Indeed, during the Gillard Government re-shuffle in December 2011, the Department of Prime Minister and Cabinet was given responsibility for developing cyber security policy, not just its coordination, together with additional staff.

During this time (from 2004 to 2008), Des also supervised me as a Ph.D. candidate, and through his persistence and insistence ensured my occasionally flagging spirits were continually revived. Undertaking a Ph.D. part-time and while engaged in a busy job, there could have been no better ally and mentor than Des Ball. He helped get me through my first book in 1990[7] and helped me get through my Ph.D. in 2008.[8] In discussing the benefits of having Des as a thesis supervisor with others, whether for a Masters or a Ph.D., there is unanimity that he is the very best. He is exceptional. He strives for excellence and simply accepts that being average is not good enough. He sets a high benchmark for research and writing that inspires others. He helps his students excel.

We continued to discuss cyber issues at our regular meetings over lunch at Chats café on the ANU campus during 2009 and 2010 — with Des encouraging me to write a piece for the Kokoda Foundation's *Security Challenges* journal on the need for closer regional cyber security cooperation, while Des penned an article on China's cyber warfare capabilities.[9] Des argued that China has the most extensive and most practised cyber warfare capabilities in Asia. He stepped his readers through how these capabilities had been developed since the mid-1990s, which intelligence and military organisations were involved, and the capabilities that had been demonstrated in defence exercises and in attacks on computer systems and networks in other countries. As Des cautioned, however, it is difficult to determine the origin of these attacks — whether by official agencies or private citizens, or as he refers to them, 'Netizens'. Such is his thoroughness that Des goes to the trouble of finding out the Chinese term for Netizens and sharing that with his readers: *'wang min'*.

Des also highlighted that China's own computer systems and networks were highly vulnerable, which he concludes has led to the adoption of a pre-emptive strategy, as practiced in Chinese Army exercises, which would see cyber attacks conducted at the very beginning of a conflict. Des also points out that Chinese offensive cyber capabilities are fairly rudimentary. While they can launch denial-of-service attacks, deface web sites, erase data, post misleading information, and develop basic viruses, there is no evidence to suggest the Chinese can penetrate highly secure networks or manipulate critical data. Des' assessment is that the Chinese could not, today, bring down selected command and control, air defence or intelligence networks and databases of advanced adversaries, nor manipulate the data in those networks.

As ever, Des provided a well thought out and well-constructed argument where he concluded there was no evidence that Chinese cyber-warriors could penetrate highly secure networks or covertly steal or falsify critical data. Des rated China's information warfare capabilities as inferior for at least the next ten years; although, he did caution that the threat of a Chinese-initiated cyber war meant Australia's national security agencies needed to strengthen their protective capabilities and be ready for retaliatory and offensive operations. He did point out, however, that Australia was among the top ten targets for China's cyber-intelligence operations, and that China seemed to be behind the theft of emails from Parliament computers, which was reported in the media in March 2011.

In November 2011, the Project 2049 Institute released a report on the Chinese People's Liberation Army (PLA) Signals Intelligence and Cyber Reconnaissance Infrastructure.[10] That report generated quite a deal of interest, even more so after Des had commented on the possibility that the PLA may have consolidated computer and network attack missions with electronic warfare into an integrated Network Electronic Warfare activity under the Fourth Department, responsible for electronic countermeasures. Des had earlier pointed out that the PLA gave the Fourth Department responsibility for Electronic Warfare and the Third Department's responsibility for Signals Intelligence, as well as specialised Intelligence Warfare militia units. Des also observed that the Chinese military and intelligence agencies relied on elements of the corporate sector, not just state-owned organisations but also "private" companies.[11]

There is another important aspect of Des Ball's contribution to the cyber discussion, and which further reflects the extent of his overall contribution to the strategic and security debate more generally. As detailed earlier in this volume, Des is a founding member of the Steering Committee of the Council for Security Cooperation in the Asia-Pacific (CSCAP), and co-chair of the Australian CSCAP Committee. While Des has reached across the breadth of the security agenda in addressing regional matters, he has recently focused on cyber security and during the Steering Committee meeting in Kuala Lumpur in June 2010 was party to the agreement to form a Study Group on Cyber Security. The Study Group is co-chaired by the CSCAP committees of Malaysia, India, Singapore and Australia, and is expected to report its findings to an ASEAN Regional Forum (ARF) meeting in 2012.

In his own inimitable way, Des has yet again been an initiator of change — this time in a regional cooperation sense that might well lead to an ASEAN Regional Forum cyber security strategy that ensures a secure and safe online environment for all regional nations through effective cyber security measures that address both the domestic and international dimensions. These are but some of the examples of Des' influence on the cyber debate in Australia, in the region, and around the world. There will undoubtedly be many others in the months and years to come.

Notes

1. While it was indeed a statue that Des climbed, the first time I heard the story, it was a flagpole that he had climbed — which probably added more to the aura and mystique of the man when I first met him than climbing a statue.
2. See Gary Waters, *Gulf lesson one – the value of air power: doctrinal lessons for Australia* (Canberra: Air Power Studies Centre, 1992) and; Desmond Ball *The Intelligence War in the Gulf*, Canberra Papers on Strategy and Defence no. 78 (Canberra: Strategic and Defence Studies Centre, Australian National University, 1991).
3. Commonwealth of Australia, "Testimony of Professor Desmond Ball to the Joint Standing Committee On Treaties, Reference: Pine Gap", Official Committee Hansard, Parliament of the Commonwealth of Australia, Parliament of the Commonwealth of Australia, 9 August 1999.
4. Gary Waters and Desmond Ball, *Transforming the Australian Defence Force (ADF) for Information Superiority*, Canberra Papers on Strategy and Defence no. 159 (Canberra: Strategic and Defence Studies Centre, 2005).
5. The book that I referred to earlier in which Kim Beazley kindly wrote the foreword just prior to being appointed as the Australian Ambassador to the United States. See Desmond Ball, Gary Waters and Ian Dudgeon, *Australia and Cyber-Warfare* (Canberra: ANU E-Press, 2008).
6. Commonwealth of Australia, *Australia's National Security: A Defence Update 2007* (Canberra: Department of Defence, 2007).
7. Gary Waters, *RAAF air power doctrine: a collection of contemporary essays* (Canberra: Strategic and Defence Studies Centre, Australian National University, 1990).

8. Gary Waters, "Networking the ADF for Operations in the Information Age" (Ph.D dissertation, Australian National University, 2008).
9. Gary Waters, "The Case for a Regional Cyber Security Action Task Force", *Security Challenges* 7, no. 1 (Autumn 2011): 1–10 and; Desmond Ball, "China's Cyber Warfare Capabilities", *Security Challenges* 7, no. 2 (Winter 2011): 81–103.
10. Mark A. Stokes, Jenny Lin and L.C. Russell Hsiao, "The Chinese People's Liberation Army Signals Intelligence and Cyber Reconnaissance Infrastructure" (Washington DC: Project 2049 Institute, 2011).
11. See Desmond Ball, "China's Cyber Warfare Capabilites".

19

PRESSING THE ISSUE

Hamish McDonald

Sir Arthur Tange was a figure inspiring terror at the Department of Defence in his time as its secretary. As he set about incorporating three separate service ministries and sundry defence supply agencies into Defence, the leaks and outraged newspaper articles by newly retired military brass came in a steady stream. Tange's eye for backsliders and subverters of his authority roamed ceaseless over Russell Hill and its outposts. A group of bureaucrats who took their sandwiches out onto the central lawn, under the central memorial to American help in the Second World War, were stunned when a window flew up, and Tange leaned out to order them off.[1]

At the same time, Tange was the chief keeper of secrets. Having been head of the External Affairs department as well, he knew them all. Through the Whitlam years he'd fought hard to persuade his Labor political masters not to blow the United States alliance before they fully understood all its ramifications.

But who to trust with that information? Parliament House, lit up like an ocean liner across Lake Burley Griffin, was a ship springing leaks. The raid by Attorney-General Lionel Murphy and his Commonwealth Police on the Australian Strategic Intelligence Organisation (ASIO) headquarters in Melbourne, the leak about the Australian Secret Intelligence Service

(ASIS) help for the Central Intelligence Agency (CIA) in its subversion of Allende's left-wing government in Chile, the weaving of the Pine Gap joint intelligence base into the 1975 dismissal narrative — all had contributed to a sharp polarisation between believers and sceptics, between defenders and investigators.

In its brief life, from the beginning of the 1970s to the end of the 1980s, the weekly newspaper, *The National Times*, was a leader of the sceptics and investigators. Its journalists and contributors including Brian Toohey, Evan Whitton, Paul Kelly, Marian Wilkinson, Andrew Clark, Bill Pinwill and Deborah Snow set out to challenge conventional wisdoms in many fields. The secret workings of defence and intelligence were natural subjects. Over the 1970s came the opening-up of the wartime Ultra/Enigma signals intelligence (SIGINT) activity, the revelations that Australia possessed its own SIGINT agency in the Defence Signals Directorate (DSD), its own external intelligence outfit in ASIS, the exposure of murky CIA operations in Southeast Asia by Alfred McCoy and others, the hardening of the Suharto regime in Indonesia, and more attention to the background of the Vietnam involvement and the changing nuclear weapons balance.

As we learned on the job about these areas, desperately trying to find new and startling local angles, an academic career was starting in parallel at the Australian National University. The name Desmond Ball became increasingly quoted in stories about the above subjects.

For a year, between assignments as correspondent in Jakarta and Tokyo, I worked in Sydney for the paper, and one of my first assignments was to write a profile of Tange. When I eventually walked into Tange's office, late one Friday afternoon as the 5pm rush of bureaucrats to their weekenders got under way, it was with a great deal of nervousness. I was 30 years old. As well as being physically and psychologically imposing, Tange was surrounded with the aura of having mingled with the great and powerful for decades. He waited for the impudent presence of *The National Times* like a lion in its lair.

As we settled down to the interview, Tange threw up a few barbs before the meeting turned into an enthralling two-hour talk about episodes of his career. One of them was a shot at Ball. "You look at an article by someone like Desmond Ball and check the footnotes, and they're full of references to newspaper articles by Paul Kelly or Evan Whitton," Tange grumbled.

If there was sometimes a circular quality to the relationship between Des Ball and journalists, remember the context of the information flow of the times. No Internet, no mobile phones, no Twitter, no blogs. There might have been the occasional thud of a manila envelope of photocopies landing on the front lawn of a Brian Toohey or Laurie Oakes, the occasional call from a nervous, anonymous person, feeding coins into a public phone booth. But generally journalists and academics working in defence and international relations worked on the outside of high walls around the most interesting and sensitive areas of interest.

Journalists who got close enough to see the inner workings were often invited inside the walls. Some of the foreign correspondents posted in Southeast Asia were officially informed about the existence of ASIS, and encouraged to drop in at its then headquarters in St. Kilda's Victoria Barracks, signposted as "Central Planning", when on home leave to have a friendly chat about the persons and events they encountered. Some correspondents decided not to report certain matters, in the national interest. Creighton Burns, the correspondent of *The Age* in Singapore during *Konfrontasi*, later admitted withholding his knowledge that Australian Special Forces were engaged in operations inside Indonesia's territory in Borneo. There were many academic counterparts; Toohey notes, "tame academics who sang for their supper".

The cosy relationship broke down through the 1970s with the disillusionment over Vietnam, the arrival of a younger generation of journalists, some of them former student activists, and a wave of counter-cultural magazines and newspapers inspired by the British satire boom. *The National Times* was an effort by a stodgy old newspaper company to latch on, its attacks on shibboleths counter-balanced by articles on the best reds to cellar, road tests of Volvo cars, and adventurous travel. The attitudes around the defence and foreign policy establishments were changing, but the walls remained, with many zealous defenders. The approach adopted by *The National Times* was often the battering ram — repeating the same clutch of embarrassing facts about the Nugan Hand bank, the Mr Asia drug syndicate, the mysterious American warnings about "blowing the cover" at Pine Gap in the hope that something would give.

Often it did, but as often as not, the breakthroughs came in the United States, whose secrets Tange and others were anxiously trying to protect. At *The National Times*, we subscribed to a glossy American magazine called *Aviation Week & Space Technology*, avidly scanning its pages for news about military satellite launches and space-based intelligence systems that might have some bearing on the bases in Australia.

Des Ball, working on his game changing Ph.D. thesis and gathering material for his book *A Suitable Piece of Real Estate*, was part of the education of this generation of journalists. Deborah Snow recalls him as "an unusual academic who broke the mould". Indeed her first encounter was arriving at a Canberra house party to find Des sprawled on a sofa in a state of undress, smoking on a hand-rolled cigarette of some sort, while a female friend caressed his feet. Ball had none of the snootiness about journalism that was more common at that time, and recognised what journalists could do in opening up debates, putting out information that would oblige politicians and departments to respond. He was accessible and generous with his time, often at what others would consider inconvenient hours. Toohey said his biggest contribution has been "intelligent analysis" provided in a timely way to improve the quality of reporting.

One example in my case: in 1997 on my return from many years out of Australia to re-join *The Sydney Morning Herald*, I went out to cover the closing press conference of the AUSMIN talks — the annual ministerial meeting between Australia and the United States on defence and foreign policy — held at the HMAS Watson shore base in Sydney. The final communiqué was bland, but on the way out an official pointed me to a sentence mentioning that an Australian officer would be posted to a United States command centre in Colorado. It was 7pm on a Friday evening by the time I got back to the Herald. I thought of Des Ball and found him at home in Canberra. He knew exactly what it was about, and was able to give me a cracking story about Australia getting real time access to the intelligence stream coming out of Pine Gap.

Ball would not have been able to get that knowledge without continued access to military minds. As Snow notes: "Personally, he has been highly unconventional, but he has moved in some of the most rigidly conventional milieux in the world." A vast and eclectic knowledge about defence technology, and mastery of technical detail (even though Des was late to embrace computers, the internet and the mobile phone himself) won him respect from defence officials.

To the irritation of some in Russell Hill who, according to Brian Toohey, tried to get Ball declared persona non grata by the United States, Ball continued to have access to American defence circles, working with such outfits as the RAND Corporation and Henry Kissinger's office. This was happening even as the Australian Security and Intelligence Organisation (ASIO) continued to closely monitor Ball's contacts, in the apparent suspicion of subversive activity and links with foreign intelligence agencies. His ASIO file, obtained by Ball recently, is a dossier of stunningly banal activity in suburban Canberra. By then, Ball and ANU colleague David Horner had been given access to the archive of Venona intercepts by former ASIO director-general David Saddlier, to produce their book on KGB activities in Australia.

Another reason is that while Des Ball questions secrecy, he is not a pacifist or disarmer, but a believer in armed deterrence, and never showed much sympathy for the Soviet Union or the People's Republic of China. His main body of work has been directed at the dangers of that deterrence being undermined by the secrecy set up to protect it. His work on the danger of uncontrolled escalation in nuclear war was one part, leading to hurried changes in American war-fighting doctrine. His opening of the purposes of Pine Gap, Nurrungar and Northwest Cape bases revealed them as part of a stable nuclear balance between the United States and the Soviet Union (at least the latter two).

The paradoxical result was that the American bases became easier for Australian political leaders to justify to their parties and the public. They might have incorporated Australia into the United States nuclear war-fighting system, but they contributed to safeguards against accidental nuclear war. They made many Australians feel a new importance in the biggest strategic game of all. Some defence analysts argued it gave Australia bigger bargaining chips in the United States alliance, though successive governments have felt it necessary to keep up the insurance premiums with dispatch of forces to far-flung operations.

Like its British counterpart, Australia's DSD has sought to keep a veil over activities since the wartime Ultra operations and the early post-1945 interceptions of KGB traffic. Americans have a much shorter perspective on the utility of secrets. As noted to me by Rod Barton, a former Defence science and intelligence specialist who became a United Nations weapons inspector in Iraq, the kind of satellite photography that was a critical intelligence tool in the 1970s has been freely available to all via *Google Earth* for some years.

So bringing the signals intelligence story forward into contemporary milieu has been another preoccupation, which has brought Ball into collaboration with journalists. Indeed, scarcely a visit to Ball's house goes by without him bringing out an envelope of photographs of aerial arrays, radars and satellite dishes at some foreign military installation.

As discussed elsewhere in this volume, for many years Ball has followed the remote wars of insurgency between the Burmese Army, known as the *Tatmadaw*, and the dozen or so armed ethnic forces along the borders with Thailand and China, making many field trips.[2] On one of these trips, which I accompanied in 2007, Ball ranged up and down small towns, meeting informants of all kinds, constantly taking notes of military and paramilitary activity on both sides of the Salween River that formed the border. On our way back through Bangkok, we had dinner with two colonels in Thai army intelligence, who seemed deeply appreciative of his knowledge and advice — imparted frequently in talks at their training schools.

A particular focus has been on signals intelligence, and in early 2010 Ball reported that the *Tatmadaw* had obtained field radio sets from an Australian supplier and managed to unlock their frequency-hopping function.[3] As well as circumventing Canberra's arms embargo, it made interception of signals by the Karen and other insurgents difficult, if not impossible.

In 1999–2000, Des Ball suggested we collaborate in a book about the killing of the five Australian TV newsmen at Balibo in October 1975, during the Indonesian covert invasion of Portuguese Timor. I had gained some knowledge of the Indonesian operation during my time as correspondent in Jakarta, and had met several of the protagonists. I had put this together in a long piece in *The National Times* in August 1979. As the Suharto regime fractured in the late 1990s, new sources of material had opened up on the Indonesian side, and more Australians involved in the Indonesia relationship were willing to talk.

Facing renewed pressure from the bereaved families of the newsmen, the Keating and Howard governments had commissioned two investigations by the senior career government lawyer Tom Sherman, which elucidated more evidence and context from witnesses, particularly among Timorese, but left a feeling among the families and their supporters that trails had not been followed and the glaring conclusion — that the newsmen had been captured and executed by Indonesian special forces — side-stepped.

My 1979 article had included some information about DSD's interception of Indonesian military radio messages around the Balibo attack. Des Ball would be bringing much more information about this side. So began a very fruitful collaboration, involving many hours around the table in the kitchen of his Canberra home, and on my part a lot of cold calls to serving and retired military personnel who had been part of the intelligence chain from DSD's monitoring stations at Shoal Bay and Toowoomba to the "customers" receiving the "end product" in Canberra.

Some were co-operative. Some not ("You've got the wrong man," said one major, before ringing off. I never found out if this meant he had not been involved, or that it was wrong to expect him to talk.) Some tried. One old DSD operator agreed to meet at a coffee shop near her base, but innocently told her commanding officer about the meeting on the way out. As I sat waiting in the café, the manager called me over to his telephone: a colonel was on the other end, telling me the meeting was off and a general warning about to be sent out around Defence.

In a hot January in Canberra, I camped in the Ball household, and we brainstormed the book, me typing into my laptop as we formulated the narrative. It was the easiest writing task either of us had ever experienced, on my part helped by Des Ball's encyclopaedic recall of source materials that meant few stops for reference. A curious role reversal sometimes happened. Journalists are supposed to be the ones who push the story to the limits of the evidence, academics to hang back from conclusions until sourcing and collateral is forthcoming. In writing this book, I often found Des the one pushing the tale to a more dramatic statement. On the suggestion of the late John Iremonger at the publishers Allen and Unwin, the title chosen was *Death in Balibo, Lies in Canberra*. I'd thought of 'The Balibo Intercepts', but that was deemed "too Ludlumesque". Iremonger had worked as a staffer for a Whitlam minister, and felt angered and betrayed at the idea of a war crime against Australians (or at least Australian residents in the case of three of the newsmen) being covered up.

The failure to save the newsmen could have been seen as the result of a succession of communication gaps. Had the advance warning of the Indonesian operation given to the Australian Embassy in Jakarta been matched with the media reporting revealing the likely whereabouts of the TV crews, preventive steps could have been taken. Des Ball supplied information of a two-part intercept by the DSD, in which the commander of the Indonesian operation inside Portuguese Timor, Colonel Dading Kalbuardi, was said to have radioed Jakarta two days ahead of the attack asking what to do about foreign journalists, and to have received the reply that no witnesses should be allowed. The conclusion of such an intercept having been made was that either through negligence or design, no alarm was raised and the newsmen left to their fate.

The findings of our book, and a letter to the then defence minister, John Moore, by the DSD operator blocked from speaking to me, led to a reference to the Inspector-General of Intelligence and Security (IGIS). The then IGIS, Bill Blick, pulled out all the intercepts relating to Balibo, but could not find the 14 October 1975 two part message, though there was one relating to coverage by Indonesian journalists. In 2007, a long campaign by lawyers representing the bereaved families found a legal footing to force a coronial inquiry into the deaths — one of the murdered newsmen, Brian Peters, had been a resident of New South Wales (NSW). And so, over four months that year, a path-breaking inquest was held at the NSW Coroner's Court on busy Parramatta Road, opposite the University of Sydney.

Copies of the Ball-McDonald book were in the trollies of material wheeled in by teams of lawyers. The Commonwealth had its own senior counsel and junior, supported by a senior civilian DSD official, to supervise the disclosure of secret material, revealed to the court and a limited number of lawyers, with the public and press sent outside. A long retired DSD chief was interviewed in his sick bed down in a NSW South Coast town by lawyers assisting the coroner, with DSD officials in attendance, and testimony given to the court in camera.

Both of us were called to the witness stand, Des speaking by phone link. Pressed for the sourcing about the two-part intercept, Des could not pin it down, except to say it was an accepted account repeated by multiple sources in defence and intelligence circles. It was visibly seen as a victory for the DSD camp. The coroner made no finding against Australian agencies, but conclusively overturned the Sherman findings by ruling the five had been deliberately killed by Indonesian forces and local allies, with the names of two Indonesian soldiers sent to the federal government for possible prosecution. (As of April 2012, four and a half years later, the Australian Federal Police have yet to conclude whether a prosecution case can be mounted).

It can be conjectured how the information got to Des. For it to have resulted from a DSD intercept would have required a sanitisation of the DSD archives, and a memory loss by the numerous surviving DSD operators, who generally have very vivid memories of that day. Conceivably it would have come from other intelligence sources, and wrongly attributed to an intercept. For his part, the Indonesian chief of the Timor operation, General Benny Murdani, denied the exchange took place. I prefer to stick with the Scottish verdict of "not proven" rather than the English "not guilty".

There were other shortcomings in the inquest that nag me even now. One was the failure to check out allegations (in the writings of Jill Jolliffe, on which the court relied heavily) that the Special Air Service had been tasked with an attempt to pull the newsmen out of danger. Another was the implausible story that the Prime Minister, Gough Whitlam, was not informed of the deaths until he arrived back in Canberra from Sydney, four days after officials circulated the intelligence.

A decade on, Des Ball continues to educate us journalists. In Beijing, after the first Chinese manned space flight, Des sent details and a diagram of how the vehicle left in space after the return of the manned capsule turned into a surveillance satellite, trailing antennae. As the "War on Terror" continued, Des was able to supply updates on the technological battle of data mining, voice-recognition, and other aspects of the deadly hide-and-seek between al-Qaeda and Western intelligence agencies. Long may Des Ball continue to push us.

Notes

1. See Hamish McDonald, "Rudd seems to be shying away from necessary battles over defence", *The Sydney Morning Herald*, 3 May 2008.
2. See Desmond Ball, *Burma's Military Secrets: Signals Intelligence (SIGINT) from the Second World War to Civil War and Cyber Warfare* (Bangkok: White Lotus, 1998); Desmond Ball, *The Boys in Black: The Thahan Phran (Rangers), Thailand's Para-military Border Guards* (Bangkok: White Lotus, 2004); Desmond Ball and David Mathieson, *Militia Redux: The Or Sor and the Revival of Para-militarism in Thailand* (Bangkok: White Lotus, 2007) and; Desmond Ball and Nicholas Farrelly, "Burma's Broken Balance", *CSCAP Regional Security Outlook 2012*, edited by Brian Job (Singapore: CSCAP, 2011), pp. 18-23.
3. Desmond Ball and Samuel Blythe, "Radio Active:" Myanmar Seeks Communications Upgrade", *Jane's Intelligence Review 1*, September 2010, pp. 22–25.

BIBLIOGRAPHY

Acharya, Amitav. *Whose Ideas Matter? Agency and Power in Asian Regionalism*. Ithaca: Cornell University Press, 2009.
Austin, Greg, and Alexey D. Muraviev. *Red Star East: The Armed Forces of Russia in Asia*. St. Leonards: Allen and Unwin, 2000.
Babbage, Ross, Desmond Ball, J.O. Langtry and Robert O'Neill. *The Development of Australian Army Officers for the 1980s*. Canberra Papers on Strategy and Defence, no. 17. Canberra: Strategic and Defence Studies Centre, Australian National University, 1978.
Ball, Desmond. "The Blind Men and the Elephant: A Critique of Bureaucratic Politics Theory". *Australian Outlook* 28, no. 1 (April 1974): 71–92.
———. "Deja Vu: The Return to Counterforce in the Nixon Administration". California Seminar on Arms Control and Foreign Policy no. 46. Santa Monica, California, December 1974.
———. "American Bases in Australia: The Strategic Implications". *Current Affairs Bulletin* 51, no. 10 (March 1975): 4–17.
———. "United States Strategic Doctrine and Policy with Some Implications for Australia". In *The Strategic Nuclear Balance: An Australian Perspective*, edited by Robert O'Neill. Canberra: Australian National University, 1975.
———. ed. *The Future of Tactical Airpower in the Defence of Australia*. Canberra: Strategic and Defence Studies Centre, Australian National University, 1976.
———. "Equipment Policy for the Defence of Australia". In *The Defence of Australia — Fundamental New Aspects*, edited by Robert O'Neill. Canberra: Australian National University, 1977.
———. "The Costs of the Cruise Missile". *Survival* 20 no. 6 (November/December 1978): 242–47.
———. "Allied Intelligence Cooperation Involving Australia During World War II". *Australian Outlook* 32, no. 2 (December 1978): 299–319.
———. "Developments in US Strategic Nuclear Policy Under the Carter Administration". *SDSC Working Paper* 17. Canberra: Strategic and Defence Studies Centre, 1979.

——. "The MX Basing Decision". *Survival* 22, no. 2 (March/April 1980): 58–65.

——. "Soviet ICBM Deployment". *Survival* 22 no. 4 (July/August 1980): 167–70.

——. *A Suitable Piece of Real Estate: American Installations in Australia*. Hale and Iremonger: Sydney, 1980.

——. "Conclusion". In *Problems of Mobilisation in the Defence of Australia*, by Desmond Ball and J. O. Langtry. Manuka: Phoenix Defence Publications, 1980.

——. *Politics and Force Levels: The Strategic Missile Program of the Kennedy Administration*. Berkeley: University of California Press, 1980.

——. *Can Nuclear War Be Controlled?* Adelphi Paper, no. 169. London: International Institute for Strategic Studies, Autumn 1981.

——. "US Strategic Forces: How Would They Be Used?". *International Security* 7, no. 3 (Winter 1982/83): 31–60.

——. "Counterforce Targeting: How New, How Viable?". *Arms Control Today* 11, no. 2 (February 1981): 1–9, reprinted in *The Use of Force: International Politics and Foreign Policy*, edited by Robert J. Art and Kenneth N. Waltz, 2nd ed. Lanham, MD: University Press of America, 1983.

——. "The Role of Strategic Concepts in US Strategic Nuclear Force Development". In *National Security and International Stability*, edited by Bernard Brodie, Michael D. Intriligator and Roman Kolkowicz. Cambridge, MA: Oelgeschlager, Gunn and Hain, 1984.

——. "Nuclear War at Sea". *International Security* 10, no. 3 (Winter 1985–86): 3–31.

——. "Soviet Strategic Planning and the Control of Nuclear War". In *The Soviet Calculus of Nuclear War*, edited by Roman Kolkowicz and Ellen Propper Mickiewicz. Lexington, MA: Lexington Books, 1986.

——. "Toward a Critique of Strategic Nuclear Targeting". In *Strategic Nuclear Targeting*, edited by Jeffrey Richelson and Desmond Ball. Cornell: Cornell University Press, 1986.

——. *A Base for Debate: The US Satellite Station at Nurrungar*. Sydney: Allen and Unwin, 1987.

——. *Crisis Stability and Nuclear War, A Report published under the auspices of the American Academy of Arts and Sciences and the Cornell University Peace Studies Program*. Ithaca, NY: Cornell University, January 1987.

——. "The Use of the Soviet Embassy in Canberra for Signals Intelligence (SIGINT) Collection". *SDSC Working Paper* no. 134. Canberra: Strategic and Defence Studies Centre, 1987.

——. *Australia's Secret Space Programs*. Canberra Papers on Strategy and Defence, no. 43. Canberra: Strategic and Defence Studies Centre, 1988.

——. *Pine Gap: Australia and the US Geostationary Signals Intelligence Satellite Program*. Sydney: Allen and Unwin, 1988.

———. "Soviet Signals Intelligence: Vehicular Systems and Operations". *Intelligence and National Security* 4, no. 1 (January 1989): 5–27.

———. "Controlling Theatre Nuclear War". *British Journal of Politics* 19, no. 3 (July 1989): 303–27.

———. *Soviet Signals Intelligence (SIGINT)*. Canberra Papers on Strategy and Defence, no. 47. Canberra: Strategic and Defence Studies Centre, Australian National University, 1989.

———. *Soviet Signals Intelligence (SIGINT): Intercepting Satellite Communications*. Canberra Papers on Strategy and Defence, no. 53. Canberra: Strategic and Defence Studies Centre, Australia National University, 1989.

———, ed. *Aborigines in the Defence of Australia*. Canberra: Australian National University Press, 1991.

———. *Building Blocks for Regional Security: An Australian Perspective on Confidence and Security Building Measures (CSBMs) in the Asia-Pacific*. Canberra: Strategic and Defence Studies Centre, 1991.

———."Improving Communications Links Between Moscow and Washington". *Journal of Peace Research* 28, no. 2 (1991): 135–59.

———. " 'Provocative Plans': A Critique of US Strategy for Maritime Conflict in the Pacific". *SDSC Working Paper* 79. Canberra: Strategic and Defence Studies Centre, Australian National University, 1991.

———. *Soviet SIGINT: Hawaii Operation*. Canberra Papers on Strategy and Defence, no. 80. Canberra: Strategic and Defence Studies Centre, 1991.

———. *The Intelligence War in the Gulf*. Canberra Papers on Strategy and Defence, no. 78. Canberra: Strategic and Defence Studies Centre, 1991.

———. "Strategic Culture in the Asia-Pacific Region". *Security Studies* 3, no. 1 (Spring 1993): 44–74.

———. *Signals Intelligence in the Post-Cold War Era: Developments in the Asia-Pacific Region*. Singapore: Institute of Southeast Asian Studies, 1993.

———. "Tasks for Security Cooperation in Asia". In *Security Cooperation in the Asia-Pacific Region*, edited by Desmond Ball, Richard Grant and Jusuf Wanandi. Washington: Center for Srategic and International Studies, 1993.

———. "Trends in Military Acquisitions in the Asia/Pacific Region: Implications for Security and Prospects for Constraints and Controls". *SDSC Working Paper* no. 273. Canberra: Strategic and Defence Studies Centre, 1993.

———. "Arms and Affluence: Military Acquisitions in the Asia-Pacific Region". *International Security* 18, no. 3 (Winter 1993/94): 78–112.

———. Interview by Stewart Harris, National Library of Australia, transcript, 26 October 1994.

———. "A New Era in Confidence Building: The Second-Track Process in the Asia-Pacific Region". *Security Dialogue* 25, no. 2 (1994): 157–76.

———. "Trends in Military Acquisitions: Implications for Security and Prospects for Constraints/Controls". In *The Making of a Security Community in the Asia-*

Pacific: Proceedings of the Seventh Asia-Pacific Roundtable, edited by Bunn Nagara and K. S. Balakrishnan. Kuala Lumpur: Institute of Strategic and International Studies, 1994.

———. "Signals Intelligence (SIGINT) in Pakistan". *Strategic Analysis* 18, no. 2 (May 1995): 195–214.

———. "Signals Intelligence in India". *Intelligence and National Security* 10, no. 3 (July 1995): 377–407.

———. "Signals Intelligence in China". *Jane's Intelligence Review* 7, no. 8 (August 1995): 365–70.

———. "Signals Intelligence in North Korea". *Jane's Intelligence Review* 8, no. 1 (November 1995): 506–10.

———. "Signals Intelligence in Taiwan". *Jane's Intelligence Review* 11, no. 1 (November 1995): 28–33.

———. "Signals Intelligence (SIGINT) in Sri Lanka". *Strategic Analysis* 18, no. 8 (November 1995): 1077–108.

———. *Signals Intelligence (SIGNIT) in South Korea*. Canberra: Strategic and Defence Studies Centre, Australian National University, 1995.

———. *Signals Intelligence (SIGINT) in South Korea*. Canberra Papers on Strategy and Defence, no. 110. Canberra: Strategic and Defence Studies Centre, Australian National University, 1995.

———. "Over and Out: Signals Intelligence in Hong Kong". *Intelligence and National Security* 11, no. 3 (July 1996): 62.

———. "Developments in Signals Intelligence and Electronic Warfare in Southeast Asia — Part 1". *EW Bulletin* 9 (August 1996): 1–11.

———. "Arms Acquisitions in the Asia Pacific: Scale, Positive and Negative Impacts on Security and Managing the Problem". In *The Emerging Regional Security Architecture in the Asia-Pacific Region*, edited by Thangam Ramnath. Kulala Lumpur: Institute of Strategic and International Studies, 1996.

———. "CSCAP: Its Future Plase in the Regional Security Architecture". In *Managing Security and Peace in the Asia-Pacific*, edited by Bunn Nagara and Cheah Siew Ean, pp. 289–325. Kuala Lumpur: Institute of Strategic and International Studies, 1996.

———. "Maritime Cooperation, CSCAP and the ARF". In *The Seas Unite: Maritime Cooperation in the Asia Pacific Region*, edited by Sam Bateman and Stephen Bates. Canberra: Strategic and Defence Studies Centre, 1996.

———. *Signals Intelligence (SIGINT) in South Asia: India, Pakistan, Sri Lanka (Ceylon)*. Canberra Papers on Strategy and Defence, no. 117. Canberra: Strategic and Defence Studies Centre, Australian National University, 1996.

———. "The Joint Patrol Vessel (JPV): A Regional Concept for Regional Cooperation". *SDSC Working Paper* no. 303. Canberra: Strategic and Defence Studies Centre, 1996.

———. "SIGINT strengths form a vital part of Burma's military muscle". *Jane's Intelligence Review* 10, no. 3 (March 1998): 35–41.

———. *Burma's Military Secrets: Signals Intelligence (SIGINT) from the Second World War to Civil War and Cyber Warfare*. Bangkok: White Lotus, 1998.

———. "Burma and Drugs: The Regime's Complicity in the Global Drug Trade". *SDSC Working Paper* 336. Canberra: Strategic and Defence Studies Centre, 1999.

———. "Multilateral Security Cooperation in the Asia-Pacific Region: Prospects and Possibilities". *RSIS Working Paper* 2. Singapore: RSIS, 1999.

———. "Regional Maritime Security". In *Oceans Governance and Maritime Strategy*, edited by David Wilson and Dick Sherwood. Sydney: Allen and Unwin, 2000.

———. *The Council for Security Cooperation in the Asia Pacific: Its Record and Its Prospects*. Canberra: Security and Defence Studies Centre, 2000.

———. "Silent Witness: Australian Intelligence and East Timor". *Pacific Review* 14, no. 1 (March 2001): 35–62.

———. "The New Submarine Combat Information System and Australia's Emerging Information Warfare Architecture". *SDSC Working Paper* no. 359. Canberra: Strategic and Defence Studies Centre, 2001.

———. "Information Warfare (IW) in Asia: Signals Intelligence (SIGINT), Electronic Warfare (EW) and Cyber-Warfare". Paper prepared for the CASIS 2002 Conference on The New Intelligence Order: Knowledge for Security and International Relations, Ottawa, 26–28 September 2002.

———. "China and Information Warfare (IW): Signals Intelligence (SIGINT), Electronic Warfare (EW) and Cyber-Warfare". Paper prepared for ASC '03: Asian and Chinese Security Issues in the Decade 2001–11, New Delhi, 25–29 January 2003.

———. "Security Developments in the Thailand-Burma Borderlands". Sydney: Australian Mekong Resource Centre, 2003.

———. "Security Trends in the Asia-Pacific Region: An Emerging Complex Arms Race". *SDSC Working Paper* no. 380. Canberra: Strategic and Defence Studies Centre, Australian National University, 2003.

———. "The Implications of New Technology". In *The Regime of the Exclusive Economic Zone: Issues and Responses. A Report of the Tokyo Meeting*, edited by Mark Valencia, pp. 62–70. Honolulu: East-West Center, 2003.

———. *The Boys in Black: The Thahan Phran (Rangers), Thailand's Para-military Border Guards*. Bangkok: White Lotus, 2004.

———. "China and Information Warfare: Signals Intelligence, Electronic Warfare and Cyber-Warfare". In *Asian Security and China, 2000–2010*, edited by K. Santhanam and Srikauth Kondapalli, pp. 115–41. New Delhi: Shipra Publications, 2004.

———. "Intelligence Collection Operations and EEZs: The Implications of New Technology". *Journal of Marine Policy* 28, no. 1 (2004): 67–82.

———. "The Probabilities of On the Beach: Assessing 'Armageddon Scenarios' in the 21st Century". *SDSC Working Paper* no. 401. Canberra: Strategic and Defence Studies Centre, 2006.

———. "Burma's Nuclear Programs: The Defectors' Story", *Security Challenges* 5, no. 4 (2009): 119–31.

———. Interview by Nicholas Farrelly, *The Australian National University Mentor Interview Series*, transcript, 18–19 May 2011.

———. "Tensions and Arms Racing in Northeast Asia". Paper delivered to the IISS-Asia MacArthur Asia Security Initiative Workshop, Singapore, November 2011.

———. "China's Cyber Warfare Capabilities". *Security Challenges* 7, no. 2 (Winter 2011): 81–103.

———. "Defence Security Architecture in East Asia". Paper prepared for a lecture at the Sultan Hassanal Bolkiah Institute of Defence and Strategic Studies (SHHBIDSS), Brunei Darussalam, 8 March 2012. (Copy of manuscript provided by Des Ball to author.)

———. "Reflections on Defence Security Architecture in East Asia". *RSIS Working Paper* 237. Singapore: RSIS, 2012.

———. *Northeast Asia: Tensions and Action-Reaction Dynamics*. Adelphi Paper. London: International Institute of Strategic Studies, forthcoming.

———, and Amitav Acharya. *The Next Stage. Preventive Diplomacy and Security Cooperation in the Asia-Pacific Region*. Canberra Papers on Strategy and Defence, no. 191. Canberra: Strategic and Defence Studies Centre, 1999.

———, and Ross Babbage. *Geographic Information Systems: Defence Applications*. Brassey's Australia, Rushcutters Bay, 1989.

———, and Sam Bateman. "An Australian Perspective on Maritime CSBMs in the Asia-Pacific Region". *SDSC Working Paper* no. 234. Canberra: Strategic and Defence Studies Centre, 1991.

———, and Sam Bateman. "An Australian Perspective on Maritime CSBMs in the Asia-Pacific Region". In *A Peaceful Ocean? Maritime Security in the Pacific in the Post-Cold War Era*, edited by Andrew Mack. Sydney: Allen and Unwin, 1993.

———, and Samuel Blythe. "Radio Active: Myanmar Seeks Communications Upgrade". *Jane's Intelligence Review* 1 (September 2010): 22–25.

———, and Edwin Coleman. "The Land-mobile ICBM System: A Proposal". *Survival* 19, no. 4 (July/August 1977): 155–63

———, and Nicholas Farrelly. "Burma's Broken Balance". *CSCAP Regional Security Outlook 2012*, edited by Brian Job. Singapore: CSCAP, 2011.

———, and Nicholas Farrelly. "Soldiers of political fortune". *East Asia Forum Quarterly* (December 2011): 33–34.

———, and Nicholas Farrelly. "Eastern Burma: Long wars without exhaustion". In *Diminishing Conflicts in Asia and the Pacific: Why Some Subside and Others Don't*, edited by Robin Jeffrey, Edward Aspinall and Anthony Regan. London: Routledge, 2012.

———, and Nicholas Farrelly. "Interpreting 10 Years of Violence in Thailand's Deep South". *Security Challenges* 8, no. 2 (2012): 1–18.

———, and Euan Graham. "Japan's Airborne SIGINT Capabilities". *SDSC Working Paper* no. 353. Canberra: Strategic and Defence Studies Centre, 2000.

———, and David Horner. *Breaking the Codes: The KGB's Network in Australia, 1944–1950*. Sydney NSW: Allen and Unwin, 2000.

———, and Pauline Kerr. *Presumptive Engagement: Australia's Asia-Pacific Security Policy in the 1990s*. Sydney: Allen and Unwin, 1996.

———, and Gary Klintworth. "China's Arms Buildup and Regional Security". In *China as a Great Power: Myths, Realities and Challenges in the Asia-Pacific Region*, edited by Stuart Harris and Gary Klintworth. Melbourne: Longman Australia 1995.

———, and Chong Guan Kwa, eds. *Assessing Track 2 Diplomacy in the Asia-Pacific Region: A CSCAP Reader*. Canberra: Strategic and Defence Studies Centre, 2010.

———, and J. O. Langtry. "Conclusions: National Development and National Security". In *A Vulnerable Country: Civil Resources in the Defence of Australia*, edited by J. O. Langtry and Desmond Ball. Canberra: Strategic and Defence Studies Centre, 1986.

———, Cliff Lord and Meredith Thatcher, eds. *Invaluable Service: The Secret History of New Zealand's Signals Intelligence (SIGINT) during Two World Wars*. Auckland: Resource Books Ltd, 2011.

———, and Andrew Mack, eds. *The Future of Arms Control*. Sydney: Australian National University Press, 1987.

———, and Andrew Mack. "The Military Build-Up in Asia-Pacific". *The Pacific Review* 5, no. 3 (1992): 197–208.

———, and Andrew Mack. "The Military Build-Up in the Asia-Pacific Region: Scope, Causes and Implications for Security". *SDSC Working Paper* no. 264. Canberra: Strategic and Defence Studies Centre, 1992.

———, and David Mathieson. *Militia Redux: The Or Sor and the Revival of Paramilitarism in Thailand*. Bangkok: White Lotus, 2007.

———, and Hamish McDonald. *Death in Balibo, Lies in Canberra*. Sydney: Allen and Unwin, 2000.

———, Anthony Milner, and Brendan Taylor. *Track II: Mapping Track II Institutions in New Zealand, Australia and the Asian Region*. Wellington: The Asia-New Zealand Foundation, 2005.

———, Anthony Milner and Brendan Taylor. *Track 2 Diplomacy in Asia*. Canberra: Strategic and Defence Studies Centre, 2006.

———, Anthony Milner and Brendan Taylor. "Track 2 Security Dialogue in the Asia-Pacific: Reflections and Future Directions". *Asian Security* 2, no. 3 (2006): 174–88.

———, and Jeffrey T. Richelsen, eds. *Strategic Nuclear Targeting*. Ithaca, NY: Cornell University Press, 1986.

———, and Russ Swinnerton. "A Regional Regime for Maritime Surveillance, Safety and Information Exchanges". *SDSC Working Paper* no. 278. Canberra: Strategic and Defence Studies Centre, 1993.

———, and Russ Swinnerton. "A Regional Regime for Maritime Surveillance, Safety and Information Exchanges". *Maritime Studies* 78 (September/October 1994): 1–17.

———, and Robert C. Toth. "Revising the SIOP: *Taking War-Fighting to Dangerous Extremes*". *International Security* 14, no. 4 (Spring 1990): 65–92.

———, Gary Waters and Ian Dudgeon. *Australia and Cyber-Warfare*. Canberra: ANU E-Press, 2008.

———, and Robert Windrem. "Soviet Signals Intelligence (SIGINT): Organization and Management". *Intelligence and National Security* 4, no. 4 (October 1989): 621–59.

Bateman, W. S. G. "Strategic and Political Aspects of the Law of the Sea in East Asian Seas". Ph.D. dissertation, Australian Defence Force Academy, University of New South Wales, Canberra, 2001.

Beazley, Kim C. *The Defence of Australia 1987*. Canberra: Australian Government Publishing Service, 1987.

Bermudez Jr., Joseph S. *Shield of the Great Leader: The Armed Forces of North Korea*. St. Leonards: Allen and Unwin, 2001.

Bruneau, Richard A., and Scott G. Lofquist-Morgan. "Verification Models for Space Weapons Treaties: A Flexible, Layered Approach as a Negotiating Tool". In *Building the Architecture for Sustainable Space Security*. Geneva: United Nations Institute for Disarmament Research 2006.

Capie, David, and Paul Evans. *The Asia-Pacific Security Lexicon*. Singapore: Institute of Southeast Asian Studies, 2007.

Chatters IV, Edward P. and Brian J. Crothers. "Space Surveillance Network". *AU-18 Space Primer*, pp. 249–58. Maxwell: Air University Press, September 2009.

Cheema, Pervaiz Iqbal. *The Armed Forces of Pakistan*. St. Leonards: Allen and Unwin, 2002.

Commonwealth of Australia. *Australian Defence*. A White Paper presented to Parliament by the Minister for Defence, the Hon. D. J. Killen. Canberra: Australian Government Publishing Service, 1976.

———. "Answers To Questions Upon Notice, Defence-related Facilities: Foreign Involvement". Question No. 1253, 10 October 1978.

———. "Question on Notice: Defence: the Pine Gap Facility". Question from Senator D. Margetts to the Minister for Defence, Senator Robert Ray. Question no. 1625, Hansard, Senate, 19 September 1994.

———. "Testimony of Professor Desmond Ball to the Joint Standing Committee On Treaties, Reference: Pine Gap". Official Committee Hansard, Parliament of the Commonwealth of Australia, Parliament of the Commonwealth of Australia, 9 August 1999.

———. "Testimony of Professor Paul Dibb to the Joint Standing Committee On Treaties, Reference: Pine Gap". Official Committee Hansard, Parliament of the Commonwealth of Australia, Parliament of the Commonwealth of Australia, 9 August 1999.

———. *Intelligence Services Act 2001*. Australian Government ComLaw, No. 152, 2001. Available at <http://www.comlaw.gov.au/Details/C2005C00695>.

———. "Defence: Pine Gap". Question from T. Plibersek MHR to the Minister representing the Minister for Defence. Question No. 286. Answers to questions on notice, Hansard, House of Representatives, 28 May 2002.

———. "Department of Defence Submission, Response to Issues Paper, Joint Standing Committee on Foreign Affairs, Defence and Trade Inquiry into Australia's Defence Relations with the United States". Canberra: Department of Defence, May 2005.

———. *Australia's National Security: A Defence Update 2007*. Canberra: Department of Defence, 2007.

———. "Joint Defence Facility Pine Gap". Answers to questions on notice, Hansard, House of Representatives, 16 June 2008.

———. *Defending Australia in the Asia Pacific Century: Force 2030, Defence White Paper 2009*. Canberra; Department of Defence, 2009.

———. "Australia-United States Exchange of Letters Relating to Harold E. Holt Naval Communications Station". *AUSMIN 2010*. Canberra: Department of Foreign of Affairs and Trade, 2010.

Cossa, Ralph. "The ASEAN Regional Forum: Moving Towards Preventive Diplomacy". In *Assessing Track 2 Diplomacy in the Asia-Pacific Region: A CSCAP Reader*, edited by Desmond Ball and Kwa Chong Guan, pp. 219–26. Canberra: Strategic and Defence Studies Centre, 2010.

CSCAP. "Study Group on Facilitating maritime security cooperation in the Asia Pacific". Concluded working and study group, Council for Security Cooperation in the Asia-Pacific <http://www.cscap.org/index.php?page= facilitating-maritime-security-cooperation-in-the-asia-pacific>

———. "Study Group on Naval Enhancement in the Asia-Pacific". Concluded working and study group, Council for Security Cooperation in the Asia-Pacific <http://www.cscap.org/index.php?page=Naval-enhancement-in-the-Asia-Pacific>.

CSCAP Study Group on Facilitating Maritime Security Cooperation in the Asia-

Pacific. "Memorandum 6 — The Practice of the Law of the Sea in the Asia Pacific". Council for Security Cooperation in the Asia-Pacific, December 2002.

Dibb, Paul. *Review of Australia's Defence Capabilities: Report to the Minister for Defence*. Canberra: Australian Government Publishing Service, 1986.

———. "America has always kept us in the loop". *The Australian*, 10 September 2005.

Dorling, Phillip. "Australia and the US agree on a spy satellite deal". *Sydney Morning Herald*, 7 February 2011.

Dorn, Walter A. *The Case for a United Nations Verification Agency: Disarmament Under Effective International Control*. Working Paper 26. Canadian Institute for International Peace and Security, July 1990.

———. *Tools of the Trade? Monitoring and Surveillance Technologies in UN Peacekeeping*. New York: United Nations Department of Peacekeeping Operations, September 2007.

Evans, Paul. "Building Security: The Council for Security Cooperation in the Asia Pacific (CSCAP)". *The Pacific Review* 7, no. 2 (1994): 125–39.

Evans, Gareth and Paul Dibb, *Australian Paper on Practical Proposals for Security Cooperation in the Asia Pacific Region*. Canberra: Department of Foreign Affairs and Trade, 1993.

Fealy, Greg, and Virginia Hooker, eds. *Voices of Islam in Southeast Asia: A Contemporary Source Book*. Singapore: Institute of Southeast Asian Studies, 2006.

Findlay, Trevor. *A Standing United Nations Verification Body: Necessary and Feasible*. Compliance Chronicles 1, December 2005.

Fraser, Malcolm. "Our star spangled manner". *The Age*, 7 June 2012.

———. "Politics, Independence and the National Interest: The legacy of power and how to achieve a peaceful Western Pacific". 2012 Gough Whitlam Oration, Sydney, 6 June 2012.

Ghamari-Tabrizi, Sharon. *The World of Herman Kahn*. Cambridge: Harvard University Press, 2005.

Graham, Euan. "Japan's Sea Lane Security, 1940–2004: A Matter of Life and Death?". Oxon: Routledge/Nissan Institute, 2006.

Hall, Richard. *The Rhodes Scholar Spy*. Milsons Point: Random House Australia, 1991.

Haynes, John Earl and Harvey Klehr. *Venona: Decoding Soviet Espionage in America*. New Haven: Yale University Press, 1999.

Healey, Denis. *The Time of My Life*. London: Michael Joseph, 1989.

Huxley, Tim. "The ASEAN States' Defence Policies 1975–81: Military Responses to Indochina?". *SDSC Working Paper* no. 88. Canberra: Strategic and Defence Studies Centre, 1984.

———. "The ASEAN States' Internal Security Expenditure". *SDSC Working Paper* no. 122. Canberra: Strategic and Defence Studies Centre, 1987.

——. "Brunei's Defence Policy and Military Expenditure". *SDSC Working Paper* no. 166. Canberra: Strategic and Defence Studies Centre, 1988.

——. "The Political Role of the Singapore Armed Forces' Officer Corps: Towards a Military-Administrative State?". *SDSC Working Paper* no. 279. Canberra: Strategic and Defence Studies Centre, 1993.

——. *Defending the Lion City: The Armed Forces of Singapore*. St Leonards: Allen & Unwin, 2000.

Ireland, Judith. "US marines not a 'US base' on Australian soil: Smith". *The Age*, 4 April 2012.

Jaramillo, Cesar, ed. *Space Security 2011*. Ontario: Project Ploughshares, 2011.

Jasani, Bhupendra. "International Satellite Monitoring Agency: Has the time come for its establishment?". Proceedings of Workshop on Safeguards Perspectives for a Future Nuclear Environment, Cernobbio Villa Erba, Italy, 14–16 October 2003.

Job, Brian, L."Track 2 Diplomacy". In *Asian Security Order. Instrumental and Normative Features*, edited by Muthiah Alagappa, pp. 279–341. Stanford: Stanford University Press, 2003.

Job, Brian L. "Track 2 Diplomacy: Ideational Contribution to the Evolving Asian Security Order". *Assessing Track 2 Diplomacy in the Asia-Pacific Region*, edited by Desmond Ball and Kwa Chong Guan, pp. 112–61. Canberra: Strategic and Defence Studies Centre, ANU, 2003/2010.

Joint Committee on Foreign Affairs and Defence. *Threats to Australia's Security: Their Nature and Probability*. Canberra: Parliament of Australia, 1982.

"Joint Space Operations Center". Fact Sheet. Vandenberg Air Force Base, 6 June 2008.

Joint Standing Committee on Treaties. "Dissenting Report — Australian Greens, Report 121 of the Joint Standing Committee on Treaties". Canberra: House of Representatives Committee, October 2011.

Kraft, Herman Joseph S. "The Autonomy Dilemma of Track Two Diplomacy in Southeast Asia". *Security Dialogue* 31, no. 3 (2000): 343–56.

Langtry, J. O. "Geostrategic Imperatives". In *The Northern Territory in the Defence of Australia: Strategic and Operational Considerations*, edited by J. O. Langtry and Desmond Ball. Canberra: Strategic and Defence Studies Centre, 1991.

——, and Desmond Ball. *Controlling Australia's Threat Environment: A Methodology for Planning Australia's Defence Force Development*. Canberra: Strategic and Defence Studies Centre 1979.

——, and Desmond Ball, eds. *A Vulnerable Country: Civil Resources in the Defence of Australia*. Canberra: Strategic and Defence Studies Centre, 1986.

——, and Desmond Ball, eds. *The Northern Territory in the Defence of Australia: Strategic and Operational Considerations*. Canberra Papers on Strategy and Defence no. 73. Canberra: Strategic and Defence Studies Centre, 1991.

Large, Scott F. National Reconnaissance Office, Memorandum. Subject:

Declassification of the "Fact of" National Reconnaissance Mission Ground Stations and Presence Overseas". 24 September 2008.

Lockheed Martin. "Lockheed Martin Space Fence Radar Prototype Tracking Orbiting Objects". Press release, 8 March 2012. Available at: <http://www.lockheedmartin.com /us/news/press-releases/2012/march/0306-ms2-space-fence-radar-prototype-tracking-orbiting-objects.html>.

Lowry, Robert. *The Armed Forces of Indonesia*. St. Leonards; Allen and Unwin, 1996.

McDonald, Hamish. "Rudd seems to be shying away from necessary battles over defence". *The Sydney Morning Herald*, 3 May 2008.

Nautilus Institute. "Australian Defence Satellite Communications Station, Geraldton". *Australian Defence Facilities, Australian Forces Abroad Briefing Book*. Available at <http://nautilus.org/publications/books/australian-forces-abroad/defence-facilities/australian-defence-satellite-communications-station-geraldton/>.

O'Neill, Robert, ed. *The Defence of Australia: Fundamental new aspects — Proceedings of a conference organised by the Strategic and Defence Studies Centre, the Australian National University, October, 1976*. Canberra: Strategic and Defence Studies Centre, 1977.

Pownall, Angela. "US looks to space base in WA". *The West Australian*, 2 July 2011.

Richelson, Jeffrey T. "Technical Collection and Arms Control". In *Verification and Arms Control*, edited by William C. Potter. Lexington: Lexington Books, 1985.

———. *America's Space Sentinels: DSP Satellites and National Security*. Lawrence: University Press of Kansas, 1999.

———. "Out of the Black: The Declassification of the NRO". National Security Archive Electronic Briefing Book No. 257, 18 September 2008, at <http://www.gwu.edu/~nsarchiv/NSAEBB/NSAEBB257/index.htm>.

———, and Desmond Ball. *The Ties That Bind: Intelligence Cooperation between the UKUSA Countries — the United Kingdom, the United States of America, Canada, Australia and New Zealand*. Sydney, London and Boston: Allen and Unwin, 1985.

Rolfe, James. *The Armed Forces of New Zealand*. St. Leonards: Allen and Unwin, 1999.

Rosenberg, David. *Inside Pine Gap: The Spy Who Came In From the Desert*. Prahran: Hardie Books, 2011.

Selth, Andrew. "A Reply to Des Ball — Burma's Nuclear Programs: A Need for Caution". *Security Challenges* 5, no. 4 (2009): 133–37.

Sheldon, Simon. "Evaluating Track II Approaches to Security Diplomacy in the Asia-Pacific: The CSCAP Experience". *The Pacific Review* 15, no. 2 (2002): 167–202.

Soesastro, Hadi, Clara Joewono and Carolina G. Hernandez, eds. *Twenty Two Years of ASEAN ISIS: Origin, Evolution and Challegnes of Track Two Diplomacy*. Jakarta: CSIS, 2006.
Stokes, Mark A., Jenny Lin, and L.C. Russell Hsiao. "The Chinese People's Liberation Army Signals Intelligence and Cyber Reconnaissance Infrastructure". Washington, D.C.: Project 2049 Institute, 2011.
Taylor, Brendan and Anthony Milner. "Track 2: Developments and Prospects". In *Assessing Track 2 Diplomacy in the Asia-Pacific Region: A CSCAP Reader*, editd by Desmond Ball and Chong Guan Kwa, pp. 179–90. Canberra: Strategic and Defence Studies Centre, 2010.
Thatcher, Meredith and Desmond Ball, eds. *A National Asset: Essays Commemorating the 40th Anniversary of the Strategic and Defence Studies Centre*. Canberra Papers on Strategy and Defence, no. 165. Canberra: Strategic and Defence Studies Centre, 2006.
United Nations. "Report of the Secretary-General, The Implications of Establishing an International Satellite Monitoring Agency". New York: United Nations Department for Disarmament Affairs, 1983.
United Nations Office for Disarmament Affairs. *Verification in All Its Aspects, Including the Role of the United Nations in the Field of Verification*. New York: United Nations Department for Disarmament Affairs, 2008.
United States Air Force Space Command. *History of Air Force Space Command, January–December 1988*. Peterson AFB: AFSPACECOM, n.d.
United States–China Economic and Security Review Commission. *Occupying the Information High Ground: Chinese Capabilities for Computer Network Operations and Cyber Espionage*. 7 March 2012.
United States Defense Support Program (DSP) Satellites. "U.S. Air Force Fact Sheet". Los Angeles Air Force Base, 23 February 2011.
United States Department of Defense. "Veteran's Day Message: Message by Secretary of Defense Robert M. Gates". Washington, D.C., 8 November 2010.
United States Department of State. "Memorandum of Understanding between the Department of Defense of the United States of America and the Department of Defence of Australia concerning joint production, operations, and support of Wideband Global Satellite Communications". Washington, D.C., 14 November 2007.
──────. "Agreement between the Government of Australia and the Government of the United States of America relating to the Operation of and Access to an Australian Naval Communication Station at North West Cape in Western Australia". Washington, D.C., 16 July 2008.
United States House Armed Services Subcommittee. "U.S.A.F. testimony in the House Armed Services Subcommittee on Strategic Forces Hearing". Satellite Spotlight, 16 March 2011.

United States House of Representatives. "Statement of the Honorable Erin C. Conaton Under Secretary of the Air Force, Department of the Air Force Presentation to the Subcommittee on Strategic Forces Committee on Armed Services". *Air Force Space Posture*. United States House of Representatives, 15 March 2011.

Ushioda, Setsuko. *Satellite-Based Multilateral Arms Control Verification Schemes and International Law*. Ph.D. dissertation. Institute of Air and Space Law, McGill University, Montreal. 1992.

Wanandi, Jusuf. "ASEAN ISIS and Its Regional and International Networking". In *Twenty Two Years of ASEAN ISIS: Origin, Evolution and Challenges of Track Two Diplomacy*, edited by Hadi Soesastro, Clara Joewono and Carolina G. Hernandez, pp. 31–42. Jakarta: CSIS, 2006.

Waters, Gary. *RAAF air power doctrine: A collection of contemporary essays*. Canberra: Strategic and Defence Studies Centre, 1990.

———. *Gulf lesson one — The value of air power: Doctrinal lessons for Australia*. Canberra: Air Power Studies Centre, 1992.

———. "Networking the ADF for Operations in the Information Age". Ph.D. dissertation. Australian National University, 2008.

———. "The Case for a Regional Cyber Security Action Task Force". *Security Challenges* 7, no. 1 (Autumn 2011): 1–10.

———, and Desmond Ball. *Transforming the Australian Defence Force (ADF) for Information Superiority*. Canberra Papers on Strategy and Defence, no. 159. Canberra: Strategic and Defence Studies Centre, 2005.

Wattanayagorn, Panitan, and Desmond Ball. "A Regional Arms Race?". In *The Transformation of Security in the Asia/Pacific Region*, edited by Desmond Ball. London: Frank Cass, 1996.

Weeks, Stanley B., and Charles A. Meconis. *The Armed Forces of the USA in the Asia-Pacific Region*. St. Leonards: Allen and Unwin, 1999.

West, Nigel. Venona: *The Greatest Secret of the Cold War*. Chicago: Trafalgar Square, 2001.

Whitlam, Gough. Speech to the Parliament of Australia, Canberra, 4 April 1974.

Wiant, Jon A. "Burma's Military Secrets: Signals Intelligence (SIGINT) from 1941 to Cyber Warfare". *Studies in Intelligence* 44, no. 1 (Spring 2000): 95–96.

You, Ji. *The Armed Forces of China*. St. Leonards: Allen and Unwin, 1999.

Jack, Desmond, Raelene and Dorothy Ball in Timboon, Victoria, 1965.
Source: Desmond Ball

Desmond Ball with Jol Langtry, 1975.
Source: Strategic and Defence Studies Centre, Australian National University

Desmond Ball, Takashi Tajima, Christopher Bentham (Director, IISS), Gregory Treverton (Deputy Director, IISS), Robert Litwak, Avi Plascov, ---, Pauli Jarvenpaa and Sharahram Chubin at an IISS Workshop, United Kingdom, 1980.
Source: Desmond Ball

Desmond Ball at the entrance to the Pine Gap station, July 1984.
Source: Strategic and Defence Studies Centre, Australian National University

Fredor Mediansky, Desmond Ball and Paul Dibb at a SDSC Conference at the ANU, c. 1984.
Source: Darren Boyd

Desmond Ball at a book launch, 16 December 1985.
Source: Darren Boyd

Desmond Ball with President Jimmy Carter, Atlanta, Georgia, 1985.
Source: Strategic and Defence Studies Centre, Australian National University

Desmond Ball, John Geering and Peter Ginger, 6 February 1990.
Source: Strategic and Defence Studies Centre, Australian National University

Desmond Ball and David Horner in South Korea, September 1992.
Source: Darren Boyd

Desmond Ball with Leszek Buszynski, Ralph Gerard Ward and Kenneth Peacock, 1992.
Source: Strategic and Defence Studies Centre, Australian National University

16th Council for Security Cooperation in the Asia Pacific (CSCAP) Steering Committee meeting, Canberra, December 2001.
Source: Strategic and Defence Studies Centre, Australian National University

Desmond Ball with Ron Huisken and Ray Furnell at a media briefing on the Iraq War, March 2003.
Source: Strategic and Defence Studies Centre, Australian National University

Desmond Ball at a Thai Border Patrol Police anniversary celebration, 2007.
Source: I-Ling Tseng

Desmond Ball at a music shop in Chiang Mai, northern Thailand, looking for Border Patrol Police songs, 2009.
Source: I-Ling Tseng

Desmond Ball in Thailand, 2009.
Source: I-Ling Tseng

Desmond Ball in his office in the Hedley Bull Centre, Room 4.46, 2010.
Source: I-Ling Tseng

Desmond Ball in Waley, 2010.
Source: Phil Thornton

Desmond Ball with Robert Ayson and Shahriman Lockman at a dinner in Kuala Lumpur after the 25th ASEAN-ISIS Asia-Pacific Roundtable, 2 June 2011.
Source: Sheryn Lee

Desmond Ball with Anthony Milner
at a regional security dialogue, 2011.
Source: Sheryn Lee

Desmond Ball in Takua Pa, 2011.
Source: I-Ling Tseng

Desmond Ball and his very good friend Colin Ploughman.
Source: I-Ling Tseng

Desmond Ball in Japan, 2011.
Source: I-Ling Tseng

Desmond Ball and David Mathieson in Thailand researching Thai security organisations.
Source: Colin Ploughman

Desmond Ball with Benjamin Schreer, Sheryn Lee, Anthony Milner, Nicholas Farrelly, Brendan Taylor, and John Blaxland over lunch at Chats Café, the Australian National University, 10 August 2012.
Source: Sheryn Lee

www.ingramcontent.com/pod-product-compliance
Lightning Source LLC
Chambersburg PA
CBHW062008220426
43662CB00010B/1277